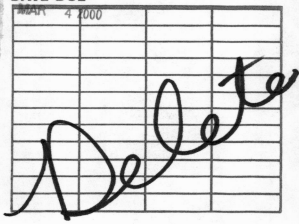

THE LABOR MOVEMENT IN WISCONSIN
A HISTORY

THE LABOR MOVEMENT IN WISCONSIN

A HISTORY

By Robert W. Ozanne

The University of Wisconsin–Madison

Madison, Wisconsin
THE STATE HISTORICAL SOCIETY OF WISCONSIN
1984

Library of Congress Cataloging in Publication Data:
Ozanne, Robert W.
The Labor Movement in Wisconsin.
1. Trade unions—Wisconsin—History.
2. Labor and laboring classes—Wisconsin—History.
3. Labor disputes—Wisconsin—History.
4. Industrial relations—Wisconsin—History.
I. Title.
HD6517.W5093 1984   331.88'09775   84-8824
ISBN 0-87020-227-8

PREFACE

The direct origins of this book lie in the surge of enthusiasm for state and local history aroused by the National Bicentennial Celebration of 1976. At that time the executive board of the Wisconsin State AFL–CIO expressed to me its interest in a book that would give an account of the development of labor unions in the state. With financial support from the Wisconsin American Bicentennial Commission, work was begun.

Labor union interest in Wisconsin labor history is of long standing. In 1950 the Wisconsin State Federation of Labor gave to the State Historical Society of Wisconsin a grant to begin acquiring local union records–minute books, reports, financial statements—and to tape record interviews with Wisconsin labor leaders. It was supplemented by a grant from a Rockefeller Foundation-funded Committee on Studies in American Civilization. A priceless contribution to that effort was the donation to the Historical Society of a microfilm of the complete files of the International Brotherhood of Pulp, Sulphite and Paper Mill Workers, rich with accounts of unionism in the Wisconsin paper industry. Without the positive response of dozens of local unions and central bodies which have deposited their minute books in the State Historical Society, this history would not have been written.

Among published works, the most useful for the purpose of this book was *The Development of the Labor Movement in Milwaukee,* by Thomas W. Gavett. Gavett's book is so good, in fact, that had he written a companion volume on the labor movement outside of Milwaukee, there would have been no need for the present work. For the history of the two Kohler strikes, the most important source was Walter Uphoff's *Kohler on Strike: Thirty Years of Conflict.* The account of the Oshkosh Woodworkers' strike is based on the article by Lee Baxandall in the *Green Mountain Quarterly* of May, 1976. *Factories in the Valley: Neenah-Menasha, 1870–1915,* by Charles N. Glaab and Lawrence H. Larsen, provided an excellent description of the origins of papermaking in Wisconsin.

Local newspaper reports from the magnificent collections of the State Historical Society of Wisconsin constituted virtually the sole source for many of the early labor-management disputes, especially in smaller Wisconsin cities. Union publications, as would be expected, provided information on both labor disputes and internal union activities. The annual convention proceedings of the Wisconsin State Federation of Labor and the Wisconsin State Industrial Union Council (CIO) formed the backbone of information on finances, membership, internal politics, and policies of the labor movement. The State Historical Society in Madison houses these documents. The periodical publications (usually monthly) of international unions were used extensively.

v

Among unpublished sources, the State Historical Society's collection of the minutes from local central bodies, local unions, and executive boards of state organizations were utilized. For information on the period since 1920, oral history tapes and transcripts from both the State Historical Society and the Archives of Labor and Urban Affairs at Wayne State University in Detroit were important.

Interviews with dozens of Wisconsin union officers and with a smaller number of management employees provided valuable information not otherwise available. One of those interviewed, former AFL regional director Charles Heymanns, also permitted use of his extensive files.

The discussion of the important role of the Socialists in the Wisconsin labor movement owes much to the Ph.D. thesis of Frederick I. Olson, "The Milwaukee Socialists, 1897–1941." The WSFL role in the Farmer-Labor Progressive Federation, 1935–1940, came largely from the Ph.D. thesis of Lester F. Schmidt, "The Farmer–Labor Federation: The Study of a United Front Movement Among Wisconsin Liberals, 1934–1941." Studies of trade unionism and labor relations in various Wisconsin cities, generated by the author's students over the years, were likewise useful.

Employer policies toward unions and the work force are an essential part of labor history. In most histories, authors are limited to the employers' public pronouncements to newspaper reporters, usually during strike situations. In this history, however, a number of employers provided an inside view of management's labor relations policies.

The greatest resource for management policy was the personal and business papers of David Clark Everest, long-time president of the Marathon Paper Corporation. Everest was not only the president of Marathon but also the secretary–treasurer of an employer group made up principally of Wisconsin papermaking companies, the Western Paper Manufacturers Association. As a result, his papers give, in intimate detail, the labor relations policies and practices of many Wisconsin employers. Everest's papers are in the State Historical Society, as are those of another paper company employer, Edward P. Sherry, owner of the Flambeau Paper Company at Park Falls.

Two Wisconsin employers generously gave the author access to labor relations files in their offices. The Kimberly–Clark Corporation provided the minutes of its Mill Councils, 1920–1937. These minutes remain in the possession of the company. It also made available interviews with past personnel officials who added much to an understanding of the evolution of company personnel and labor relations practices. The Consolidated Water Power and Paper Company of Wisconsin Rapids made available its files on collective bargaining, 1919–1937. This material remains in the possession of the company.

In the late 1950's, the Department of Economics of the University of Wisconsin, which since the turn of the century has pioneered in labor studies, afforded me research time to devote to the history of unions and of corporate labor relations policies. Since 1976 the School for Workers of the University of Wisconsin Extension Division has provided major financing for the book.

An important objective of this history has been to stress geographical coverage across the state. Residents of Rhinelander, Nekoosa, and Marinette, as well as Beloit, Kenosha, and of course Milwaukee, to name but a few of the localities included, will find herein episodes in local unionism going back beyond the memories of their most senior citizens.

Despite the effort to achieve broad coverage, there are omissions. Not every city or town which has been the site of union activity is named, and of the state's 1,100 local unions, only a selected few have received detailed discussion. The names of many local labor leaders, important to their communities and among their fellow unionists, have had to be left out. It is my hope that these omissions will be corrected by others in the future, and that this book will serve to stimulate the interest that already exists in the study of local labor history.

* * *

Because this book was many years in preparation even before the Bicentennial grant, I am deeply indebted to many persons. Research assistants who worked on the paper industry unionism did their work in late 1950's to the middle 1960's. These graduate students were Louis Bean, Keith Voelker, Lloyd David, Edward Garvoille, and Harry Graham. After a hiatus of a dozen years, other research assistants worked during the period 1976 through 1980. They were Douglas Earle, Michael Terris, Barbara Morford, Neil Basen, and an undergraduate volunteer, Greta Van Susteren. Among the research assistants, I am most indebted to Barbara Morford, who not only worked on a number of chapters but also put special emphasis on the subject of women in the labor movement. In addition, her knowledge of photography was useful in selecting many of the historical photographs.

Typing is an essential part of any book. For their conscientious and patient assistance I wish to thank especially Betty Reis, Debra Kleist, Nancy Kluever, and for the final rush with its endless revisions, Gale F. Spangler. Office co-ordinator Eleanor Nugent shepherded the work through many a clerical crisis.

ROBERT W. OZANNE

May, 1984

CONTENTS

ILLUSTRATIONS
follow pages 52 and 148

PART I

The Early Years of Unionism

Past and Present Sites of
Union Activity in Wisconsin

Superior

Ashland

Niagara

St. Croix River

Park Falls

Rhinelander

Tomahawk

Menominee R.

Flambeau River

Wisconsin River

Merrill

Menominee Mich.

St. Croix River

Brokaw

Wausau

Peshtigo

Marinette

Schofield

Chippewa Falls

Eau Claire River

Mosinee

Wolf River

Shawano

Eau Claire

Chippewa River

Green Bay

De Pere

Stevens Point

Wisconsin (Grand) Rapids

Kaukauna

Kimberly

Port Edwards

Nekoosa

Menasha

Appleton

Fox River

Neenah

Two Rivers

Manitowoc

Oshkosh

Ripon

La Crosse

Fond du Lac

Sheboygan

West Bend

Wisconsin River

Madison

Waukesha

West Allis

Milwaukee

Cudahy

South Milwaukee

Edgerton

Janesville

Racine

Beloit

Kenosha

CHAPTER 1

The First Unions, 1847–1886

THE EARLIEST UNIONS in the United States were formed on the East Coast by urban craftsmen, such as shoemakers, carpenters, and printers. These skilled workers were joining unions by 1800, long before the advent of railroads, power machinery, and factories, and decades before the white settlement of Wisconsin began.

Wisconsin Territory was created and opened to settlement in 1836, after the Black Hawk War of 1832 resulted in confinement of Wisconsin Indians to a few small reservations, many of whom subsequently moved further west. With the Indian cessions it became safe for settlers to homestead in Wisconsin, and land titles became available. The attractions of the new territory to the settlers were many and varied, and most were linked with the later development of labor unions.

The southern half of Wisconsin was prairie, dotted with patches of deciduous trees. The prairie was considered prime land for raising wheat. In rapid succession settlers from the Eastern states and from overseas—Germany, Holland, and the Scandinavian countries—turned the prairie into a vast wheatfield, and Wisconsin became a major grain exporter. The northern half of the state was covered with forests of mixed hardwoods and conifers. But in certain areas, such as those along the Wolf and Wisconsin rivers, there were many square miles of white pine, the most precious of all woods, soon to become the source of a lumbering empire and later to become the base of one of Wisconsin's largest manufacturing industries, papermaking.

The Lake Michigan port cities of Kenosha, Racine, Milwaukee, and Sheboygan served the farmers as wheat-exporting centers. To transport wheat and flour, the services of coopers (barrelmakers) were needed. Rivers were dammed to power the newly built gristmills, which ground the wheat. Foundries employing skilled molders were necessary to repair the gristmills as well as to produce the plows and reapers with which the farmers worked the land.

The leading port city, Milwaukee, had 20,000 inhabitants by 1847. It was there that the first Wisconsin unions were founded. Two of the earliest unions were formed by the bricklayers in 1847 and the carpenters in 1848. These were the building trades essential to house the city's residents and to build its docks, stores, and warehouses. Transportation was also a prime need. The unions connected with its development were the Ship Carpenters and Caulkers Association, which called the first successful strike in Milwaukee in 1848, and the Sailors Union, formed in 1851. Four hundred railroad construction workers struck for back pay in 1853, but did not form a permanent union. Other pre–Civil War trade unions, whose members worked to meet the needs of Milwaukee's inhabitants, were the Shoemakers, formed in 1848; the Tailors, 1850; and the Cigar Makers, 1852. Printers founded the Typographical Union in 1852 and affiliated with the International Typographical Union as Local 23 in 1859. It is the only one among these earliest unions that has had a continuous existence to the present.[1]

Labor unions commonly came into being because workers needed an organization to advocate their demands for better conditions. Workers in Milwaukee had two general complaints. They wanted more money, and they desperately wanted a shorter workday than the generally standard twelve hours. To achieve better wages, the unions demanded a restriction on the number of apprentices, who were often paid less than half the experienced journeyman's wage. Some unions also demanded the prohibition of women in the trade. This was true of the Tailors Union, the Cigar Makers, and especially the Typographical Union. Their grievance arose because employers universally paid lower wages to women and children than men. In the United States during this period, strikes were of brief duration because unions were small, there were no citywide union organizations to collect funds for strike benefits, and few unions were affiliated with national organizations. When employers hired out-of-town replacements for striking workers, the local union would offer free rail tickets to get the strikebreakers out of town. But the unions could not compete with the Milwaukee and Saint Paul Railway, which in 1872 offered free passes to Milwaukee for strikebreaking printers to aid the city's newspapers during the printers' strike of that year.[2]

By the end of the Civil War, unions were making substantial wage gains. Rapid inflation encouraged workers to join unions, and the labor shortage of that period lent them increased bargaining strength. But during the post–Civil War depression, unemployment destroyed the unions by eliminating their ability to threaten to strike.

The Long Depression, 1873–1878

Before 1900, individual unions seldom had a continuous life. They arose in times of prosperity, but in periods of depression found themselves helpless to achieve wage increases or to shorten the working day. Such was the fate of the Coopers, one of the larger unions in Milwaukee during the 1860's and the early 1870's. Their product was wooden barrels for shipping flour, and Wisconsin in 1870 was at the peak of its wheat-growing stage. Milwaukee was a center for milling and exporting grain and was the location of the E. P. Allis Company, a specialist in milling machinery. The union conducted almost constant strikes, mostly unsuccessful, during the 1870's. The strikes took their toll, and the union disintegrated in 1878.[3]

During the "long depression," which lasted from 1873 until 1878, no new unions were founded and most existing ones became inactive or expired. An exception was the Iron Molders Union. Perhaps the insatiable demand for the potbellied stove and the woodburning kitchen range kept the foundry industry afloat even though industrial demand vanished during the depression. Both the Milwaukee Molders Local 125, which had been founded in 1865, and the Racine and Kenosha Local 131, founded in 1867, remained very much alive despite the recession. On August 15, 1876, the two Wisconsin Molders Unions, joined by Local 23 from Chicago, held an areawide picnic at Racine. Trains brought four hundred members and their families from Local 125 in Milwaukee, plus a band and one thousand workers from Local 23 in Chicago. The Racine and Kenosha Local 131 were hosts, and the mayor of Racine addressed the affair.[4]

Among the early unions that had their start in Milwaukee was one that spread eastward to become, for a time, the nation's largest union. It was an organization of shoemakers, the Knights of St. Crispin, founded in 1867 by a Milwaukee shoemaker, Newell Daniels, and several of his fellow workers.

The Knights of St. Crispin began as an effort to protect the skilled workman from the competition of "green hands," or unskilled laborers drawn into the trade by the advent of industry mechanization. The Knights spread rapidly beyond the borders of Wisconsin, a state where shoemaking was not a large trade, to such eastern shoe centers as Lynn, Massachusetts. Its membership soon reached 50,000, making it for a short time the largest union in the country, and Daniels held the national offices of treasurer and grand scribe. A primary goal of the union was to redistribute income by making labor scarce, and to achieve that end, the eastern chapters conducted large strikes. In Wisconsin there were ten lodges, one as far north as Ashland. Daniels and his fellow workers set up a cooperative workshop in Milwaukee. When the workshop went under in 1873 due to the financial panic, the Knights of St. Crispin vanished from that city.[5] Daniels continued, however, to be active in the Milwaukee labor movement.

In the midst of the long depression an event of national consequence awakened the country to the worsening status of labor–management relations. Without union guidance, industrial unrest took on a new and formidable form. A series of riots in the more industrialized states of the East shook the nation's industrial and governmental structures. In July, 1877, after a third wage cut on the Baltimore and Ohio Railroad, spontaneous strikes broke out in Maryland and spread westward as far as St. Louis. Federal troops were sent into Maryland and West Virginia. At Pittsburgh, when railroad workers refused to move Pennsylvania Railroad trains, National Guard troops threw down their arms and joined the strikers. Soon strikers, idlers, and troops alike were looting and burning freight cars and threatening loyal guardsmen who had retreated into the roundhouse. In Cleveland, Fort Wayne, and Chicago serious disturbances occurred. In some instances factory workers joined the railroad employees.[6]

Because it was less industrialized, Wisconsin completely avoided the 1877 riots. The traumatic events nevertheless made a lasting impression on Wisconsin industrialists and government officials. As in other states, the Wisconsin National Guard was modernized and readied for possible use in future labor–management disputes. The next nationwide labor conflagration was the great eight-hour day struggle of 1886, and in that conflict Milwaukee was a full participant.

The Eight-Hour Day Explosion of 1886

During this period the list of worker complaints was always long, but heading every list was the length of the work week and the daily hours. Laborers in the post–Civil War building trades worked ten to twelve hours a day, printers ten, railroaders often twelve, and factory workers ten to twelve. All worked a six-day week.

In 1866 and 1867 a pied piper, Richard Trevellick, traveled the Midwest preaching the message of the eight-hour day. In 1867 he met with Milwaukee working men at City Hall. Workers in Milwaukee already were primed for Trevellick's message: two years earlier they had organized a Labor Reform Association, whose name later was changed to the Eight-Hour League. The movement spread to other Wisconsin cities, and a bill to limit the workday to eight hours was already under consideration in the state legislature, having been introduced by assemblymen from Milwaukee, Racine, and Fond du Lac. Trevellick and other Eight-Hour Leaguers wanted a straightforward law banning all work after eight hours.

Their expectation was that it would not be necessary to raise hourly rates, since the abrupt shortage of labor occasioned by the passage of the law would force wages rapidly upward and raise take-home pay above the former total for a ten-hour day. Following this same reasoning, Wisconsin employers, fearing the wage effect of a compulsory eight-hour-day law, proposed crippling amendments to the bill. The final bill presented for, consideration concerned women and children only. It stated that eight hours should constitute a day's work for women and children in all manufacturing establishments except those where worker and employer agreed to the contrary or where worker and employer agreed on a term of work (called a contract) by the week, month, or year. Since the employer was not required to hire anyone who insisted on the eight-hour day, the law was obviously a dead letter. It also contained a provision stating that children under eighteen and women were not to be "compelled" to work more than eight hours per day. Children under fourteen were prohibited from working more than ten hours a day, but the law provided no enforcement machinery. The legislature, dominated by farmers who had an unfavorable view of anyone who worked only eight hours a day sided with employers and voted for the emasculating amendments. The law took effect on July 4, 1867.[7]

Wisconsin labor learned from this experience that obtaining shorter hours must depend solely on their own efforts. In Milwaukee, the massive strikes of 1886 were the result.

Between the end of the long depression, in 1879, and May of 1886, union membership in Milwaukee rose to new heights. Defunct unions came to life with unexpected militance. Cigar makers, building trades workers, printers, and railroad workers all participated in militant strike actions. By now there were new unions in the factories, especially those involving iron and steel. Two large factory unions were those of the Iron Molders, which, as we have seen earlier, represented foundry workers in many of Milwaukee's growing metalworking plants, and the Amalgamated Association of Iron and Steelworkers, which represented 800 workers at the new North Chicago Rolling Mills plant at Bay View, a suburb located southeast of the Milwaukee downtown area. The Steelworkers struck over the issue of hours in 1881, and in 1882 won wage increases resulting from a nationwide strike that included 35,000 men in six states.[8] Other reactivated unions were the Coal Heavers, Tanners and Curriers,

Brewery Workers, Shoemakers, Lake Seamen's, Flour Barrel Coopers, Tight Barrel Coopers, Trunkmakers, Custom Tailors, and Butchers.

The unions grew strong in the 1880's because prosperity returned. With it came a shortage of skilled labor, which meant workers could strike without losing their jobs. In addition to wage restorations and wage increases, they again took up the call for reduced hours.

The renewed demand for the eight-hour day was put forth in the 1880's by the precursor of the American Federation of Labor, the Federation of Organized Trades and Labor Unions of the United States and Canada, founded in 1881. This new national labor organization was not in itself either large or powerful, but in 1884 it ushered in a new era of labor tactics: it set May 1, 1886, as a target date for all unions to establish an eight-hour day through collective bargaining where possible, through strikes if necessary. In some cities workers were too poorly organized to respond to the eight-hour-day call, but in Chicago and Milwaukee the challenge was taken seriously. Milwaukee in 1886 had two local labor federations which assumed leadership in attempting to establish an eight-hour day. The larger comprised those unions affiliated with a national organization, the Knights of Labor. In Milwaukee the Knights supported the eight-hour day despite the fact their national leader, Terence Powderly, warned against striking to achieve it. The second federation was the newly organized Milwaukee Central Labor Union, consisting of unions affiliated with the Federation of Organized Trades and Labor Unions.

In early 1886 a new Eight Hour League was formed, made up of delegates from the Knights of Labor and from the Central Labor Union. Wisely, the first target was to get the City of Milwaukee to pass an eight-hour day for municipal workers. A mass meeting attended by 3,000 trade unionists helped to persuade the Milwaukee Common Council on March 16, 1886, to become the first major employer to establish the eight-hour day. This example encouraged unions in the private sector to successfully demand the same treatment. With the inducement of the eight-hour day, there was a rush of workers into unions across the city. The Reliance Assembly of the Knights of Labor, composed of E. P. Allis workers, admitted 618 Polish laborers in one day alone, raising its membership to 1,600. A new union of Plasterers was formed, as was a Teamsters Union.[9]

Early in April, tobacco manufacturers across the city granted the eight-hour day, as did one of the city's largest employers, the Reliance Works owned by E. P. Allis. However, Allis also cut the pay to eight hours. This reduction was accepted by the Eight Hour League, but it brought denunciation from the Reliance employees, who expected ten hours' pay. By

May 1, workers in 200 establishments had presented eight-hour demands, but only twenty-one firms had conceded. So strong was union pressure that some firms which did not grant the eight-hour day closed down, idling 7,000 workers.[10]

The unions had scheduled a parade to demonstrate support of the eight-hour movement for Sunday, May 2. Tension mounted. The mayor of Milwaukee had earlier reported to the National Guard that the city's pawnshops had sold all of their secondhand arms. Governor Jeremiah M. Rusk, visiting Milwaukee in late April, was apprehensive enough to secretly supply the new Milwaukee National Guard headquarters on Broadway Street with increased ammunition. The entire Milwaukee police force plus four companies of infantry and artillery and the Light Horse squadron readied for immediate action.

The Sunday parade attracted about 2,500 marchers, led by bands and drum corps. Demonstrators carried the red flags of the Socialists and the tricolor flags of the Eight Hour League. The parade took place without any violence. The next three days, however, were marked by tumult. On Monday, workers who had caught the eight-hour day excitement, but whose employers had remained immune, were reluctant to go back to work. Early Monday morning about 1,000 brewery workers, members of the Knights of Labor who were striking for a wage increase, marched to the Falk Brewery to induce workers who had accepted a compromise offer to quit work. Reluctantly, Falk employees left work at noon, on orders of the District Assembly of the Knights.

The same morning several hundred Polish laborers marched down the tracks of the Milwaukee and St. Paul Railroad, convincing one group after another to join them. The first to do so were the shovelers in the coal sheds; next, the molders walked out of the railroad's foundry. The same tactics brought the workers out of the machine shop and the paint shop. Ultimately, 1,300 men were marching toward the heart of the city. Fights broke out wherever workers refused to walk out. Patrol wagons only momentarily stopped the crowd. Next in their path was the huge Reliance Works. There, Allis employees turned water hoses on the marchers. Police joined the fray as rocks began to fly. Driven back, the crowd changed direction, picking up more followers at the North Chicago Rolling Mills plant in Bay View. The demonstrators finally disbanded about 4:00 P.M.

Many skilled workers represented by unions already had received the eight-hour day or a compromise settlement. The street crowds were dominated now by unskilled workers who had received nothing, but who were determined not to be left out. Prominent among them were the Polish workers. More recent immigrants than the Germans, the Poles held the lowest paid and most physically demanding jobs in the city.

On Tuesday morning, members of the Polish Assembly of the Knights of Labor marched from St. Stanislaus Church to the North Chicago Rolling Mills, shutting down factories on their way. The combined forces of the sheriff and chief of police were unable to stop the march, and the sheriff requested the mobilization of the National Guard. Over 2,000 men reached the plant's office and presented demands for the eight-hour day and a wage increase. The company rejected both demands but agreed to discuss any other complaints. The head of the Polish Assembly, as well as Robert Schilling, head of both the Milwaukee and Wisconsin Knights of Labor, counseled moderation. But the crowd roared back that it would be satisfied with nothing less than the eight-hour day. Several companies of the National Guard arrived, scattering the demonstrators. Trains then brought in the Kosciusko Guards, whose members were Polish. At first heartened, the crowd's mood soon changed and the demonstrators threw rocks at the Guards.

The company telegraphed its Chicago office for permission to make concessions. When the reply was negative, the crowd threw more rocks at the soldiers. The Rolling Mills employees poured out, joining the crowd. The soldiers and Kosciusko Guards moved inside the company gates. When hostility increased, the guards began firing above the heads of the crowd and the plant was shut down. The demonstrators dispersed.

Trade union leaders, meanwhile, joined Milwaukee Mayor Emil Wallber in efforts to quell the disturbances and restore law and order. The Knights' leadership, now trying to avoid any connection with the riots, volunteered to patrol the streets to protect life and property, provided the National Guard was withdrawn. The leader of the Central Labor Union, Paul Grottkau, wanted to calm tempers. Speaking in German to a meeting of 1,500 workers at the Milwaukee Garden, he proposed the creation of a citywide union executive board to bargain with employers and requested that other unionists patrol the streets. Reporters who did not understand German misinterpreted the speech as an appeal to violence.

On the morning of May 5, a crowd of 1,000 again set out for the Bay View Rolling Mills. The crowd soon reached the mills, now defended by the National Guard. Major George P. Traeumer, the National Guard Commander, telephoned Governor Rusk, who replied, "Fire on them!" After issuing several warnings, Traeumer gave the order to fire. Five persons were killed and another half-dozen were wounded.

The nervousness of the governor and major undoubtedly stemmed from the tragic event that had taken place at an eight-hour-day demonstration in Chicago the night before: the historic Haymarket Square bomb incident. There, toward the end of a labor meeting addressed by the mayor, Police Inspector John Bonfield ordered his squadron of 200 to break up the meeting. When the police attempted to do so, an unknown person threw a bomb, killing seven policemen and wounding many other people. Newspapers across the country headlined the event. In Milwaukee as in Chicago, a reactionary mood set in, and innocent union officials were the targets. Employers seized upon public feeling and withdrew the eight-hour concessions. On the evening of May 5, as the demonstrations came to an end, the police rounded up twenty men for rioting or inciting to riot. One of them was Paul Grottkau.

A grand jury was convened for the purpose of investigating whether the labor organizations had used unlawful means. On June 2, the jury indicted fifty-two men. The charges had been expanded to include conspiracy to boycott, thus involving the head of the Knights of Labor, Robert Schilling. The jury that tried Schilling was unable to agree after twenty-three hours of deliberation. Before he could be retried, a different district attorney was elected with the support of a new political party set up by Schilling (described in more detail below). On a motion of the new district attorney, the court dismissed Schilling's indictment and those of other Knights accused of conspiracy. Six defendants were given short prison sentences, two were fined, nine acquitted, and charges against others were dismissed. The stiffest prison sentence was given to Grottkau, who attributed it to the vindictiveness of his labor rival, Schilling, and his political henchman, the newly elected district attorney. These trials, which took place in late 1886 and early 1887, marked the end of the labor truce between the Knights of Labor and the Central Labor Union.

After the May disturbances, the press directed their attacks not only against organized labor but also against Milwaukee's Polish community. Since 1870, Polish immigration had risen in this predominantly German city. As mentioned earlier, Germans and Yankees held the skilled jobs, while Poles were left with the unskilled jobs in foundries, breweries, meat packing plants, and railroad construction. They often began as sewer diggers, hod carriers, and ice cutters—all seasonal jobs. During the 1870's the Polish laborers were accused of being strikebreakers when they did not join a strike of coal heavers. In the eight-hour-day movement of 1886, however, they joined the unions, particularly those of the Knights of Labor, which set up separate Polish and German sections.

The riots prejudiced employers against Poles. The *Daily Sentinel,* in a story headed "No Poles Need Apply," described the firing of Poles by railroad companies, which then hired non-Poles. The article concluded: "A good many of those who struck to have their hours reduced to eight have been successful in reducing them to nothing."[11] The press also attacked other recent immigrants: "A few hundred Poles and Bohemian laborers, mostly new importations who are not American citizens, have undertaken to run the city."[12]

The Polish community fought back, but the only effective action it could take was to boycott businesses run by members of the Kosciusko Guards, who were regarded as betrayers. At that time there was one Polish alderman, Theodore Rudzinski. He had addressed several strike rallies urging moderation, and because he was visible, he bore the brunt of the Milwaukee establishment's ire. The Common Council censured him for willfully inciting to riot. Governor Rusk joined in with the only action he was able to take, cancelling Rudzinski's commission as a notary public. The Milwaukee *Sunday Telegraph* suggested that he and other Poles were from "the dregs, the scum, the filth and the sewers of the old country. Such of their classes as are already here must be kept out of official positions, no matter how small they may be."[13] The attacks on Rudzinski were interpreted by Polish residents as attacks on all and they consequently united to support him. He was one of the six People's Party candidates elected to the State Assembly in November, 1886.

The creation of the People's Party was actually the work of Robert Schilling and his supporters, but it received the support of Grottkau and the Central Labor Union in the period of temporary unity that resulted from the eight-hour-day fight. The party was surprisingly successful in the November elections. The State Master Workman of the Knights of Labor, Henry Smith, was elected to Congress. The People's Party candidate for state senator and six of its twelve Milwaukee County candidates for assemblymen won seats. In addition, the party's county victory brought in Schilling's supporter as district attorney. One factor in the party's success was the strong feelings shared by Milwaukee's Polish citizens.

The eight-hour-day strikes and riots of May, 1886, produced a groundswell of pro-union feelings among the mass of Milwaukee workers. The long-run effects on the union movement were, however, mainly negative. Labor was blamed for much of the violence. Employers stiffened their resistance to unionism, and withdrew the eight-hour concessions they had made before and during the riots. Effective July 14, the Milwaukee city council repealed the eight-hour ordinance it had passed in March. The entire labor movement was set back temporarily. The Central Labor Union disintegrated, and the Knights of Labor suffered a rapid decline in membership nationally, as well as in Milwaukee, from which they never recovered. In the AFL unions the decline was temporary, and they gradually revived. Entire unions, such as the Knights' famous Gambrinus Assembly of brewery workers, went over in a body to the four-year-old American Federation of Labor in 1890.

The eight-hour day movement was by no means dead. In Chapter 3 we will continue with the next Wisconsin episode in that story. Before doing so, we will turn to look at the early development of unionism in a major state industry—the lumber empire.

CHAPTER 2

Labor in the Lumber Industry, 1881–1898

Strike in Eau Claire

U NDER THE SLOGAN "Ten Hours or No Sawdust," Jerry Sullivan, an employee at the steam mill of the Eau Claire Lumber
Company, led 2,000 sawmill workers out on strike in the summer of 1881,
five years before the great Milwaukee eight-hour strikes. Directed by Sullivan and a union committee of twenty-four men representing nine Eau
Claire area mills, the strike began on Monday morning, July 18, 1881.
Three hundred eighty men walked out en masse after reporting for work.
They formed a procession and marched to each of the other mills, trigger-
ing new walkouts at each. That afternoon, a crowd of 1,200 workers gathered to listen to speeches by union leaders given in both English and
"Scandinavian."[1]

Grievances were many. Topping the list was the twelve-hour day; also
prominent was the contract system of hiring. In the spring, workers were
hired for the season, which lasted into the fall, on the basis of a contract
drawn up by the employer. Besides the twelve-hour day, the contract's
terms included a holdback on wages of as much as 20 per cent, to be for-
feited if the worker did not finish out the season. Wages at Eau Claire in
1881 ranged from $1.00 to $1.25 for the twelve-hour day. Setting up a
company store, as well as paying wages in "due bills" or scrip instead of
cash, were techniques frequently used to exploit workers. The existence of
"due bills" meant that wages were payable only at the close of the logging
or sawmilling season. In the meantime, workers had to make all their essential purchases at the company store, which extended them credit. For
workers who needed cash, the employer would discount due bills by 10 per
cent or more. At the company store, prices were high and quality often
low. In 1890 the Wisconsin legislature made due bills negotiable; workers
could cash them with parties other than their employers. Even so, the
worker might have to take a discount of up to 20 per cent.[2]

The first week of the strike was, from the standpoint of the union, remarkably successful. Strikers prevented "scabs" from working. The

mayor ordered all saloons closed. There was no violence. The Wisconsin Bureau of Labor Statistics reported that the city was in the possession of the strikers. Growing nervous, the mayor wired Governor William E. Smith for troops to aid in keeping the peace. The governor, vacationing on Lake Superior, appeared personally in Eau Claire on Friday, July 29. He immediately wired the adjutant-general to send troops. The next day eight companies, 376 men in all, reported for duty, each with twenty rounds of ammunition.[3]

Despite the absence of violence, after the arrival of the troops the sheriff arrested five union leaders, including Sullivan. Other leaders fled the town, effectively destroying the strike's leadership. Saturday afternoon Governor Smith gave a public speech in which he said he had not called up the troops to force sawmill workers to work twelve hours a day, but only to allow those who wished to work such hours to do so. Ignoring the unilateral aspect of the so-called contract, he stated that the men should abide by their contractual obligations and that in calling out the troops he was doing his duty to uphold the laws and constitution of the state.[4]

With the strike leaders in jail or having fled, the mills reopened on Monday, operating with limited crews and under the protection of the state troops. Each day through Thursday, more replacements and returnees manned the mills. At this point the strike was called off. Many strikers already had left to find work elsewhere.

This was the first occasion in Wisconsin in which state troops had been called out on strike duty, and it raised a considerable controversy. The Oshkosh *Northwestern* called it "a sad day for the people when it becomes necessary to thrust the bayonet into the faces of the citizens, and especially of the laboring class. It looks as though the governor had been governed more by fear than discretion, and more by the representations of a few interested employers than by a free consultation with the employed."[5]

According to the *Madison Daily Democrat,* Governor Smith's action in calling out the militia to deal with Eau Claire strikers brought widespread state and even national press criticism from the Green Bay *Gazette,* the La Crosse *Chronicle,* the Jefferson *Banner,* the Beloit *Free Press,* the New York *Sun,* and the New York *Herald.*[6]

Supporting Governor Smith's use of troops were the Eau Claire *Free Press* and the Commissioner of the Wisconsin Bureau of Labor Statistics, Frank A. Flower, whose report, published three years after the event, described it as follows:[7]

> At Eau Claire they [the state troops] met two thousand men armed with guns, clubs, pistols, crow-bars and mill tools—large, horny-

handed and resolute fellows, accustomed to hard work and hard us-
age, and fearless of danger.

Demagogues, who had never worked a stroke, incited the men to
attack the militia, declaring that it was an insult to Eau Claire to send
soldiers there to keep the peace, an insult to free citizens and a menace
to workingmen. One well-known local politician mounted a box and
advised the mill men to attack the militia at the moment when Col. C.
P. Chapman, in charge of the third battalion, was picketing the public
park. The men in Col. Chapman's command had service belts from
each of which plainly protruded twenty rounds of fixed ammunition.
This seemed to have greater influence on the half-frenzied mob, the
most turbulent of whom were not strikers or workingmen, but bum-
mers—than the appeals of the politicians, and no collision took
place. . . .

The lesson taught by this strike to the lawless classes, who are
never union men or workingmen, was salutary. It demonstrated that
after crowds of rioters have defied civil authority and overridden the
sheriff, they have not yet secured control of the country nor subju-
gated a community of peaceable citizens; and that those who have
grievances, or wrongs to redress, must resort to courts and peaceful
methods, not to riotings and destruction of property and life. The
state possesses abundant power to protect both, which responds
quickly to the command of the governor.

There had been nothing in the newspaper accounts of the strike to support Flower's inflammatory accusations against the Eau Claire lumber
mill strikers. One Eau Claire paper, the *Daily Leader,* denied that there
was any destruction of property whatsoever.[8]

Although the 1881 sawmill strike was unsuccessful, in the sense that the
short-lived union was defeated, in 1882 the Eau Claire area mills reduced
the workday from twelve to eleven hours. Many future strikes were to
occur over the same issue—reduction of hours.

Strike Actions in Subsequent Years

In this era lumber strikes affected a substantial portion of the state's
workers, for lumbering was by far the largest industry in Wisconsin. As
late as 1889, it employed over one-fourth of all industrial workers in the
state. The nearest industry in size comprised the various railroads, which
employed only 6 per cent of the industrial labor force.

Several distinct occupations were involved in lumbering. The first was
logging, primarily a winter trade. Because logging camps were remote and
frequently shifted location, their labor force was individualistic and mi-
grant. Consequently, unionism never developed in the camps. "Boom-
ing"—floating the logs to the mill—required considerable skill, but it, too,

never became unionized except occasionally, as part of related sawmill strikes. Union growth occurred primarily in the cities, where there were sawmills, sash and door plants, and a variety of woodworking industries such as coopering, butter pails manufacturing, and, of course, the construction trades.

The next large wave of lumbering industry strikes occurred in 1885 and 1886 in the mills of the Menominee River Valley, on both the Michigan and Wisconsin sides. The strike actions were triggered by a ten-hour-day law, passed by the Michigan legislature, which took effect September 23, 1885. As was true of other such laws, it was not valid if individual workers agreed by contract with the employer to waive the ten-hour provision. The result was that employers simply presented their workers with a statement waiving the provision, and required them to sign the statement as a condition of employment. The workers immediately went out on a strike that lasted until October 5, when the employers indicated that they would agree to a ten-hour day for the 1886 season, but would continue the eleven-hour day for the remainder of 1885. The strike was resumed ten days later, when Michigan employers tried to get their men to sign a waiver agreeing to an eleven-hour day for as long as they were employed.

Although the strike only began when the Michigan law became effective in September, union organizing had been going on since July at Marinette and Peshtigo in Wisconsin, and Menominee in Michigan. Union goals were the reduction of working hours, payment of wages in cash, and adequate time for dinner. The Menominee River Laboring Men's Protective and Benevolent Union was affiliated directly with the Knights of Labor. Its president was an able man, J. H. Fitzgibbons, who established a union newspaper, the *Menominee River Laborer*. Robert Schilling, whom we have met before as a leader of the Knights of Labor in Milwaukee, visited Marinette twice in September 1885, setting up four Knights lodges in Marinette and three in Peshtigo. According to the Marinette *Eagle,* on September 9, "The Hon. Robert Schilling addressed the union at a gala evening complete with procession and band," and on September 24, Schilling and A. G. von Schaick, manager of the L.W. and V.S. Lumber Company, addressed a gathering of 3,000 people at Turner Hall.[9]

In the Marinette-Menominee strike, 2,500 men left their jobs. On October 15, millowners locked out all workers in an effort to force acceptance of the eleven-hour day. The lockout failed to achieve its purpose; many workers left the area rather than agree to eleven hours. The employers then negotiated with the unions, and the ten-hour day, plus cash payment of wages, were secured for the Menominee River Valley. Schilling personally participated in the final negotiations at Marinette. According to the Wisconsin Bureau of Labor Statistics, 90 other Wisconsin sawmills throughout the state adopted the ten-hour day, but another 120 mills retained the long hours.[10]

A third strike wave hit the lumber mills of Ashland and Washburn in 1890, when 1,400 men went on strike under the leadership of the North Wisconsin Millmen's Union, an affiliate of the American Federation of Labor. The strike leader was William O'Keefe, an AFL organizer who was also the publisher of the Ashland *Daily News*. The settlement that ended the strike established a workday of ten and a half hours.

In 1892, strikes broke out among mills on the Wisconsin River. They began on July 25 at the Gilkey–Anson Company sawmill at Merrill, where twenty-four men asked for a raise from $1.60 per day to $1.75. The request was granted to nineteen of the men, who nevertheless struck on behalf of the other five workers. Two days later a thousand men were out on strike against seven of the town's eight mills.[11] Robert Schilling arrived and negotiated the strikers' demands. The final settlement granted the ten-hour day and pay on a weekly basis.[12]

Following the Merrill settlement, strikes for reduction of hours broke out at Stevens Point, Wausau, and Schofield. At the end of August, six mills at Rhinelander struck and received the ten-hour day. By the end of September, mills in every town on the Wisconsin River, with the exception of Tomahawk, had succeeded in establishing the ten-hour workday. William O'Keefe, who had led the Ashland strikes, also led the Rhinelander strikes.[13]

Not all lumber strikes were successful. In late April, 1892, a strike began in La Crosse when the John Paul Lumber Company discharged three union leaders. In 1873 La Crosse had been the site of the first recorded lumber strike for the ten-hour day. That action had been unsuccessful; the union leaders were blacklisted and replaced. By 1892, however, La Crosse mills were operating at ten hours, and it was union leaders' dismissal that incited the strike. Mr. Collins of the "grand labor council" negotiated for the union in an effort to gain reinstatement for the three men,[14] but the union soon gave in to company pressure. The first left town; the second left the union. When the third agreed that he would not neglect his work to circulate and talk to the men about the union, John Paul consented to take him back. The union nevertheless persisted in its demand that no man could be discharged without good cause, and on May 1 asked for a wage increase. The employers, all members of the Lumbermen's Exchange, stood together. Two thousand men were out for almost two weeks, but then went back to work under the previous conditions. The Knights of Labor was active in the La Crosse action. Terence Powderly, national Grand Master of the Knights, was expected to appear in support of the workers, but the strike collapsed before he could reach the city.[15]

Except for the northwest section of the state, Wisconsin lumber workers had won the ten-hour day by 1892. Labor's next struggle would be for the nine-hour day, generally, and in the building trades for the eight-hour day. At Marinette, where workers first had won the ten-hour day, they struggled for the eight-hour day in 1892, but were unsuccessful.

The sawmill strikes in general had a great impact on shortening the working day, but they had less effect on other grievances, such as the complaints against pay in scrip, the company store, and the withholding of pay until the end of the season. A list of cities and towns with the dates of their strikes shows the widespread character of the workers' protest against long hours in the sawmills: La Crosse, 1873; Eau Claire, 1881; Marinette, 1885; Porterville, 1886; Ashland, 1890; La Crosse, 1892; Wisconsin River, 1892; Merrill, 1892; Stevens Point, 1892; Wausau, 1892; Schofield, 1892; Flanner, 1892; Manawa, 1892; Rhinelander, 1892; Eagle River, 1892; Woodboro, 1892; Eau Claire, 1892; Marinette, 1892; Chippewa Falls, 1898; Rice Lake, 1899; Marinette, 1899; Sheboygan, 1899–1900; Marinette, 1903 and 1904.

The Oshkosh "Conspiracy"

With 40,000 inhabitants in 1898, Oshkosh was the state's second largest city, although it was far smaller than Milwaukee. Its industry was almost wholly dependent on wood. It was the first city to exploit in a major way the state's rich resource of white pine. As the pines along the the Wolf River disappeared into the city's sawmills, the millowners converted to products requiring more skill, especially sashes and doors, making Oshkosh the world capital of the sash and door industry in the 1890's.

A strike of considerable proportions took place in the late spring and summer of 1898 among the city's 2,000 woodworkers. Between 1,300 and 1,600 members of the Amalgamated Woodworkers struck for fourteen weeks, and a historic conspiracy trial ensued.[16]

Before looking at the conduct of this strike, it is important to note significant differences between the Oshkosh woodworkers' walkout and the earlier sawmill strikes. The ten-hour-day strikes had been almost spontaneous affairs. The Oshkosh strike was planned carefully by the Amalgamated Woodworkers union which formally affiliated with a local central council and with the national AFL union. The union's general secretary,

Thomas Kidd of Chicago, assumed general direction of the strike. The chief organizer of the Wisconsin State Federation of Labor, Frank J. Weber, assisted the Woodworkers both before and during the strike. Even the national AFL president, Samuel Gompers, came to Oshkosh during the strike to bolster striker morale. In contrast to Eau Claire, Marinette, and the Wisconsin River cities, where labor had no central organizing bodies and no mature unions, Oshkosh had had a central council of unions since 1892. The city, in fact, hosted the State Federation of Labor convention in 1894. It was second not only in population, but also in unionization, according to Weber, in a May visit to Oshkosh, just prior to the strike.

The Oshkosh labor movement earlier had produced a sophisticated paper, the *Labor Advocate,* edited during 1893 and 1894 by Dr. Hiram Franklin Hixson, who held a Ph.D. in psychology from Ashland College in Ohio, and had done further work at Johns Hopkins University, where he studied under the distinguished psychologist G. Stanley Hall.[17] Hixson had then turned his talents to assisting the trade union movement as an editor, organizer, and political campaigner. He was president of Oshkosh's Federal Labor Union, and his interest in the Woodworkers was important for their organizing activities. While campaigning for the People's Party in the fall of 1894 (the campaign is described in Chapter 1), he contracted typhoid fever after addressing a rally in West Superior, Wisconsin. He left the train to enter the hospital at Chippewa Falls, and died there a few days later. His body was sent to Oshkosh, where trade unionists and other citizens turned out in large numbers to pay their respects. It was then sent to his birthplace in Kansas for burial.[18] The executive board of the Wisconsin State Federation, of which Hixson was a member, passed a resolution of condolence at his death.

The 1898 Oshkosh strike was motivated by desperation on the part of the workers and marked by good management on the part of the strike leadership, under the direction of Thomas Kidd. The basic grievances were wages and job security. Repeated wage cuts had been made during the depression which had begun in 1893. Workers had to endure the cuts because of high unemployment, but when building construction revived in 1898, they were determined to redress their condition.

The union demands were set forth in a letter addressed to the city's seven woodworking companies: Paine Lumber Company; R. McMillen and Company; Radford Bros. and Company; Williamson, Libby Company; Foster Hafner Mills; the Morgan Company; and Gould Manufacturing Company. Because of the flavor of the times that it offers, the letter is quoted here in full:[19]

Office of Woodworkers' Council,
No. 20 Main Street,
Oshkosh, Wis., May 12th, 1898.

Gentlemen:—Prior to the recent panic the wages of your employees were not any too high, but since the advent of the panic there have been repeated reductions so that we are now receiving compensation that makes it practically impossible for us to make ends meet. We did not attribute the small wages to any willful desire on your part to take unfair advantage of the employees, but believed it to be entirely due to the ruinous competition that prevailed throughout the country. Knowing, however, that times have improved of late we trust you will see your way to accede to the propositions which we herewith submit.

The Woodworkers' Council of Oshkosh, which represents the employees of your establishment, asks for:—

1. A general advance in wages of 25 per cent and in such cases where the advance will not make the lowest wage $1.50 per day, then we ask that the wage be raised accordingly, so that all over 18 years of age will receive, at least, $1.50 per day.

2. Believing that a woodworking factory is no place for the employment of either women or girls we respectfully ask that female labor be abolished.

3. We think that it would tend to promote harmony and the interests of your firm, as well as our own, to have our union recognized so that hereafter only members in good standing shall be employed by your firm and we ask that you concede this point.

4. We further request that wages be paid weekly, and no more than three days' wages to be retained on pay day.

We ask for an answer to the above four propositions by Saturday night at 6 o'clock. The undersigned will be at Trades Council Hall, 20 Main St., at the above time to receive such reply as you think wise to send in answer to these requests.

Very respectfully yours,
Oshkosh Woodworkers' Council,
Representing Unions 29, 49, 57 and 63.
per M. H. Kimball, Sec.

The demand that women be prohibited from working was due to the past five years' experiences, when men who were heads of households had been replaced by women and girls at much lower wages. The demand for weekly pay was in accordance with state law, in contrast to the employers' practice of paying only once a month. Recognition of the union was, of course, essential to maintaining any semblance of collective bargaining.

The seven employers, at the request of the State Board of Arbitration, submitted typical payrolls showing the number of men, boys, and girls at each pay level for a ten-hour day. The payroll for the Paine Lumber Company, dated May 14, 1898, showed that most of the men earned between $1.00 and $1.25, the boys around 70 cents, and the girls about 50 cents, for a ten-hour day.[20] The large proportion of boys and girls under eighteen—185 were employed at Paine, as compared to 539 men—and their low wages indicate the seriousness of their threat to adult jobholders. Moreover, the union attorneys, during the subsequent conspiracy trial insisted that the Paine payroll presented to the State Arbitration Board was false, substantially overstating wages.

During the early weeks of the strike, worker morale was high. Picketing at the seven plants was vigorous but nonviolent. The employers tried but failed to persuade a judge to issue an injunction against the strike. On June 1, 1898, the AFL president, Samuel Gompers, spoke in Oshkosh. He promised the strikers the backing of the AFL and threatened the employers with a national boycott of Oshkosh sashes and doors. Yet neither Gompers' appearance nor the efforts of the State Board of Arbitration could alter the employers' refusal to negotiate.

As the strike dragged on, the union stepped up its efforts to completely shut down the mills. Using to their advantage the reluctance of the police to confront them, women took their husbands' places at the front of the picket line, loading their aprons with eggs or stones and carrying long clubs in their hands. Urged on by cheers from the men, they boldly chased would-be scabs from the mill entrances.

Oshkosh was a city divided. The south side of the river was the working-class district where the strikers—Poles, Bohemians, and Germans—lived in ethnic neighborhoods. The mills, with acre upon acre of stacked lumber, lined both sides of the river. North of the river lay the business sections, the employers' homes, the professional and business classes, and many of the skilled Anglo–Saxon workers.

On the evening of June 23, strikers gathered outside the high fence of the McMillen plant and pelted the scabs, police, and deputies with eggs, stones, clubs, and assorted missiles. Someone inside the fence turned a firehose on the strikers. Angered, they charged the gate and broke through. One of the first through the gate was James Morris, a 16-year-old worker at the Paine plant. The man who had used the hose picked up a large oak club and struck Morris a fatal blow on the head. The coroner's verdict was skull fracture. The union gave him a martyr's funeral during which 1,300 strikers formed the procession to the cemetery.

The police were evidently in sympathy with the strikers and would not intervene against the crowds. The sheriff asked the governor to send in the

National Guard. Four hundred soldiers, two Gatling guns, and forty-three cavalrymen were ordered in immediately. Under the command of an Oshkosh insurance company executive, the Guard had orders to shoot to kill. The south side was occupied territory, while the Gatling guns guarded plant entrances.

The McMillen Company, on whose property the youth had been killed, settled with the strikers, granting a 15-cent-per-hour raise and barring women, but not recognizing the union. The other employers stood firm. After restoring order, the National Guard left. A month of quiet followed, but on August 3 two of the biggest firms, Paine and Morgan, reopened. Mass picketing resumed. The women's squadrons reappeared and threw eggs, salt, and rocks. The police, no longer tolerant of the women's activities, jailed nine of them. The union had long since run out of strike funds. On August 14, a thousand union members attended a meeting and voted to continue the strike, but this was only a gesture. Six days later, the fourteen-week strike was called off. The settlement terms were largely a defeat for the union: no written contract, no recognition of the union, a wage increase within a few weeks, no winter layoff, returning workers would not be penalized for union membership. Women and children were not mentioned. Despite the settlement, union leaders were blacklisted.

The Conspiracy Trial

Even before the strike ended, the district attorney had charged three union leaders with conspiracy to injure the Paine Lumber Company, based on the complaint of George Paine, president. The three defendants were Thomas Kidd, general secretary of the Amalgamated Woodworkers and the strike leader, and George Zentner and Michael Troiber, two Paine employees who were union picket captains.

Labeling a strike for improved wages and working conditions a "conspiracy" was a tactic American management used to obtain court sanction for breaking up unions by imprisoning their leaders. The Philadelphia Bootmakers Union, which in 1803 conducted one of the earliest recorded strikes in America, was destroyed by a conspiracy verdict. In an equally famous case in Chicago in 1894, Eugene Debs and other officers of the American Railway Union were tried for conspiracy to violate the newly passed Sherman Anti-Trust Act. In the Debs case, a brilliant young railroad attorney turned labor lawyer, Clarence Darrow, won a surprising acquittal of this charge for his client, although Debs still served six months in prison for contempt of court. Four years later, in the Oshkosh conspiracy trial, Darrow accepted the role of chief attorney for the union.

His defense of the Oshkosh union leaders was similar to his defense in
the Debs trial and, later, his defense of the leadership of the Western Federation of Miners. Darrow's summary argument in the Oshkosh trial, ex-
cerpted below, lasted seven and a half hours and was delivered without
notes. He defended the strikers' right to urge fellow workers to join
them:[21]

> I take it that in a free country, in a country where George M. Paine
> does not rule supreme, every person has a right to lay down the tools
> of his trade if he shall choose. Not only that, but in a free country
> where liberty of speech is guaranteed, every man has a right to go to
> his fellow man and say, "We are out on strike. We are in a great battle
> for liberty. We are waging war for our fellow men. For God's sake,
> come with us and help." Has it come to that point in America, under
> the guarantee of the freedom of speech and under the Constitution,
> that a free man cannot go to his neighbor and implore him not to
> work? If a jury or a court should write a verdict like that, it would be
> the death knell to human liberty.

He accused Paine of attempting to crush the unions by dealing individually with workers:[22]

> Now, gentlemen, I want to say a few words in relation to the labor
> question, which is really the controversy involved in this case. . . .
> Back of all this prosecution is the effort on the part of George M.
> Paine to wipe these labor organizations out of existence, and you
> know it. That's all there is of it. . . . George M. Paine says, "I will
> not meet your union; I will not meet your committee. If one of you
> have anything to say, come to me alone and talk." And they did go
> alone, and what did they get? Gentlemen, what did they get?

And he addressed the issue of child labor:[23]

> I do not care whether the little children went into the factory the day
> before they were fourteen or the day after. It is a disgrace to the civili-
> zation in which we live that they were there at all. These children,
> without a day's schooling, not for a few hours in the day, but bound
> to rise before light during more than six months in the year, bound to
> go home after dark during more than six months in the year, while
> their tender flesh and bones should be forming freely to make citizens
> worthy of a great land. These children, instead of having the sunshine
> and the light and the play that children ought to have, instead of en-
> joying the benefits of the common schools of this republic, are set to
> work in this mill for ten hours of every day.

In his final words to the jury, he urged them to "render a verdict in this
case which will be a milestone in the history of the world, and an inspiration and hope to the dumb, despairing millions whose fate is in your
hands."[24] The jury stayed out fifty-five minutes and brought back a verdict of not guilty.

Enduring Effects

The impact of the Oshkosh Woodworkers' strike was long-lasting. Despite the strong efforts of the workers, the skilled leadership of Kidd, and the appearance of both Gompers of the AFL and Frank Weber of the State Federation of Labor, the employers prevailed. The lesson apparently was that unions were too weak to protect their workers. A year later the Woodworkers threatened a strike but could not obtain sufficient support. The union rapidly disintegrated and did not reappear for twenty years. The labor shortages and inflation of World War I temporarily revived the organization, but Paine management defeated a strike in 1920 and blacklisted union leaders once again. The fear of labor organization at Paine carried through the great period of union growth in the 1930's and 1940's. Not until 1956 did a labor organization, the Carpenters and Joiners Union, gain recognition at Paine's Oskosh plant, and it did so by a slim margin of 7 votes out of 400 in a National Labor Relations Board election.

Woodworkers in other Wisconsin cities were equally dissatisfied with low wages and bad working conditions. Lacking the large firms that characterized Oshkosh, their strikes were shorter and did not attract the state and national attention of the Oshkosh strike and conspiracy trial. Menasha, an early woodworking center, experienced strikes in 1885, 1896, 1897, and 1899, and a temporary shutdown in 1904. The 1885 strike led to the formation of Knights of Labor assemblies during one of Robert Schilling's trips to the Fox River Valley, but the assemblies did not survive. The Amalgamated Woodworkers Union conducted the strikes of the 1890's.[25]

The city of Two Rivers was another woodworking center. On May 21, 1900, workers at the Hamilton Manufacturing Company struck, demanding a union shop for Amalgamated Woodworkers, Local 95. On the same day, employees of the Frank Eggers Veneering Company walked out in sympathy with the Hamilton strikers. The State Board of Arbitration attempted to arrange a meeting between the two managements and the union, but management refused.[26]

During these years of labor discontent in the lumber industry, the eight-hour-day movement had continued in Milwaukee. Events involving the unions in that city and also in Beloit constitute the next episode in Wisconsin labor history.

CHAPTER 3

Injunction and Open Shop: Milwaukee and Beloit, 1901–1906

A S WE HAVE SEEN, the great eight-hour-day strikes in Milwaukee in May of 1886 were part of a national eight-hour-day movement initiated by the Federation of Organized Trades and Labor Unions. In December, 1886, this organization became the American Federation of Labor (AFL). Despite the failure of the 1886 strikes in Milwaukee, Chicago, and elsewhere, the AFL was encouraged by the enormous worker support given them and therefore continued to urge selected unions to bargain and strike for the eight-hour day. In November, 1889, the Milwaukee Carpenters District Council, made up of Locals 30, 228, 290, and 318, took the lead by setting May, 1890, as the date for initiating an eight-hour workday for carpenters. The Milwaukee Federated Trades Council, which had been organized in February, 1887, as the AFL successor to the then-defunct Milwaukee Central Labor Union, began new agitation among its craft union members. On April 17, 1890, the city's Common Council, primarily due to pressure by FTC unions, passed an ordinance restricting municipal workers to eight hours. Samuel Gompers, president of the AFL, visited Milwaukee to stir up enthusiasm.

By May 2, 1890, most small contractors of carpenter labor had conceded the eight-hour day without a strike. Wages rose from 17.5 to 22.5 cents per hour, and the carpenters gained a thousand new members. Other building trades experienced similar results.[1] The manufacturing plants of the city continued, however, to work ten- and twelve-hour days. The long depression that marked the years 1893 to 1898 blocked further union moves for shorter hours. So severe was the depression that many unions disintegrated. One was the Machinists Lodge 66, which disbanded in 1894 and was not reorganized until 1897.

The Milwaukee Machinists' Strike

In 1897 the AFL decided to renew its nationwide drive for shorter hours. This time the International Association of Machinists was selected

26

to lead the movement. In realistic fashion, the Machinists set as their first goal the nine-hour day, since a direct reduction from ten to eight hours was unlikely. In self-defense, the employers formed the National Metal Trades Association and entered into negotiations with the Machinists over reduction of hours. In 1900 they reached what was known as the Murray Hill Agreement, which provided for the nine-hour day to begin on May 20, 1901, in those factories across the country which were members of the National Metal Trades Association and which were represented by the Machinists.

The Murray Hill Agreement appeared to be a milestone in peaceful labor–management relations. But as the agreed date for introducing the nine-hour day approached, local unions like Lodge 66 of Milwaukee found that the employers intended to cut weekly pay commensurate with the 10 per cent reduction in hours. The International Association of Machinists considered this a repudiation of the agreement and ordered a nationwide strike. In Milwaukee the members of the three lodges, 66, 300, and 301, all heeded the strike call. The minutes of Lodge 66 for the meeting of May 20, 1901, reported that all Machinists had walked off the job at Filer and Stowell; Kempsmiths; Pawling and Harnischfeger; Browning, Pfeiffer and Smith; and Milwaukee Harvester. Almost all workers, 99 per cent, were out at Lutter and Giess; 90 per cent were out at E. P. Allis and at Milwaukee Electric; 75 per cent were out at Nordberg Manufacturing Company and at Kearney and Trecker.[2] In the suburb of Cudahy, ninety out of 101 machinists walked out at the Bucyrus Steam Shovel and Dredge Company.[3]

On a national basis, the strike effort was a long one. The resistance of employers in Milwaukee and elsewhere was strengthened by the leadership of the National Metal Trades Association, which made no concessions. The International Association of Machinists spent $154,000 on strike benefits, but after seven months was forced to call off the strike.[4] Its struggle with the national employers' association was to continue for another thirty years.

In Milwaukee the strike lasted only eight weeks and ended in defeat for the workers, largely because both there and in Cudahy the employers tried a strikebreaking tactic new to Wisconsin: the injunction. Because injunctions were court orders and because the workers had no experience either with them or with asserting their legal rights, they obeyed the orders without protest. (Later, as we shall see, they learned to resist.) The injunction was a restraining order, issued by a judge, forbidding workers and union officers from carrying out particular activities in connection with a strike.

For example, in Cudahy the injunction prohibited picketing. One of the injunctions issued in Milwaukee was even more restrictive. The language of the court concerning strike action at the Vilter Manufacturing Company was specific:[5]

> It is ordered, That until the further order of this court, the above named defendants and the International Association of Machinists, and each and every of its members, and subordinate lodges Nos. 66, 300 and 301 of the Grand Lodge of the International Association of Machinists, and each and every member of the said lodges or associations . . . be and they are hereby enjoined and restrained from congregating or being upon or about the sidewalks or streets or alleys or places adjoining or adjacent to the premises of said plaintiff hereinafter described, or upon or about said premises. . . .
>
> And from compelling anyone in the employ of or seeking employment from said plaintiff, to listen to any arguments of the said defendants or their coconspirators or pickets, or any of them, against his will.
>
> And from persuading or inducing, in any manner, any person to join in the organization or furtherance of any conspiracy to compel this plaintiff to give up or abate in any way, its control of its factory and business. . . . Dated Milwaukee, June 22, 1901. HUGH RYAN, *Court Commissioner, Milwaukee County, Wis.*

The Machinists' experience in 1901 demonstrated the stiffening attitude of employers in the face of workers' demands for better conditions. With the pickup in business activity that began around the turn of the century, following the end of the depression of 1893–1898, union growth mushroomed nationally. According to the U.S. Department of Labor's *Historical Statistics,* membership doubled between 1898 and 1903. But that growth was equaled by the development of employers' resistance toward labor, as illustrated by events in Beloit in 1903.

The Open Shop Drive in Beloit

In the spring of 1903 Beloit, with a population of 14,000, was proportionately perhaps the best union-organized city in the state. With the help of two organizers, George Mulberry, fifth vice-president of the International Association of Machinists, and Robert Hogan, organizer for the American Federation of Labor, union membership rose from 200 in three unions in June, 1901, to 2,000 members in twenty-one unions two years later.[6] Not only were the building trades and the industrial plants unionized, but such service trades as bartending, tailoring, and retailing were well organized. Union cards were displayed in store windows. Customers bought union goods from union clerks. In accordance with their Retail Clerks' Union contract, the leading grocery stores in the city closed at 6:00

P.M. and the leading meat markets closed at 6:30 P.M. The Retail Clerks had over a hundred members.[7]

The Iron Molders Union was especially strong. In 1902 the Molders successfully struck the Fairbanks–Morse Company to protest what they considered the unfair discharge of a molder. After three weeks the company reinstated the man and the strike was called off. In March, 1903, a Molders walkout at the N. B. Gaston Sons' Scale Works forced the firm to comply with the union's demand for a minimum of $3 a day, which was already in force at other plants.[8]

The banner union in Beloit however, was the International Association of Machinists, with 525 members in 1903. At its national convention in Milwaukee on May 6–9, 1903, the International voted full support, including strike benefits, to the demands that Beloit Machinists had put forth earlier at the Berlin Machine Works: a nine-hour day, a minimum of 26.5 cents per hour, and no more than one apprentice for every five machinists. The company ignored the demands, and on May 9 the union men went out at the Berlin Works, closing down operations.

Week after week the company made no concessions. On July 6, the State Board of Arbitration proposed a compromise. The minimum wage demand was to be cut to 25 cents; for every nine hours of work the company would pay the equivalent of nine and a half hours; and there would be no change in the number of apprentices. The company's president replied to the compromise proposal:[9]

> Please accept my thanks for your suggestion as I appreciate your efforts. We shall have to refuse to accept the proposition, however, as the time has gone by for treating with the unions. Their treatment with us during the strike does not warrant our wishing to be connected in any way with the union or to treat with them as a body. If we ever start again, it shall be on the line of individual contract and no other.

The strike was called off after sixteen weeks. The men returned on an individual basis, with no union contract.

What happened to the Machinists happened to all Beloit unions. Within a year the powerful Beloit union movement had been destroyed. Union cards were removed from all stores. Union labels were removed from both city newspapers. Union after union gave up its charter. The trade union paper, the Beloit *Labor Journal,* collapsed. Its editor, AFL organizer Robert Hogan, left town. Working hours of some establishments were lengthened to include Saturday afternoons. The word "union" was seldom heard.

What had happened? What was the source of the anti-union campaign? On June 16, 1903, the secretary of the Chicago Employers' Association had visited Beloit and organized an association of employers, whose chief purpose was the elimination of unions. Such associations nationally were making a crusade of the open-shop movement. Technically, the term "open shop" meant that the employer would hire workers regardless of whether they were or were not affiliated with a union. In practice, "open shops" usually discriminated against union members and adamantly refused to recognize unions.

The Beloit Employers' Association became part of the rapidly growing national open-shop movement which would dominate American labor relations until passage of the National Labor Relations Act in 1935. Commonly referred to as the "Wagner Act," it, made illegal most of the practices of open-shop employers. To increase its effectiveness in 1903, the Beloit Employers' Association converted the organization into one called the Citizens' Alliance. The new group accepted small employers and even persuaded non-union workers to join. Its membership soon reached a thousand. The devastating effect it exerted upon the union movement is demonstrated by the declining membership rolls of several typical unions in the city. The Chicago Employers' Association representative compared the membership figures when he wrote up the Beloit story:[10]

BELOIT UNION MEMBERSHIP, 1903 AND 1904

Spring of 1903		Winter of 1903–04
400	Federal Labor Union	0
525	Machinists	106
84	Clerks	0
99	Teamsters	0
90	Garment Workers	0
46	Painters and Decorators	0
51	Electrical Workers	11
46	Shoe Workers	0
1,341		117

Employers all over the country joined in the movement. It attracted not only employers but also members of the professions—clergymen, academic professors, and lawyers whose support lent respectability to an otherwise partisan activity. The president of Harvard University, Charles Eliot, praised the strikebreaker as an American hero, preserving individual liberty.[11] A Milwaukee attorney, Joseph V. Quarles, who as a federal judge was to play a strong role in the Milwaukee Molders' strike of 1906, wrote a widely distributed pamphlet extolling the open shop.

The union movement nationally, which had seen such rapid growth from 1898 through 1903, was stopped in its tracks by the employers' offensive. In Beloit the effects were especially long-lived. Several unions managed a rather feeble organization during World War I, but soon faded. Beloit remained an open-shop town until the great upsurge of unionism in the mid-1930's.

The Molders' Strike in Milwaukee

Milwaukee was again the setting for the next episode in Wisconsin labor–management relations. In 1906 the Iron Molders Union struck for shorter hours and a pay increase. The effort began in May, when 1,200 workers walked out. The strike, which lasted almost two years, ended in defeat for the Molders, who, in light of the tactics resorted to by the employers, never stood much chance of success. One employer alone, Allis–Chalmers, spent $21,700 for the services of the Burr–Herr detective agency. One agent, planted at Burr–Herr Detective Agency by the union, testified the agency offered him $10 per person to beat up strikers. The union's attorney, William B. Rubin, recorded over 200 assaults on union members. Indeed, Peter Cramer, a union leader, died of injuries sustained in such an attack. Of the many strikebreakers imported by the companies, fifty-three were brought to court for breaking various laws; fifty-one were convicted, thirty-six of them on charges of carrying concealed weapons.[12] In a 1906 issue of the *Iron Molders Journal,* the union wrote:[13]

> Six months have passed since our members in this district were forced to strike for the shorter workday and fair conditions. During this time our members have proved themselves true blue, and no doubt have convinced the foundrymen that they have the staying qualities which are characteristic of our members throughout the country.
>
> Flattering inducements have been held out, tempting offers have been made. Our members are arrested and hauled into court on the flimsiest of charges; injunctions galore have been granted, damage suits have been instituted, and we are now charged with the violation of two of the injunctions; a number of us have been cited to appear in court to show cause why we should not be punished for contempt.
>
> All this has failed to weaken our ranks, but, on the contrary, has made us more determined than ever to carry on the struggle until victory is won.

The injunctions referred to in the union statement were a major feature in the strike dispute. The employers sought and obtained court orders with broad prohibitions against, among other things, picketing or even peaceful efforts to persuade fellow workers to join the strike. One injunction prevented molders in other plants from refusing to make castings based on patterns sent out by the Allis–Chalmers Company, which was being struck.

This time the unionists reacted: they appealed two of the injunctions to higher courts. Ultimately they were successful, but the legal procedures consumed two years. The court's ruling, at the end of that time, permitted peaceful picketing and the peaceful persuasion of strikebreakers to join their forces. But the appeals' rulings came too late, for by that time the strike had been lost.

The Molders' strike of 1906, like the Milwaukee Machinists' strike of 1901, demonstrated a serious flaw in union structure: bargaining and strikes were conducted by narrow craft unions which generally enrolled only a portion of the work force. For example, the ninety machinists who struck the Bucyrus Company in 1901 constituted less than one-fourth of the total company work force. Throughout the strike, skilled laborers in unions such as the Molders and the Patternmakers continued to work, as did of course the unskilled workers who belonged to no union. During the Molders' strike in 1906, the Machinists continued to work. A business agent of the Machinists, John J. Handley, who later became secretary–treasurer of the Wisconsin State Federation of Labor, lamented the craft division among the metal trades unions:[14]

> A word of warning, boys, get under cover before the crash comes, for it's going to be one general movement of the metal trades. The molders are on strike for the nine-hour day while the machinists are working, through no fault of ours, as we did all in our power to affiliate all metal trades into a federation long before the molders' issue arose, and now the movement is being advocated by those who held it back at that time.
>
> The issue involved in the iron molders' strike is of the most far-reaching importance, not only to the trade concerned, but to the industrial and social wellbeing of the city and state. The reduction of the hours of daily labor has long been recognized as a just, logical and necessary step for the protection of labor against displacement by machinery and for the maintenance and advancement of the standard of living.

Pride of craft was one of the historic strengths of the trade unions affiliated with the AFL. It was craft loyalties that enabled the federation to survive and grow during the period when the Knights of Labor fell part. But as Handley pointed out, in 1906 craft unionism prevented workers in the same plant from presenting a united front to the employers.

Organization by craft frequently meant that an unskilled worker had no union to join. Milwaukee Lodge 66 of the Machinists excluded the unskilled by admitting only workers who made $2.25 or more per day. According to the lodge minutes, as far back as 1892 a prospective member was denied a union card because he failed to earn the required wage.[15]

The repressive tactics perfected by employers during the Molders' strike of 1906–1907 proved effective in blocking unionization for five years. It was 1910 before the membership of the Wisconsin State Federation of Labor exceeded that of 1905. But the federation did grow, and managed to put together a statewide labor movement. The development of the State Federation is the subject of our next chapter.

CHAPTER 4

A Statewide Labor Movement

AT THE TIME of the 1886 eight-hour-day struggle in Milwaukee, the Knights of Labor was a much larger organization than its rival, the Milwaukee Central Labor Union. The Union fell apart in 1887 and was replaced in the same year by a new city trade union organization, the Federated Trades Council chartered by the AFL. Both the Knights and the FTC lost membership between 1887 and 1890. Reviving prosperity, however, and a new eight-hour-day movement, instigated by the building trades unions that were affiliates of the new American Federation of Labor (AFL), dramatically reversed the numerical relationship of the two groups. By the early 1890's the Knights of Labor, not only in Milwaukee but across the nation, was in a severe decline.

Creation of the Wisconsin State Federation of Labor

In 1893 the aggressive leadership of the Federated Trades Council, affiliated with the AFL, moved to form a statewide labor movement, the Wisconsin State Federation of Labor (WSFL). The council sent invitations to all Wisconsin unions to attend its constitutional convention in Milwaukee on June 6–8, 1893. Considering the slim financial resources of most unions, the response was good. Thirty-seven delegates attended, composed of twenty-two from Milwaukee, nine from Oshkosh, two from Madison, and one each from Ashland, Marinette, Racine, and West Superior. Among the delegates were representatives from city central bodies at Ashland, Milwaukee, Madison, Oshkosh, and West Superior. The unions at the first convention probably represented between 10 and 15 per cent of all unions in the state and about two-thirds of the municipal labor councils.[1]

It is interesting to note which unions were represented at this first convention, since they indicate the state of the productive arts in 1893. They included the Brewery Teamsters No. 72, Brewery Workers No. 9, Carpenters and Joiners No. 290, Cigar Makers No. 168, Coal Heavers No. 5791, Coopers No. 30, Electrical Workers Federated Labor Union, Furniture Workers, Horseshoers No. 11, Iron Molders No. 125, Lumber Vessel Unloaders, Machine Wood Workers No. 29, Plasterers, Tanners and Curriers, Trunk Makers, and the Typographical Union (Local 10, German-speaking; Local 23, English-speaking). Six central bodies were represented — Ashland, Madison, Marinette, Milwaukee, Oshkosh, and West Superior. Brewers and Cigar Makers were the most numerous unions in the state in the early years of the State Federation. Building trades were also numerous, but in Milwaukee they had a separate council and elsewhere often were not affiliated directly with their city central or state labor bodies.

What did the founders of the new State Federation expect to accomplish? Examination of the newspaper and labor paper coverage of the annual conventions of the early years of the federation provides a firsthand look at its goals, its progress, and its internal conflicts. Clearly, the two major goals were: (1) to establish a political arm of the labor movement so that workers could achieve reforms through use of the ballot; and (2) to provide mutual assistance in strikes or boycotts, and especially in organizing new unions throughout the state.

The machinery which the new organization set up to accomplish these goals was sound, though pitifully lacking in financial resources. The federation had no full-time officer, for its income was limited to one cent per member per month. For the year beginning June 11, 1894, these dues yielded $303.47, representing an average monthly affiliated membership of 2,529 statewide, most of whom were from Milwaukee.[2] There are no accurate figures on total union membership, but it may well have been around 15,000, the overwhelming majority of whom were not affiliated with the WSFL at this time.

At the first convention in 1893, the federation's officers included a part-time president, paid $5.00 per day plus transportation expenses for all days spent on federation business; a vice-president; a secretary paid $100 per year; and three trustees. This arrangement lasted only one year, at the end of which the position of state organizer (equivalent of president) was created and the title of president was dropped. The state organizer was selected by, and responsible to, an enlarged executive board of five elected members. This constitutional change did not reflect any dissatisfaction with the performance of the first president, since the same man, Frank J. Weber, was elected and re-elected as organizer for twenty-three years, until he declined to serve in 1917. The purpose of this governing structure was to prevent any individual from achieving personal political power. The Milwaukee Federated Trades Council adopted a similar form of

headless organization in the same year. At each Council meeting, the first
order of business was the election of a chairman to serve for the duration
of that meeting only.

In both bodies this form of organization was the creation of the Socialist members. The Socialists believed that former labor leaders had used
their position to build personal political machines which then traded off
political endorsements of Republicans or Democrats in return for personal favors. This new type of organization was designed to curtail the
power of the head of the organization and give as much control as possible
to the rank-and-file members. The Federated Trades Council still reflects
this policy by having each meeting conducted by a chairman elected for
that meeting only.

The Socialists Capture the Federation

The first task which the WSFL set for itself was formidable: to make
effective use of the workers' ballot. Probably less than 5 per cent of the
non-agricultural workers of the state belonged to unions in 1893. As we
noted above, only a small proportion of the unionized workers sent delegates to the founding state convention. Its numerical weakness, however,
did not deter the convention from setting forth a bold program of long-
range goals.

A fundamental part of the new federation's approach was to urge labor
support of a radical third party. The 1893 platform declared: "Our greatest mistake in the past was that we supported parties whose interest is to
uphold an industrial system which produced an arrogant plutocracy and
impoverished the masses of people."[3] The platform proposed practical
programs of reform, such as eventual universal suffrage for men and
women; immediate suffrage for all members of unions; free public education, including free textbooks; and more effective laws prohibiting child
labor. The platform added three specific labor law reform demands: effective safety standards and health regulations in factories, on railroads, and
in tenement houses; the eight-hour day; and the rescinding of anti-boycott
laws. Some of the platform planks were socialistic in nature and included
government ownership of banks, railroads, telephone and telegraph lines,
and local utilities; and government control of land and mines. They
stopped short, however, of advocating government ownership of factories
and all modes of production, which made the platform closer to the program of the country's Populist party than to that of the various socialists'.

The most significant speech delivered at this first convention was that of
Victor L. Berger, editor of the German-language *Wisconsin Vorwaerts*.

The *Vorwaerts* was one of two official organs of the WSFL, the second one being the English-language paper, the Oshkosh *Labor Advocate*. Berger's speech was important because of his great influence in the Milwaukee German community, especially among the blue collar workers who constituted the leadership of the Milwaukee unions. The speech, delivered in German and lasting from 1:00 A.M. to almost 3:00 A.M., pointed the direction along which the many Socialists in the Milwaukee union movement hoped to travel:[4]

> It is our duty, . . . in any case to promote an enlightened strong working class, which, when the time comes, will be able to take over the reins of civilization. To keep them resistant, this is the task of the unions. . . . They have no other task today. They cannot hold up the coming of Socialism, nor even hasten its coming. They should, however, enlighten the working people about the heritage which awaits it. And therefore it is also their duty to take political action, to try to achieve concessions and reforms. These will not hinder Socialism; for they are only installments and one day we want everything. Everything.

At the federation's second convention, at Oshkosh, the platform went all the way toward endorsing Socialism by adopting a plank that read: "Collective ownership for the people of all means of production and distribution."[5] This plank was a copy of the one adopted by the American Federation of Labor during the one year, 1893, when Samuel Gompers was defeated for the presidency by John McBride, a Socialist.

The statement had no immediate practical consequences so far as Wisconsin political action was concerned, since there was as yet no Socialist party in the state. The 1894 WSFL convention continued its political support of the People's party, which as we have seen above was a blend of rural and urban reformers to the left of the Republicans and Democrats. The federation voted to send five delegates to the People's party convention, which attempted to unite dissatisfied farmers, small businessmen, and workers. The labor delegates "Socialized" the People's party platform, and in the state elections of November, 1894, the party received 10,000 votes in Milwaukee, its highest total anywhere. This alliance of trade union Socialists and Populists ended in 1896, when instead of running on a separate ticket, the Populists gave their support to the Democrat, William Jennings Bryan.

At every WSFL convention, delegates took up resolutions attacking the Republican and Democratic parties and urging labor support for socialism. It is not surprising that a non-Socialist opposition arose. In 1896 the Socialist resolutions were bitterly opposed by delegates from Racine and

Superior. The Racine *News,* the paper put out by striking printers at Racine, used the following argument against the WSFL's support for socialism:[6]

> It is not right to say that trades unions shall go into politics. When you do that you cut the throat of the organization. It is hard enough to convince the laboring man that it is to his own advancement and interest to join the union of his craft, and it would be almost impossible to persuade him that it is necessary for him to change his politics.

This argument was especially valid outside Milwaukee, where local union leaders had no possibility of selling socialism. Their political strategy was to try to obtain favors for labor from vote-seeking Democratic or Republican candidates. The Building Trades Council of Milwaukee also was a center of opposition to the Socialists. At the 1896 WSFL convention at Racine, Otto Fischer of the Building Trades Council said his organization had sent him to inquire on what constitutional grounds Victor Berger, the Milwaukee Socialist editor, had been given delegate credentials.[7] Hurt by this attack, Berger never again asked for delegate credentials as an editor; when he attended state or national AFL conventions he did so as a bona fide delegate from the German Typographia Union, Local 10. The numerical advantage of the socialists in 1896 was indicated by such votes as those advocating public ownership of all means of production, which the socialists carried by 24 to 11.[8]

In July, 1897, the Social Democratic party was formed nationally and in Wisconsin. From this point on, the issue of labor support for the Socialist candidates became a controversial issue at WSFL conventions. There was also in existence an older Socialist Labor party, but the WSFL's interest was in the Social Democratic party, known, simply, as the Socialist party.

The height of anti-Socialist activity in the WSFL occurred at the 1898 convention in La Crosse on June 14–16. The Socialists presented a resolution pledging "ourselves to support the only real and true party of the working people, the Social Democratic Party of America," and stating "that our organizers and officers be instructed to do all in their power to agitate for the principles of said party." After lengthy discussion this resolution was defeated, 16 to 8. On a motion from an Oshkosh Woodworkers delegate, the opposite view was adopted: "That party politics whether they be Democratic, Republican, Socialistic, Populistic, Prohibition, or any other, shall have no place in the conventions of the Wisconsin State Federation of Labor."[9]

At the 1898 convention there was one more curious resolution in the area of political action. Although the Socialists had been the leading advocates of forming political ties, Frank Weber, who was not only the head of the WSFL but also a Socialist, submitted the following resolution: "Whereas, the platform of the WSFL was endorsed by the People's Party in 1894; and, Whereas the trade unions do not believe in political actions as wage workers; therefore, be it Resolved, that the WSFL sever its connection with all political parties." The resolution was adopted.[10] Perhaps Weber wished to demonstrate agreement with the anti-Socialist views of the majority of delegates, or he may have wished to ensure that a non-Socialist party would not receive labor endorsement.

Two years later, at the 1900 convention in Sheboygan, the Socialists arrived with a majority of delegates. With Weber's support they decisively established close ties to socialism. Delegates from the Milwaukee Federated Trades Council won support for two resolutions. The first resolution called "upon the working people to sever their connection and refuse any support to the Republican and Democratic parties . . . and to vote for socialism." The second declared that the FTC "recommend to the officers thereof [the WSFL] and to all trade unionists of the state to educate themselves along the lines of international socialism."[11]

The conflict of socialists and anti-Socialists was mirrored in elections of WSFL officers. Frederick Brockhausen, a Socialist member of the Milwaukee Cigar Makers, Local 24, challenged the incumbent secretary–treasurer, Martin Jesko, a member of Racine Cigar Makers, Local 304. On the first ballot the vote was a tie, 28–28. On the second ballot Brockhausen won 31–27, the most closely contested election in the history of the State Federation.

The consequence of the Socialist resolutions and the Brockhausen victory at Sheboygan in 1900 was a disaffiliation movement led by the defeated Jesko. The departures from the federation were mostly by delegates outside of Milwaukee: nine locals from Oshkosh, six from Racine, one each from Madison, Marinette, Green Bay, and Sheboygan, plus the Trades and Labor Councils from Oshkosh, Racine, and Green Bay. Two Milwaukee locals also left. The Socialist victory was therefore costly in the short run. From 1898 to 1900, membership in the WSFL had risen from 1,625 to 5,000. In the next year there was a loss of 200 members: the loss of 1,000 non-Milwaukee members was not quite balanced by a gain of 740 in Milwaukee. This increased the percentage of Milwaukee membership in the WSFL from 53 per cent in 1900 to 69 per cent in 1901.[12]

Meanwhile, a similar battle was going on in the Milwaukee Federated Trades Council, but the Socialists also triumphed there in December of 1899. Socialist control of both the FTC and the WSFL remained unchallenged for the next thirty-five years. But the bruising struggle caused the Socialist leadership to moderate its ideological push and to place increased emphasis on organizing new unions, providing assistance for collective bargaining, and lobbying for protective legislation.

By 1903, membership in the State Federation had grown to about 6,800 persons, which was an improvement over the previous growth rate, but pale in comparision to the 1898–1900 increase. In 1903, Milwaukee still accounted for 69 per cent of the federation's membership. Progress nevertheless had been significant in La Crosse, Manitowoc, and Green Bay, although Green Bay's growth represented only a restoration of the number of members on the eve of the 1900 convention, and Manitowoc's increased membership probably was due to the convention's being held in that city in 1903. On the other hand, La Crosse, which had had only three unions affiliated in 1900 and four in 1901, had an impressive total of eighteen unions affiliated in 1903, as well as a newly organized Trades and Labor Council that replaced the previous Central Labor Union. Membership in Sheboygan had declined since the 1900 convention; in 1903 that city accounted for only 6 per cent of Federation membership. La Crosse made up 7 per cent of the membership, and no other city had over 3 per cent.

Craft membership in the federation still was dominated by the Brewery Workers, the Cigar Makers, and the Woodworkers, which collectively accounted for 54 per cent of membership in 1903. Cooper membership was on the decline after 1901, but membership of the printing trades rose steadily throughout this period of the turn of the century, reaching 8.4 per cent in 1903. As a general trend—broken only briefly in 1901—craft membership in the State Federation was becoming more diverse.[13]

Frank Weber: Labor's Grand Old Man

The most influential leader of the new Wisconsin State Federation of Labor was Frank Weber. As president of the Milwaukee Federated Trades Council he took the lead in getting the FTC to invite all Wisconsin unions to come to Milwaukee on June 5, 1893, for the purpose of founding the Wisconsin State Federation of Labor. At that time, forty-three-year-old Weber was already a veteran unionist. At eighteen he had become a sailor on the Great Lakes and within five years had risen to the post of captain; later he sailed around the world on clipper ships. Quitting the sea, he became a ship's carpenter in Milwaukee shipyards and joined the

Knights of Labor. He then moved to the Carpenters Union and was active in the eight-hour-day movement of 1886.

During his twenty-three years as state organizer (president) of the WSFL, he furnished inspiration and knowledge for workers who wanted to unionize. The advice and encouragement he gave to first-time unionists in such towns as Oshkosh in 1898, Marinette in 1916, and Nekoosa, in 1919 was invaluable. He was an inspirational speaker at strike rallies, in Labor Day ceremonies, and at annual conventions of the WSFL.

Fortunately, he was a consummate politician, holding together diverse factions within the labor movement. These groups included: (1) the Milwaukee building trades, which were frequently open enemies of the Socialists in the FTC and the WSFL; (2) the Socialist faction that was centered in Milwaukee, especially among the Brewery Workers, Cigar Makers, and skilled metal trades; and (3) the unions outside of Milwaukee, usually anti-Socialists, with the exceptions of Sheboygan and Manitowoc. The Socialists were Weber's solid supporters, but often did not constitute a majority of the WSFL. He found it necessary on occasion to avoid issues on which the unions were divided.

From 1900 to 1917, Weber held the principal post in both the WSFL and the FTC. With the rapid growth of the State Federation after 1914, he turned the leadership of that organization over to Henry J. Ohl, Jr., whom he and the Milwaukee Socialists had been preparing for leadership for several years. Weber continued to hold the post of organizer for the FTC until 1934, when he resigned at age eighty-four.

Weber was always a fighter for groups outside of the unions who were too weak to help themselves: children, the unemployed, and exploited women. He realized early the need for protective labor legislation, such as restriction of child labor and provision for workers' compensation. He served regularly as legislative representative for the WSFL and the Milwaukee FTC. From 1886 to the mid-1890's, he was a Populist, but turned to the socialists after becoming head of the State Federation. Running as a Socialist, he served twelve years in the Wisconsin State Assembly, where he introduced key labor and other progressive legislation ten years ahead of its time.

Victor Berger: A Leader Without Portfolio

Victor Berger, whom we have noted already as a leading Milwaukee Socialist and congressman, cannot be called strictly a labor leader, since he never held any formal office except as an executive board member of the FTC and was only a frequent delegate to the conventions of the American

Federation of Labor. In regard to his influence in the Wisconsin labor movement, however, Berger may be said to have been as important as any of the titular leaders. The characteristic which differentiated the Wisconsin State Federation from other state labor movements was its Socialist orientation. Berger deserves the major credit for selling socialism to the trade union leaders of the FTC and the WSFL. Unlike many other radical leaders, he fashioned a Socialist program which was both flexible and compatible with trade union needs.

His influence on unionism in the state was not merely indirect in building a successful Socialist party in Milwaukee. He also was an active participant in the labor movement. He was present at the founding convention of the WSFL in 1893, where he delivered a speech on socialism. His newspaper, *Wisconsin Vorwaerts,* was designated the official WSFL German-language newspaper, and the Milwaukee Federated Trades Council consistently contributed money to it. From 1894 through 1896, Berger, as editor of that paper, was given full delegate credentials at WSFL conventions. In 1894 he served on the Resolutions Committee, which brought in the resolution asking for "collective ownership . . . of all means of production and distribution" that was adopted and remained in the constitution for many years.

We have already described how, at the 1896 WSFL convention, the building trades led an open attack on Berger's delegate status, which he never again requested in his capacity as editor. He did not, however, end his effort to influence the direction of either the WSFL or the FTC. When delegate majorities in both the FTC and the WSFL fell into the hands of the anti-Socialists, Berger instituted Socialist caucus meetings to capture both bodies. As a result of caucuses held in the *Vorwaerts'* offices, Socialists gained control of the FTC in 1899 and of the WSFL in 1900.[14] Socialist votes came principally from the large Brewery Workers, Local 9, and the Cigar Makers.

With both of the state's major central bodies led by Socialists, Berger transferred his trade union activities to the AFL national conventions. As a delegate, he attended seven AFL conventions between 1898 and 1910, representing either the WSFL, the FTC, or the International Typographical Union (German Typographia, Local 10).[15] At these conventions he led attacks on the president, Samuel Gompers, because Gompers was not directing American workers toward Socialism. On occasions, Berger cast almost the only vote against Gompers. His vitriolic opposition must have been an embarrassment for Frank Weber. Alhough a Socialist, Weber was a friend of Gompers and had served under him as a special AFL organizer during the 1890's.

In protest against the Socialist domination of the FTC, some anti-Socialists set up another Milwaukee central labor body, the Central Trade and Labor Union, in 1902. Weber and the council successfully appealed to Gompers for assurance that the rival would not be recognized by the AFL and the anti-Socialist rebellion was defeated. As we have seen earlier, the Milwaukee Building Trades Council was a center of opposition to the Socialists. Since 1895 the unions of the building trades had affiliated not with the FTC but with the National Building Trades Council, which was not in the AFL. The FTC therefore established a rival building trades council. The rivalry, however, was not good for either body and in 1907 the building trades finally joined the FTC and received a charter from the Building Trades Department of the AFL.[16]

In the early years of the WSFL, Berger and Weber did not see eye to eye. At the conclusion of the first convention in 1893, Berger wrote an editorial in *Vorwaerts* in which he paternalistically evaluated the new president: "His name was too often associated with the names of a few crafty workers' politicians. In any case he is now rid of this bad company. He has unconditionally the ability, and now the opportunity to do much good, if he wants to. We will hope for the best and thus do our best to support him." The editor then instructed the president: "The local Trades Council should immediately alter its constitution according to the model of the State Federation. Here Frank J. Weber can readily show if he is up to the new task or not."[17] Berger meant that the Milwaukee FTC constitution should incorporate the public ownership planks of the WSFL.

In 1894, when the WSFL adopted the AFL's short-lived Socialist platform, Berger was jubilant. But as the Socialist opposition showed its power in the WSFL during the years 1896–1898, a breach, the exact cause of which is not clear, developed between Berger and Weber. The rift was healing, though, by the time of the 1899 WSFL convention, when Berger wrote in *Vorwaerts:* "I only want to mention that Chairman Weber behaved respectfully towards us this time."[18]

After 1900, Weber appears to have been a dedicated Socialist. When in that year the FTC voted to endorse the Socialist slate in the Milwaukee spring election, some members protested to the executive council of the AFL. Weber, as a national organizer for the AFL, ignored their appeal on the grounds it was improperly addressed. Despite this assistance and Weber's twelve years as a Socialist member of the State Assembly, Berger retained doubts concerning Weber's Socialist convictions because of his long friendship with Berger's archenemy, Samuel Gompers. Due primarily to Berger's efforts, the WSFL never lost an opportunity to castigate Gompers.[19] Weber attended the AFL convention in 1919 as a delegate from the WSFL, and in his report to the 1920 convention of the WSFL, he felt obliged to explain that he had not voted against the election of Gompers because, quite simply, Gompers had run unopposed.[20]

Berger, like Robert Schilling and Paul Grottkau, had been born in Europe in 1860, in the Austro–Hungarian city of Nieder–Rehback. His parents were of the middle class. He attended the *gymnasium* (high school) and the universities of Budapest and Vienna. When his parents suffered financial reverses, he emigrated with them to the United States. After trying various odd jobs, including cowpunching in the West and metal polishing in New York, he moved to Milwaukee in 1882. There he became a teacher of German, history, and geography in the public schools. It was while he was teaching that he became a Socialist.[21]

It is interesting to note that it was Berger who converted Eugene Debs, head of the Socialist Party of America and its presidential candidate from 1900 through 1924, to Socialism. Debs was a leader of the American Railway Union and headed its 1894 strike against the Pullman Car Palace Company, for which he was sent to jail. Berger visited Debs in his jail cell, and as a result of their discussions, Debs became a Socialist. In the years ahead, however, Debs was unsuccessful in gaining Berger's support for the radical national union, the Industrial Workers of the World (IWW), which Debs had helped to found in 1905. Instead of joining his fellow Socialist in support of this new labor organization which, its founders hoped, would replace the more conservative AFL, Berger not only did not attend the secret founding convention himself, but also convinced the Socialist leaders of the Milwaukee FTC to refuse to send a delegate. He opposed the IWW because he saw it as a threat to the Socialist party and to the Socialist-controlled Wisconsin labor movement. Within two years Debs came to agree with Berger's assessment and left the IWW.

The strong opposition to the IWW, which Berger aroused in the Milwaukee Socialists who were entrenched in the FTC and the WSFL, blocked IWW efforts to organize Milwaukee workers and to capture Wisconsin's labor leadership.[22] The Socialist leaders of the WSFL warned all local central bodies not to cooperate with the IWW. At a meeting of the Superior Trades and Labor Assembly in January, 1911, one member, Louis Olson, appeared wearing an IWW button. A motion was made and seconded that he discard the button if he wished to retain his seat. The motion was defeated. Evidently, Olson had some explanation, other than support for the IWW, for wearing his button. The Assembly minutes do not state what it was, but do record that his explanation was accepted.[23]

An examination of the Chicago *IWW Lumber Workers Bulletin* indicates that although from 1918 through 1920 there were numerous reports from IWW organizers about their activities in Wisconsin, particularly in the lumber camps, there were no reports of organizing successes. On the contrary, the organizers reported most frequently that the lumber workers knew nothing of the IWW, were indifferent to unionism, and were afraid of their bosses.[24]

How did the three immigrants—Schilling, Grottkau, and Berger—achieve leadership positions in Milwaukee so soon after their arrival? One answer is that they came from the right country. In 1900 over half of Milwaukee's population of 285,000 had been born in Germany or was of German parentage. German newspapers had a substantially larger circulation than English ones.[25] Up until World War I, many children attended German-language schools. Of the German social, political, and cultural organizations that flourished in Milwaukee, the most important to Berger were the fraternal Turnverein and the Socialist political organizations. A Turnverein could be found in every German community in the United States. Besides emphasizing gymnastics, the Turnvereins offered a variety of German social, cultural, and intellectual activities.

When the Socialist party captured the principal posts in the Milwaukee city government in 1910, Berger's trade union followers were finally rewarded with important city administrative jobs. Henry Ohl, member of Typographical Union, Local 23, and future president of the WSFL, was given an important post in the City Health Commission. John J. Handley of Machinists, Local 66, and future secretary–treasurer of the WSFL, took a post in the Department of Public Works. James Sheehan, president of the FTC, was elected chairman of the County Board by its Socialist majority.[26] These men were to play a considerable role in the growth and development of the Wisconsin labor movement in the years to follow. That story constitutes the subject of Part II of this volume.

PART II

Unionism Matures

CHAPTER 5

Growth of the Wisconsin Labor Movement in the Twentieth Century

THE PATH of growth followed by the Wisconsin State Federation of Labor (WSFL) was tortuous. From 1898 to 1905, the organization more than quadrupled in size, swelling from 2,000 to 9,100. Then, experiencing the effects of the employers' open-shop offensive, by turns it stagnated or declined until 1912, when it began rising once again. A substantial increase in membership, from 11,200 in 1912 to 16,500 in 1915, resulted not so much from the formation of new unions or the expansion of existing unions as from an aggressive drive by the WSFL to convince unaffiliated unions to join the State Federation. In Wisconsin as in the rest of the nation, only the industrial boom of World War I gave new hope to the labor movement. From 1915 to 1920, average annual membership in the WSFL more than doubled, reaching almost 37,000 in the latter year, which marked the peak of growth until the 1930's.[1] Figure 2 (page 63) shows in graphic form the ups and downs of union membership.

The State Federation membership that is shown in Figure 2 did not include the entire Wisconsin labor movement. In January, 1920, the officers of the WSFL estimated that the total union membership in the state was 62,000, a figure 25,000 higher than the average WSFL membership of 37,000 for that year.[2] Who were these non-affiliated unionists? Some were members of railroad unions. Known as the "operating brotherhoods," four separate unions of railway workers—Engineers, Firemen, Conductors, and Trainmen—were not then affiliated with the American Federation of Labor. Many other local unions, whose parent organizations were AFL affiliates, did not pay dues to the WSFL for financial reasons. For many years before the 1930's, for instance, most unions in the Wisconsin paper industry were struggling to stay alive and did not have the resources to afford WSFL membership. To some unions outside Milwaukee, the WSFL, which had only one or two full-time officers, seemed too remote to be worth the cost of joining. Early in the century, a few unions objected to the Socialism of the WSFL. Even within Milwaukee, the WSFL's head-

49

quarters, of sixty locals that in 1901 were affiliated with the city's Federated Trades Council, only thirty-three were members of the WSFL, and only twenty-nine paid per capita dues that year. Among the unions not affiliated with the WSFL were Iron Molders, Nos. 125 and 166; Electrical Workers, No. 83; Carpenters, Nos. 188 and 288; Painters, No. 159; Barbers, No. 50; Butchers, No. 64; Iron and Steel Workers, No. 3; and Journeyman Tailors, No. 86.[3] Four Machinist Lodges, Nos. 66, 300, 301, and 432 were not affiliated, but were in dire condition because they were on strike for the nine-hour day.

Craft Unionism Before World War I

It is interesting to note which unions, at various times, were largest in the WSFL and in the Milwaukee Federated Trades Council. Before the explosion of industrial unionism in the mid- and late 1930's, craft unions dominated the central bodies. In 1898 the five largest unions in the WSFL were the brewery workers, with 36 per cent of the affiliated membership; the Cigar Makers, with 19 per cent; the Coopers, with 11 per cent; the Woodworkers, with 8 per cent; and the printing trades, with 5 per cent. The brewery workers were themselves divided into various locals. In Milwaukee, for example, there was Local 89, Brewery Malsters; Local 72, Brewery Teamsters; Local 213, Brewery Bottlers; Local 25, Brewery Engineers and Firemen; and Local 9, Brewery Workers. The Coopers, who made the barrels for the breweries, were in the separate Coopers International Union.[4]

As the WSFL grew, the brewery workers remained the largest affiliated group of unions until 1919, when the manufacture of alcoholic beverages was prohibited, and would not be permitted again until 1933. And yet in 1930, eleven years after the manufacture of beer had ended, the brewery workers had fallen only to fifth place; first place was occupied by the Carpenters.

If we look at the leading unionized crafts affiliated within the Milwaukee Federated Trades Council, the combined brewery workers locals in the early 1900's were not only in first place but had double the membership of the union next in size, the Typographers. In 1906, third place was held by the Iron Molders; fourth by the Lake Seamen; and fifth by the Plumbers. By 1908 the Carpenters were second and the Iron Molders had been destroyed, their number three position taken by the Machinists. The Hod Carriers were fourth, the Glass Blowers, fifth. In 1907 the third largest union in Milwaukee was that of the Theatrical Employees.[5]

Why were the brewery workers the only ones to sustain themselves, even though recognition had to come from the big employers? An important reason is that it was a consumer industry. Moreover, in 1900 their product, beer, was sold almost exclusively to blue collar workers, and a boycott of a particular brand of beer could severely hurt company sales. By contrast, the products of the Allis–Chalmers Company—milling and mining machinery and electrical generators—were sold exclusively to other manufacturers. Having little to fear from a boycott, Allis–Chalmers and other metal fabricators could feel free to attempt to stifle the unions, principally the Molders and the Machinists, which vainly tried to secure recognition. Similarly, Wisconsin's paper manufacturers were not threatened by boycotts of their products and did not hesitate to squelch attempts to unionize, as we will see in Part III of this volume.

The brewery workers had an added advantage enjoyed by no other union. From 1910 on, the growing political power of the Prohibitionists forced the brewing industry employers to seek political assistance from the trade union movement. Recognition of brewery workers' unions was, of course, a prerequisite to mobilizing labor's votes against state and national prohibition.

This group of unions was especially important to the WSFL because it maintained without interruption its affiliation with the federation. The brewery workers' loyalty to the WSFL therefore gave it great influence. It was one of the strongly Socialist unions, primarily because the industry tended to hire workmen of German origin, and those from urban Germany often brought with them their socialistic ideas. The brewery workers had a German section which conducted its lodge meetings and wrote up its minutes in German. These unionists were the essential force in keeping Socialist leaders at the helm of the WSFL. When younger workers returning from World War II became active in the brewery union, the Socialist element evaporated.[6]

In its early years, then, unionism was primarily craft unionism—among printers, cigar makers, coopers, workers in the brewery trades and in the numerous building trades. These unions constituted the pioneers and pacesetters of the labor movement. In Chapter 3, for example, we saw that the four Milwaukee carpenters unions, composing the new Carpenters District Council, won the eight-hour day in 1890. Similarly, between 1898 and 1910, Kenosha Carpenters, Local 61, by tough bargaining doubled its hourly rates, cut the workday from nine hours to eight, and gained such fringe benefits as the right to sharpen their saws on the boss's time, time and a half wages for overtime, and double time on holidays. During this period the Kenosha Carpenters had only one serious confrontation with the contractors. In the depression year of 1908, employers joined together and locked out the union, forcing acceptance of a wage cut from 50 to 47.5 cents per hour.[7] Contractors in other trades and other cities occasionally joined forces and not only demanded wage cuts but ordered workers to quit the union.

Since building trades workers owned their own tools, their union members had a resource that could tide them over crises such as lockouts. The Plumbers and the Bricklayers even established producer co-operatives to support their members during strikes. The Milwaukee Bricklayers and Masons, Local 8, stated in its constitution that in the event of a strike the officers of the union became the managers of a construction company that could "figure on work, enter into contracts, and furnish bond for the completion of such work as they may obtain."[8] In 1891 that event occurred, and one of the union's activities was to repair and construct homes for members. The local's treasury even provided the mortgage money.[9]

The correspondence of Local 8 also reveals the way it handled a perpetual problem among building trades unions: contractors who hired non-union workers and paid less than the union wage scale. In May, 1902, the corresponding secretary wrote a letter to four members who were accepting wages and hours below the union scale: "You are hereby notified to demand 50 cents per hour and 8 hours per day or you must leave the union for working against the constitution. By order of Union, No. 8."[10] And in the same month the secretary, reporting to the national office, described the union's plan for penalizing a contractor who was employing non-union masons: "If the mayor and city attorney can't stop that contractor we will stop every public job until they come to their senses. . . . As the matter now stands he [the contractor] must pull down part of the work and we shall see that he will do so if he must pull down the whole basement."[11]

In 1885, the Milwaukee Journeymen Plumbers Union conducted a prolonged strike against their employers, the Master Plumbers' Association, which held together and refused the union's demands. The journeymen, with the help of the Plumbers International Union, whose headquarters were moved temporarily to Milwaukee, established four co-operative plumbing shops in different sections of the city. The master plumbers fought back by getting their national association, then meeting in St. Louis, to deny materials to the union's co-operatives. This boycott caused some cancellations of deliveries to the co-operatives but did not stop their operations, which continued successfully for several years. The private

Metal fabricating plant, c. 1885.

Sawmill and lath mill crews, Paine Lumber Company, Oshkosh, c. 1890.
Note the smattering of women and teenaged boys.

Newspaper headlines from the last quarter of the nine-teenth century are one gauge of the extent of labor organizing and protest.

EXTRA

Five O'clock Edition.

THEY SHOOT

The Militia Open Fire on the Mob at Bay View.

Troops Swarm Kinnickinnic Valley.

Military from the Interior of the State.

No Blank Cartridges, But Shots to Kill.

Kosciusko Guards Fire Several Volleys Yet Injure Nobody.

The Bay View Rolling Mills Forced to Shut Down.

FEARS THAT THE ST. PAUL SHOPS WILL BE DESTROYED.

preserve the peace in this emergency.
"GEORGE PASCHEN,
Sheriff of Milwaukee County."

The Governor's guards, of Madison, under Maj. Helms, and the Watertown guards, of Watertown, under Capt. Salliday, were telegraphed for late in the morning, to arrive on a special train. A Gatling gun was also ordered from Madison.

At 10:30 Mayor Wallber received a telephone message from Sheriff Paschen, who with a posse of deputies was in the Kinnickinnic valley, asking for reinforcements. Gov. Rusk held a hasty consultation with the sheriff, and at once issued orders to Maj. Traeumer and Capt. Schoeffel to move. Previous to issuing the order to march, Gov. Rusk, Maj. Traeumer, Col. King and Capt. Schoeffel had a conference in regard to taking charge of the arms in the various gunshops in the city. It was decided that Mayor Wallber should ask that the gunshops should be closed, and the police take possession of each shop and as speedily as possible remove all guns, pistols, knives and ammunition to the armory for safekeeping.

The militia was armed with muskets, fixed bayonets, and twenty rounds of ball cartridges. The cavalry carried twenty rounds for carbines and fifty rounds for revolvers, besides their sabers. No blank cartridges were furnished and orders were given that if orders to fire were made, that the soldiers should shoot to kill.

A few minutes before 11 o'clock the infantry formed into line in the armory and were ordered to load their guns. Capt. Coogan then stepped before them and giving the order, "Company, attention," proceeded to make them a short speech on their duties as men. In substance, he said: "Stand firm, don't get excited, and obey orders. When you are ordered to fire, pick out your man and shoot to kill. Don't show the white feather. The bugle call sounded, the ponderous doors of the armory swung open and the Sheridan guards headed by Maj. Traeumer, Adjt. Falk and Capt. Coogan marched forth, followed by the Lincoln guards, in command of Capt. Miller. The thousands of men lining the streets in front of the armory, reaching down to Mason street, received the troops with mingled cheers and jeers. Women in the

Milwaukee Daily Journal, May, 1886

Chicago Tribune, June, 1898

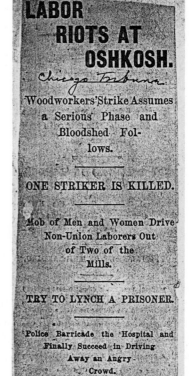

LABOR RIOTS AT OSHKOSH.

Chicago Tribune

Woodworkers' Strike Assumes a Serious Phase and Bloodshed Follows.

ONE STRIKER IS KILLED.

Mob of Men and Women Drive Non-Union Laborers Out of Two of the Mills.

TRY TO LYNCH A PRISONER.

Police Barricade the Hospital and Finally Succeed in Driving Away an Angry Crowd.

STATE TROOPS TO RESTORE ORDER

Oshkosh, Wis., June 28.—[Special.]—With one striker dead and a mob of infuriated men surrounding the hospital determined to lynch his slayer, with armed deputies by the hundred patrolling the streets, and with State troops hurrying to the scene from Milwaukee by special train, this has been

Wisconsin National Guardsmen drawn up in the yard of the E.P. Allis Reliance Works, Milwaukee, during the Eight Hour riots of May, 1886.

WHi(X3)6046

Interior of the Boone Tire Factory, Chippewa Falls, c. 1919.

Foundry workers at the Fairbanks-Morse plant, Beloit, c. 1925.

Paul Grottkau, editor of the Arbeiter Zeitung *and leader of the Central Labor Union, Milwaukee.*

Robert Schilling, editor of the Milwaukee Volksblatt *and leader of the Knights of Labor.*

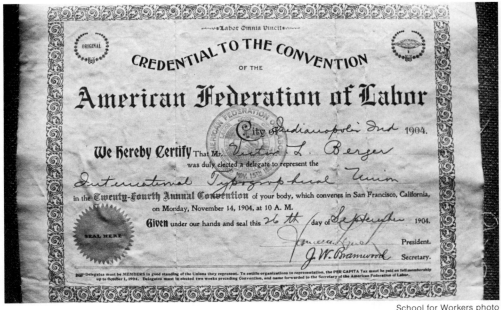

Victor L. Berger's credentials to the convention of the International Typographical Union, 1904.

United Brotherhood of Carpenters and Joiners of America, Local 1074, Eau Claire, c. 1910.

Union Labor Hall at the corner of Sixth and Juneau, Milwaukee, c. 1915, where the Federated Trades Council met.

Socialist legislators of Wisconsin, 1904–1906: Frederick Brockhausen, Frank J. Weber, Edmund J. Bernes, and Winfield R. Gaylord.

Labor Should be a Power in Congress

Outside on the Doorstep

The real man should not have to stand on the outside with his hat in his hand and humbly knock at the door.

❧ ❧ ❧

"We have too many lawyers in Congress now. It is time the voice of labor was heard. If I go to Congress there will be one man on the inside who will hear the knock of the man on the outside."— *William J. Cary, in an address to the union of Telegraph Operators.*

WHi(X3)30807

Cartoon and campaign statements from stationery of William J. Cary of Milwaukee, a telegrapher's union member elected to Congress in 1906.

Maud McCreery campaigning for woman suffrage in Brown County, 1912.

Frank J. Weber, principal founder and "grand old man" of the Wisconsin State Federation of Labor, c. 1923.

Homer Martin of the United Auto Workers addresses a UAW rally in Janesville, c. 1937.

Mayor Daniel Hoan of Milwaukee addresses a huge rally of workers during a strike against the Seaman Body Corporation and the Nash Motor Company, March, 1934.

employers finally agreed to employ only union members if the co-operative shops were sold. Dissension within the union's co-operatives had developed by that time anyway, since some members held office jobs while others were performing the manual labor. The plumbers therefore agreed to unite: they sold the co-operatives and in 1891 formed a new union, Journeymen Plumbers and Gasfitters, Local 75, the current Milwaukee local.[12]

Each craft union local was not only an organization to gain economic benefits, but a fraternal lodge which had its own social life. The Labor Temple with its friendly bar also provided daily socializing. Here, amid clouds of tobacco smoke, members played cards, thrashed out union problems, and discussed the politics of the community and nation. Upstairs there were one or more meeting halls, often rented out to fraternal lodges such as the Odd Fellows, or local ethnic societies, such as the Danish Brotherhood. The union's limited finances dictated that the Labor Temple be located in the poorer part of downtown; it was almost invariably an old building and was definitely not a place for family entertainment. It served strictly as a refuge for the male union member.

Ethnicity was an important bond which helped to unite workers. We already have mentioned the German section of the brewery workers and the Typographical Union. Local 8 of the Milwaukee Bricklayers also had both English and German sections. Figure 1 shows a page of minutes from the Bricklayers written in German script, along with a translation. The minutes tell of the union victory in the citywide eight-hour-day strike of May, 1886.

The craft union also offered a career opportunity for the male members of the family, since sons and nephews of journeymen often were favored for apprenticeship openings, much as doctors, lawyers, businessmen, and farmers helped their children become established in their parents' occupation. Take, for example, the Kings, a family of plumbers. Frank King of Milwaukee was appointed by Secretary of Commerce (later President) Herbert Hoover to a national commission of five members who drew up the first national standards for sewage treatment and water quality. Frank had three younger brothers, Tony, Peter, and Joe, who were all members of Local 75. Tony, in the mid-1930's, became the managing business agent for Plumbers and Gasfitters, Local 75, a position which he held until his death in 1966. Peter and Joe became plumbing contractors, and Peter for many years served as president of the state's Plumbing Construction Association. In the second generation of the King family, Tony's son Gordon followed his father into the plumbing trade and, like his father, later be-

FIGURE 1

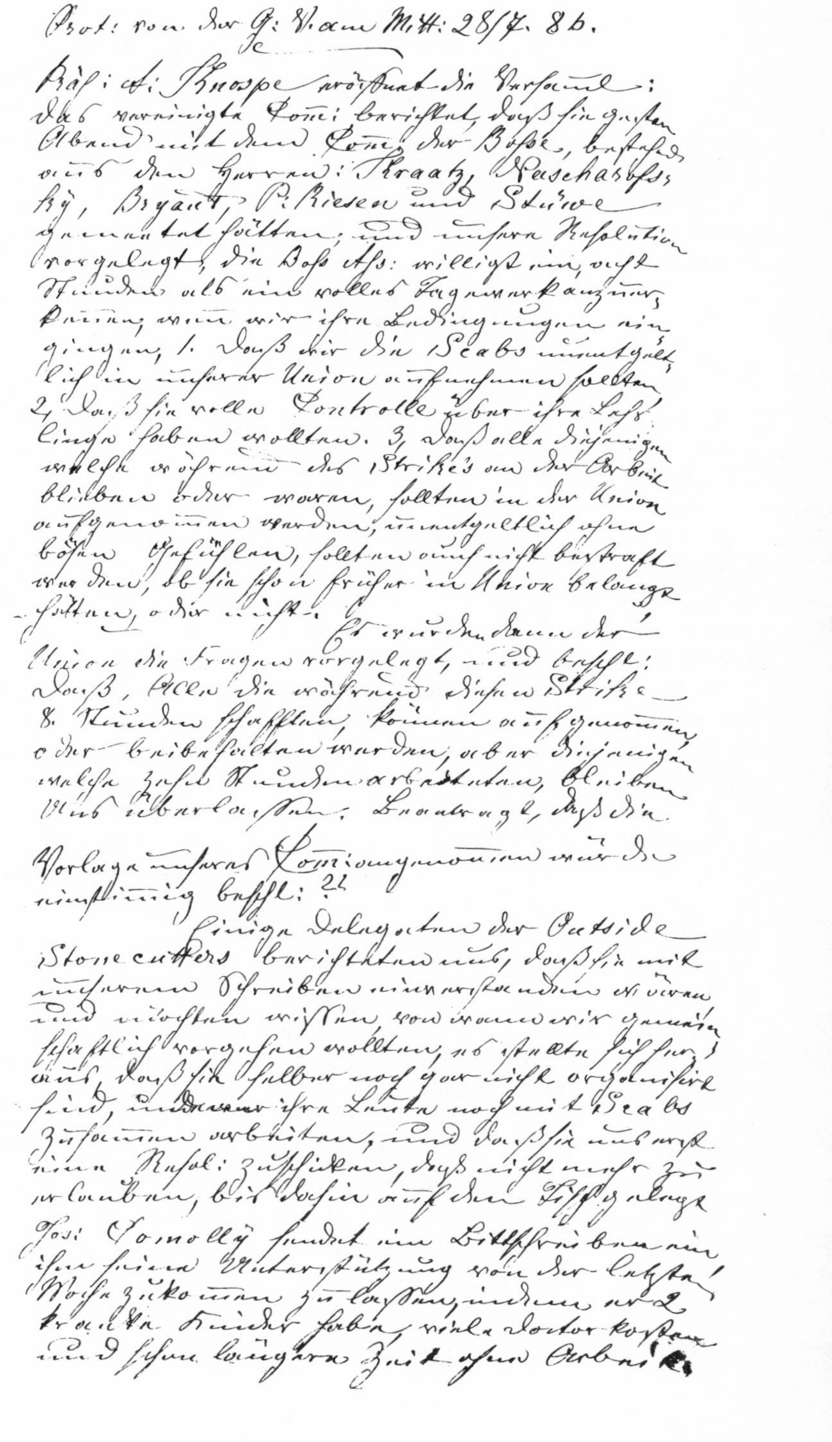

Prot: von der G: V. am Mitt: 28/7. 86.

Präs: A. Knospe eröffnet die Versamml: das vereinigte Comi: berichtet, daß sie gestern Abend mit dem Com. der Bosse, bestehend aus den Herren: Kraatz, Naschatofsky, Bryant, P. Riesen und Stuwe gemeetet hätten, und unsere Resolution vorgelegt, die Boss Ass: willigt ein, acht Stunden als einen vollen Tagewerk anzuerkennen, wenn wir ihre Bedingungen eingingen, 1. daß wir die Scabs unentgeltlich in unsere Union aufnehmen sollten 2, daß sie volle Controlle über ihre Lehrlinge haben wollten. 3, daß alle diejenigen welche während des Strike's an der Arbeit blieben oder waren, sollten in der Union aufgenommen werden, unentgeltlich ohne bösen Gefühlen, sollten auch nicht bestraft werden, ob sie schon früher in Union belonget hatten, oder nicht. Es wurden dann der Union die Fragen vorgelegt, und beschl: Daß, Alle die während dieses Strike 8. Stunden schafften, können aufgenommen oder beibehalten werden, aber diejenigen welche zehn Stunden arbeiteten, bleiben uns überlassen. Beantragt, daß die Vorlage unseres Comiteegenossen wurde einstimmig beschl: 22

Einige Delegaten der Outside Stonecutters berichteten uns, daß sie mit unserem Schreiben einverstanden wären und möchten wissen, wo wenn wir gemeinschaftlich vorgehen wollten, es stellte sich heraus, daß sie selber noch gar nicht organisirt sind, indem ihre Leute noch mit Scabs zusammen arbeiten, und daß sie uns nur eine Resol: zuschicken, daß nicht mehr zu erlauben, bis daher auf den Tisch gelegt

Jos: Connolly sendet ein Bittschreiben ein, ihm seine Unterstützung von der letzten Woche zukommen zu lassen, indem er 2 kranke Kinder habe, viele doctor kosten und schon längere Zeit ohne Arbeit

TRANSLATION: FIGURE 1

[Minutes of the general meeting on Wednesday, July 28, 1886,
Bricklayers, Local 8, Milwaukee]

President A. Knospe opens the meeting.

The consolidated committee reported that it met last night with the committee of the Bosses, consisting of Mssrs. Kraatz, Nasharofsky, Bryant, P. Riesen and Mr. Stuewe and our resolution was submitted: the delegates of the bosses agreed to recognize that eight hours work are a day's work, if we are willing to accept their conditions:

1. That we will admit the Scabs in our union without a fee.
2. That they will have complete control over their apprentices.
3. That the persons who continued working during the strike should be accepted by the Union without a fine or bad feelings. They should not be punished, regardless if they were Union members before or not.

The question was put to the Union and they decided that everyone who worked no more than eight hours during the strike could be admitted or remain in the union, but the ones who worked ten hours will be subject to our decision. A motion by the consolidated committee was made and carried unanimously.

Some delegates from the Outside Stonecutters reported that they are in accord with our letter and would like to know when we can act together; but then we found out that they themselves are not yet organized and their people are still working together with Scabs; they will send us a resolution stating they will not permit this sort of thing in the future. Until then this matter was tabled. Ch. Kraatz, Conr. Bach, Franz Nascharofsky and W. Equitz appeared in our hall and signed the resolution. The original, that was signed, states: We, the undersigned employers of masons and bricklayers of the City of Milwaukee agree to adopt eight 8 hours as working day, to all Masons a. Bricklayers belonging to the Masons and Bricklayer's Union of the City of Milwaukee.

Jos. Comolly mailed us a petition asking for assistance for the last week, since he has two sick children, many doctor bills and has already been quite a while without work.

came the managing business agent of the same local. In the third generation, Gordon's son went to college, becoming a specialist in water resources management.[13]

Until the state Workers' Compensation Law took effect in 1913, unions were often the only source of financial aid for injured and sick workers. Thus the minutes of Sheet Metal Workers Local, No. 374, in Superior (Local 42 since 1912) report the granting of sick benefits for a brother who had fallen off a scaffold and fractured a leg.[14]

Although the chief threat to the building trades unions came from the contractors' associations, unions also quarreled among themselves over jurisdiction—such as which type of work should be performed by which union—in efforts to preserve jobs for a particular local or craft. In 1912, for example, the Kenosha carpenters complained that laborers, not carpenters, were being used to plumb and hold wooden forms for concrete, and later, that members of the Sheet Metal Workers engaged in carpentry.[15] In 1905 the Superior Sheet Metal Workers charged that Carpenters Union members were installing a steel ceiling on the old town church.[16] In addition, different locals within the same craft and international union vied with one another for members. The Kenosha Carpenters objected when brother carpenters from Milwaukee worked in Kenosha and did not pay dues to the Kenosha local.

Union Growth During and After World War I

Even before the United States entered the war in 1917, the WSFL membership began to expand. In 1914, Henry Ohl, the young leader in Milwaukee's Typographical Union, Local 23, was hired by the federation to travel the state and seek the affiliation of unions which had not joined. As the membership chart (page 63) illustrates, Ohl's mission was quite successful and was repeated in successive years.

The years 1916 and 1917 marked a substantial tightening of the national labor market, sparked by huge war orders for England and France even before the United States entered the war in April, 1917. This labor shortage gave renewed courage to unions in the paper industry towns where the hated, archaic 78-hour week was still in existence. In Milwaukee, by early 1916, the Federated Trades Council had set up a special organizing committee, the Labor Forward Movement, and had appropriated $500 for its support. Meetings were held throughout the city and over 2,000 workers were recruited into new unions.[17]

The diminished demand for labor, resulting from the end of World War I and the sharp depression which began in mid-1920, changed the balance of power between unions and employers. Employers now banded together in a new open-shop crusade similar to that of 1903–1906. This time it was labeled "the American Plan," implying that unionism was synonymous with the Bolshevik Revolution in Russia. This employer offensive was very successful and robbed unions of many of their wartime and postwar membership gains.

By 1930, WSFL membership had dropped from its January, 1920, zenith of 41,000 down to 25,800.[18] Most of the decline occurred during the depression of 1920–1922. The "prosperous twenties," 1923–1929, marked an era of generally full employment. But, lacking strong unions, wages did not rise. For example, 39 cents an hour was the common labor rate paid by paper mills in the Fox River Valley over that entire period. Wages were higher in the Milwaukee metal fabricating plants, but nevertheless conditions were also hard there. Hours were long, usually nine per day for five days and four or five on Saturday. As late as 1929, the A. O. Smith Company operated parts of its auto frame plant thirteen hours at night and eleven hours each day. Unlike the early paper mills, which rotated day and night shifts, workers in the A. O. Smith night shift stayed in that slot year after year.

The decline of the labor movement during this period was particularly discouraging to Frank Weber, who served during this period as secretary of the Milwaukee Federated Trades Council. Weber attributed the downturn to the prosperity of the late 1920's. In May, 1929, he wrote, prophetically: "The labor movement . . . is being misled by the glitter of the age— fine raiments, sports and amusement—and does not see how the links for the chain that will bind to a most degraded servitude condition are being forged."[19] Perhaps "the glitter of the age" was more apparent to Weber than to the majority of workers and labor leaders, for one of his sons, Orlando, became president of the huge Allied Chemical and Dye Company and reportedly retired as a multi-millionaire.[20]

An interesting sidelight to the labor movement in this stagnant period is a capitalist venture that Weber and several other Socialists and labor colleagues turned to in early 1929. They invested in and ran a mining operation, the Butterfly Consolidated Mines, near Telluride, Colorado. William Coleman, general secretary of the Wisconsin Socialist party and an official in the Milwaukee Painters and Decorators, Local 781, left the city to spend two years as mine manager in Colorado. Beset by technical and other problems, including the drastic fall in silver prices early in the Depression, the enterprise ended in failure, closing in 1931.[21] Coleman, in a rather poignant comment on his dual role as capitalist and mine manager, wrote Weber in November, 1929: "Yes Weber we are the only hope of the entire district [Telluride] and we will soon be going over the top . . . then I want to come back to Milwaukee and take my place in the fight for a better life for the workers."[22]

At the end of this period of union decline, there was at least one attempt by Wisconsin labor to take a stand against management: a strike in 1928 and 1929 at Kenosha's Allen–A hosiery plant, conducted by the Kenosha local of the American Federation of Full-Fashioned Hosiery Workers.[23] The strike began when the company assigned each knitter two machines instead of one. A total of 330 workers went out; 370 continued to work. The company soon began hiring replacements including some strikebreakers imported from Pennsylvania. Hosiery Workers national headquarters sent in Louis Budenz to direct the strike. There was an unusual amount of violence which spread from the picket line to the cars and homes of those still working. Strikers slashed tires and planted fire bombs in garbage cans and cars. In a few cases, strikers raked their houses with gunfire. A federal judge in Milwaukee issued an injunction against the picketing and violent disturbances. Union members continued to picket. A grand jury indicted twenty-six union members, including the strike leader, Louis Budenz, of an illegal conspiracy to violate the injunction. Budenz was on the witness stand for two days when the union members were brought to trial. The jury acquitted all of the conspiracy charges.

Violence continued. On one occasion, 150 windows at the plant were broken. At the next trial, twenty-seven strikers were convicted of civil contempt and fined $100 each, plus costs. They refused to pay and were sent to jail in Milwaukee, but union rallies, held in Milwaukee, Chicago, and Kenosha, raised money to pay the fines.

Union members and their sympathizers, however, were also targets of violence. The union protested that the local government was one-sided in its administration of justice. The city attorney and the assistant city attorney were chief counsel and assistant counsel to the Allen–A company. The judge who called the grand jury which indicted the strikers was revealed to have received, and never repaid, a $20,000 loan a few years earlier from the president of a large Kenosha employer. The Allen-A company and the city of Kenosha spent thousands of dollars on private detectives. One of the private detectives' victims was the strike leader, Louis Budenz, whose hotel room was the object of stink bombs.

The Kenosha Trades and Labor Council gave the striking knitters full support. Strikers and 3,000 supporters staged a parade marching through the streets with cars and trucks carrying banners to alert the public to the union's viewpoint. Kenosha received nationwide attention when the national President of the AFL, William Green, addressed a crowd of 5,000. The WSFL sent out a statewide appeal to its members for funds. Members of the Milwaukee Hosiery Workers voted to contribute two dollars per week to the strikers.

After ten months, Budenz, realizing that the strike was lost, returned to New York. He emerged years later as the editor of the Communist *Daily Worker*. To what extent might the union defeat in this strike have turned him to the left? Kenosha workers carried on the strike for another year. It was never officially called off but the union's cause was lost. The two-machine system prevailed, and the company operated with non-union workers. Future events made clear that the Kenosha workers had not been intimidated and as the recession of the thirties began to lift, Kenosha became one of the most highly unionized cities in the state.

The Effects of the Great Depression

During the years 1929–1933, the United States succumbed to the worldwide depression. National income plummeted from 80 billion to 49 billion dollars. Official unemployment rose to 25 per cent, a figure that did not count many who worked only a few days per month. Wages were slashed repeatedly. Lifetime savings were destroyed. Thousands of banks closed their doors. Millions of people were driven to private and public charity. In Wisconsin, the economic disaster was as devastating for farm families as for city workers. In 1933, farmers desperately attempted to raise ruinously low milk prices by adapting strike tactics, hitherto confined to unions, to milk production. Under the leadership of the Wisconsin Milk Pool, groups of farmers gathered on roads leading to Wisconsin cities and dumped tons of fresh milk that had been destined for processing plants. Trains were stopped in southern Wisconsin to block milk from reaching Chicago. Governor Albert Schmedeman called out the National Guard to break the farmer's strike. The guardsmen included young urban workers, armed with baseball bats, who pursued farm boys across the open fields, recalling earlier times when sheriffs' deputies and the National Guard had broken through the unions' picket lines. The WSFL issued statements of support for the farmers.

What solutions had trade union leaders to offer in the face of this national catastrophe? The journalist Louis Adamic, overstating the case to a

certain extent, described the condition of the American Federation of Labor in strong terms:[24]

> The body is undoubtedly a sick body. It is ineffectual—flabby, af-
> flicted with the dull pains of moral and physical decline. The big in-
> dustrialists and conservative politicians are no longer worried by it.
> Indeed, the intelligent ones see in it the best obstacle—temporary at
> least—to the emergence of a militant and formidable labor move-
> ment. . . . The ten year decline of the whole organization, I think,
> has already gone too far to be rejuvenated by anybody.

While the Depression deepened, the aging executive board of the national AFL even as late as 1931 reaffirmed its opposition to unemployment
insurance or any similar federal programs to remedy the workers' condition. In Wisconsin, however, the Socialist leadership of the WSFL was
quick to recognize the magnitude of the economic crisis and worked hard
to enlist government counteraction. In 1931, with strong labor support,
the newly elected governor, Philip F. La Follette, proposed a work relief
program to aid the unemployed and to provide purchasing power to stimulate the economy—two years in advance of the New Deal's programs.
The La Follette jobs program called for construction of highway over-
passes, which his enemies dubbed "the La Follette roller coasters," at all
of the state's major railway crossings. This program provided thousands
of jobs at union wages to Wisconsin workers, yet it was little more than a
drop in the bucket compared to the magnitude of the unemployment.

The Depression brought to fruition Wisconsin labor's long crusade for
unemployment compensation (described in Chapter 8). Although unemployment drastically reduced the income of the WSFL, its leadership became more politically aggressive even as its economic strength declined.
Federation membership dropped from 25,800 in 1930 to 17,500 in 1933.[25]
Similarly, the Federated Trades Council membership in Milwaukee declined to 20,000 in 1933, reduced by 43 per cent from its peak of 35,000 in
1920.[26]

The State Federation repeatedly urged the government to take steps to
remedy the situation. In January, 1932, the executive board of the WSFL
issued a three-part statement, urging support for the La Follette legislative
relief plans, advocating a bill for the eight-hour day to give immediate
employment to more workers, and reiterating its stand favoring unemployment issurance.[27] A year later, at the bottom of the Depression, the
federation's executive board drew up a more radical list of measures to
combat the recession:[28]

> The chief problems which will claim the attention of the organized
> labor movement in the State of Wisconsin and the nation in the year

> 1933 are: Emergency relief for the unemployed, opportunity to work for those out of work, maintaining educational standards, promoting additional public works and ever increasing the functions of government, stemming further cuts in salaries, increasing wages to conform to a decent standard of living, defend and promote social legislation, prevention of a general sales tax, putting in motion unemployment reserves, and the adoption of six-hour-day and a five-day-week.
>
> The first measure to be considered by the Wisconsin legislature should be that of providing immediate relief. . . . All of these necessary funds should be raised by additional income and inheritance taxes, and, if necessary by direct capital levy.

This statement was accompanied by a not unrealistic warning of impending revolution:

> Labor is compelled to speak frankly and give warning that unless there is an immediate and radical change for the better, revolution is imminent. And when we speak of revolution, we do not mean a political revolution by ousting one political party and installing another. We mean "revolution" set in motion by hungry, dejected, and demoralized humans who seek to overthrow a government that fails to furnish them the wherewithal to live and to take them out of their misery.

While the federation was battling for measures to take care of the unemployed, its own strength was being seriously eroded by the drop in per capita payments. The quarterly meetings of the executive board from June, 1932, through May, 1933, received increased requests from locals for suspension of per capita fees because of financial hardship. The officers of the WSFL went on half pay. But the condition of the labor movement was about to change.

As President Franklin D. Roosevelt's New Deal began to take shape in the summer of 1933, the economy started to turn around. The new national policy of "freedom to organize" removed workers' fears of joining unions. The Milwaukee *Sentinel* reported in August, 1933, that John J. Handley, secretary of the WSFL, was busy enrolling new members: "Union meetings are being held here nightly and labor is invading industries which have always closed the door to unions. . . . Applications for memberships . . . are pouring into headquarters in Brisbane Hall so rapidly that officials find themselves swamped."[29] The New Deal was, in fact, a new era for labor.

Wisconsin Labor Under the New Deal: Renewed Militancy

At certain periods in the past, workers had swarmed into unions: during the Civil War and in the years 1872–1873, 1880–1883, 1885–1886, 1900–1904, and 1916–1919. On these occasions, however, employers had dug in their heels and, through concerted open-shop drives, driven the unions back, reducing them to a few crafts in the big cities and among the railroad workers. Consequently, when the New Deal began, organized labor represented only about 8 per cent of the non-agricultural work force.[30] In 1933, however, there was a great change. The United States government abandoned its normal anti-labor policy and enacted a series of measures which constituted a bill of rights for labor, including Section 7(a) of the National Recovery Act of 1933 and the National Labor Relations Act of 1935 (the Wagner Act). In addition, the federal government established social security, unemployment compensation, work relief, and other measures designed to intervene in the economy to reduce unemployment.

In Wisconsin, a sympathetic governor, Philip F. La Follette, elected to his third term in November, 1936, and a legislature with a large block of labor-endorsed members made it possible at last for the state's labor unions to establish permanent relationships with employers by passing in 1937 the Wisconsin Labor Relations Act, similar to the National Labor Relations Act. Both federal and state laws now prohibited such previous tactics of employers as spying on workers and dismissing those who led or joined unions. For the first time in American history, collective bargaining, through unions freely chosen by workers, was sanctioned by law. Both federal and state officials began to conduct investigations of labor law violations and to carry out the prosecution of guilty employers. Instead of striking for the right to enter into collective bargaining with the employer, the union could petition the federal or state government to conduct elections for recognition by secret ballot. If the union received a majority vote, the employer was legally bound to sit down with it around the bargaining table.

These new legal protections caused an unprecedented surge toward unionism. Figure 2 shows the phenomenal membership growth in the WSFL through 1936, and in the WSFL and the Wisconsin CIO-affiliated unions thereafter. Nationally, the trends were similar. From 1933 through 1936, the unions that Wisconsin workers joined were those of the American Federation of Labor (AFL), which was affiliated with the Wisconsin State Federation of Labor (WSFL). Now for the first time, workers in large plants began to form single plant unions which affiliated with the AFL as "federal labor unions," an industrial form of unionism. The plants of the Nash Motor Company (now American Motors) in Racine and Kenosha, the Seaman Body plant in Milwaukee, which made bodies for Nash cars, and General Motors at Janesville were examples of these new unions.

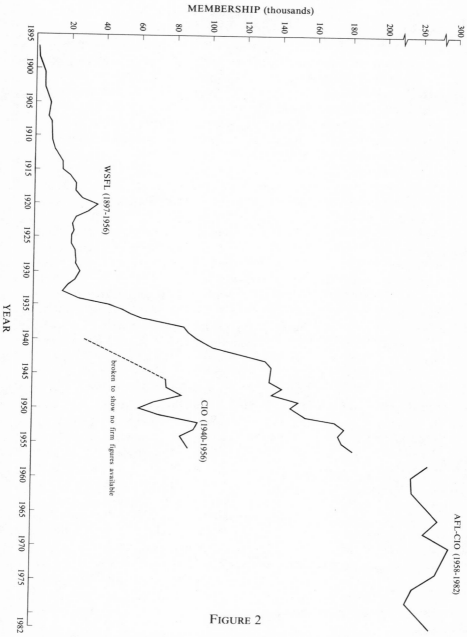

FIGURE 2

Membership of the Wisconsin State Federation of Labor (1897–1956), the Wisconsin State Industrial Council, CIO (1940–1956), and the Wisconsin State AFL–CIO (1958–1982).

The Kenosha Nash workers, assisted by Felix Olkives and Gilbert Fechner of the Kenosha Trades and Labor Council, began to unionize in the fall of 1933.[31] To avoid bargaining with them, Nash set up a company-dominated union. Then, on November 9, 1933, 200 workers on the assembly line went out on strike to protest new piece rates. In response, Charles Nash locked out all 3,000 workers at his Kenosha and Racine plants. Twelve days later, the Chicago Regional Labor Board negotiated a tenuous settlement. Nash agreed to recognize a committee, chosen by the employees, to arbitrate any disagreements over restoring strikers to their former jobs, and the union agreed to try the piece rates on a temporary basis.[32]

Meanwhile, federal labor unions had been formed under WSFL leadership at both the Nash plant in Racine and at Seaman Body in Milwaukee. Workers at these two plants were standing by, ready to support the Kenosha strike if necessary, and when the Kenosha lockout ended, both plants' workers decided to ask for a 20 per cent wage increase and strict seniority rules. After a brief sitdown strike, Federal Labor Union No. 19059 at Seaman Body won a 10 per cent wage increase and a vague statement that the company would abide by seniority. Nash immediately offered the same wage increases at the Racine and Kenosha plants, but the Racine local was not satisfied and struck on February 21, 1934, taking out 1,200 workers. The Seaman Body and Kenosha locals followed suit, idling 1,600 at Kenosha and 1,800 in Milwaukee. The Nash plants shut down completely but Seaman Body continued to operate with strikebreakers.

After six weeks of mediation, the Automobile Labor Board, a special board appointed by President Roosevelt, thought it had found an acceptable settlement. The Racine and Milwaukee locals accepted its terms, but Kenosha rejected them. Seaman workers then retracted their acceptance. Despite their acceptance Racine workers stayed out because all three locals had agreed not to settle individually. Two weeks of direct negotiations then led to settlement in which Kenosha workers received a 5 to 17.2 per cent wage increase. At Seaman, where strikebreakers had been operating the plant, the company agreed to rehire strikers before rehiring strikebreakers, overturning a company policy of first rehiring workers with dependents. The federal labor unions at each plant received sole bargaining rights.[33] Summing up their success, labor historian Sidney Fine has written that "the three locals came to be among the most powerful of the federal labor unions in the entire automobile industry. They had clearly demonstrated that in certain circumstances, at least, militancy was not without its rewards in the campaign to organize the automobile workers."[34]

In Janesville, auto workers at the two General Motors plants organized unions with the help of the WSFL, first at the Chevrolet plant in 1933 and then at the Fisher Body plant in 1934. The motivating factor was the unfairness of the piecework system.[35] There were, however, no strikes until after the massive sitdown of auto workers began at Flint, Michigan, in December, 1936. On January 5, 1937, the Janesville workers struck in support of the Flint workers. Their sitdown lasted only one day. The city manager, Henry Traxler, got the company to agree not to reopen the plant until the Flint sitdown was settled, in return for which the union agreed to evacuate the plants. Both the unions and General Motors knew that the Flint settlement would be the determining factor. A problem arose, though when an "Alliance Movement" was started in an effort to recruit General Motors workers who were opposed to the union and supported management. Both Alliance and union members wore buttons showing their respective memberships, and after the strike was settled, a "battle of buttons" broke out with union members stripping them off of the Alliance members. The sheriff, in response, closed all taverns and dance halls within ten miles of the city.[36]

The revived—and successful—determination of workers to unionize in this period is illustrated further by the strike against the Milwaukee Electric Railway and Light Company in 1934. The company, which had operated under various names over the years, had a long history of strong opposition to union-organizing efforts. In 1896, during a month-long strike of 700 workers, it put barricades around its property, imported hundreds of strikebreakers, and ultimately defeated the strike. In 1912, when the Federated Trades Council tried to organize its employees, the company promptly discharged the organizing activists. The workers then struck, but management again refused to submit to arbitration, on the grounds that to do so would constitute recognition of the union. The company did, however, set up a jointly run Employee Mutual Benevolent Association, in effect a company union, over which management gained enough control to quell another attempt, in 1919, to organize employees.

The outcome of the strike in 1934 was entirely different: it lasted only four days and ended in a union victory. The company at first attempted to block the strike, paying the Bergoff Detective Agency $39,000 to conduct strikebreaking activities, but immense popular support for the strikers swept the city. The demonstrations ended in property damage and the accidental death of a demonstrator at the car barns. The strongly pro-labor mayor, Daniel Hoan, castigated the company in scathing terms: "You are solely responsible for the riots that have so far blotched the good name of this city. . . . Your attitude toward your employees, our people, our city, our Federal Government is more arrogant than that of any ruler in the world." The company capitulated, granting full recognition to the union. It had taken more than forty years, but the street railway company was finally unionized.[37] Clearly, the nature of the times had changed.

What is today one of the largest unions in Wisconsin, the International Brotherhood of Teamsters, was, in 1935, a small and struggling group of workers. The General Drivers, Local 200, had 250 members from many scattered trucking companies around the state. Because the employers offered only open-shop contracts—meaning that their employees were not required to join the union—it was impossible to collect enough dues to run the local and to finance a strike against all employers at the same time. Instead, the union struck one company at a time. Two pickets in a car followed each truck of the largest company, the Dairy Transfer and Storage Company. When the truck stopped to make each delivery, one of the pickets stepped out and displayed a sign urging the store to refuse the delivery; if it did not refuse, the picket would remain in front of the store. At the end of the first week the company, able to make very few deliveries, signed a closed-shop contract with Local 200.

The second company targeted for picketing was Checker Express; it signed a closed-shop contract before the picketing could begin. The employers' association then agreed to the closed shop and Local 200's membership jumped from 250 to 1,500. Teamster locals were being organized in La Crosse, Eau Claire, Green Bay, Fond du Lac, and other cities, but employers tended to escape the union by locating their base of operations in the areas that had the lowest wages. In 1937 the Teamsters Union countered by forming the Wisconsin Conference of Teamsters, whose goal was to equalize wages for the over-the-road drivers. In 1938 a conference representative, Frank Ranney, met other Teamster representatives in Minneapolis and organized the first multi-state conference, which eventually became the Central States Conference of Teamsters.[38]

Tire workers across the country, meanwhile, had been organizing into federal unions. In the northwestern area of Wisconsin, the tire builders at the Gillette Rubber Company plant in Eau Claire caught the union fever, and in September, 1933, were granted a Federal Labor Union charter, No. 18684, by the AFL. Tire building was a physically demanding job, performed in excessive heat. Low wages—$13.76 per week—and wage cuts were causes for discontent, as were job insecurity, the lack of paid vacations, and the absence of lockers and shower facilities. But memories of their previous experience in union-organizing caused some workers to hang back.

In April, 1919, soon after Gillette had opened in Eau Claire, the workers formed Federal Labor Union, No. 16545, to address the grievances of fourteen-hour day shifts and a reduction in women's piece rates. One month later, the Gillette Company announced a lockout at the close of the day. The union, not to be upstaged, closed the plant at 1:00 P.M. The union asked for wages 10 per cent below the union scale, but an impasse resulted. After eight weeks the company reopened without the union. In 1933 a number of Eau Claire merchants, remembering the 1919 strike and its huge loss of income for the city, unsuccessfully tried to prevent the union from representing the Gillette workers by publishing an anti-union appeal.[39]

The 1933 organizing drive covered the men who were the auto and truck tire builders, but not the women, who made bicycle tires. Mary Navocek was the only woman member for a while. Federal Local No. 18684 and its 1936 successor, Local 19 of the United Rubber Workers of America, CIO, were to have a profound impact on the entire Eau Claire community. By the 1970's, successive collective bargaining agreements had made Eau Claire's rubber workers among the highest-paid factory workers in the city. The Gillette firm was bought by Uniroyal Inc., which grew to be Eau Claire's largest employer. Local 19 contributed many full-time staff representatives to the United Rubber Workers; one of them was Milan Stone, elected national president in 1981.

Not all of the organizing efforts in Wisconsin were successful. One of the more spectacular defeats was the strike at a Milwaukee department store, the Boston Store, in December, 1934. The Retail Clerks International Protective Association, Local 1284, had launched an organizing drive at several of the city's stores in the fall. Six hundred clerks were initiated during October. Unable to get any significant wage concessions by bargaining with the Boston Store management, the union called a strike for November 29, just at the beginning of the Christmas rush. Despite what would now be considered wage demands with a sexist differential of $25 a week for men and $20 for women, the union was well supported by the female clerks.[40]

The strike was a united effort of three unions, Clerks, Teamsters, and Building Service Employees, and on the first day 1,200 workers began picketing. There was no violence during the strike.[41] The entire Milwaukee labor movement pledged its support; on one Saturday in December,

10,000 picketeers jammed the sidewalks around the store. The League of Women Shoppers provided assistance at meetings and on the picket line. The Workers Alliance, composed of workers with the WPA (Works Progress Administration), also contributed pickets.[42]

Six federal mediators came to Milwaukee in fruitless efforts to reach a settlement. An extremely cold winter and the store's willingness to hold out through the holiday season eventually broke the strikers' morale and in mid-January the unions signed a settlement bringing a small wage increase but no union security or effective grievance procedures. The defeat set the tone for future Milwaukee department store relationships. Almost fifty years later none of Milwaukee's major department stores had been unionized.

Another exception to the general success of unionism in this period was the effort, led by the WSFL, to establish collective bargaining at the Kohler Company, a plumbing supply firm located in Kohler Village, just west of Sheboygan. In July and August, 1933, Federal Labor Union, No. 18545, was formed in what proved to be only the beginning of a thirty-year struggle for union recognition. The firm was managed by the Kohler family, industrialists in the Sheboygan area since 1873. Kohler Company workers were recruited primarily from nearby Sheboygan families.

Sheboygan workers had a long history of unionism, and the Kohler family had an equally long history of opposition to unions. In an earlier depression year, 1895, massive strikes had broken out in Sheboygan, involving a total of 4,000 workers. Strikers appeared at the Kohler plant to urge employees there to join the strike, but the Kohler workers held back and the company president, John M. Kohler, delivered a stern lecture to the crowd.[43] Two years later, members of Molders Local 286 struck the plant to protest a wage cut. The company refused to make any concessions, and the union had to abandon the strike.[44]

When an AFL Federal Labor Union (FLU) was formed in 1933, the company responded by setting up a rival company union, the Kohler Workers Association (KWA). The company stated its willingness to meet with the FLU, but made it clear that it was equally willing to meet with other individuals and members of the KWA. Henry Ohl, WSFL president, and Walter Kohler, company president, had this exchange:[45]

> Mr. Ohl: The point is that if half a dozen different people or groups of men negotiated with the Kohler Company on different bases it may bring about the situation of bargaining for different conditions. We

want to bargain in behalf of these men for standards of work to be applicable throughout the plant.

  Mr. Kohler . . . We will, of course, deal with you, but we should also continue to deal with others.

The company, it appeared, would not sign a labor agreement with anyone but would merely put company policy in writing.

Mr. Kohler:	We will make a statement of policy. We cannot give a written agreement.
Mr. Ohl:	We do not want a statement of policies at all. We want to know what you will agree to.
Mr. Kohler:	Were we to make a definite statement in a letter, that would be an agreement.
Mr. Heymanns	[Kohler employee, member of FLU No. 18545 Bargaining Committee]: No, absolutely no!

Further progress seeming hopeless, the union called a strike for July 16, 1934. The union's mass picketing prevented the company from operating. The company hired 250 deputies and armed them with tear gas and guns. It mounted machine guns on the company's roof and on the deputies' trucks. Tension rose. On the evening of July 27, a mob, estimated at 4,000 to 5,000, began stoning company buildings, breaking hundreds of windows. The deputies first used tear gas to repel the strikers and strike sympathizers, then opened fire, killing two workers and injuring forty-two. The county sheriff asked for the National Guard, and Governor Albert Schmedeman responded by sending in 600 National Guard cavalrymen on the following morning. The Guard restored order and removed the company's machine guns. The union petitioned the National Labor Relations Board for an election. The election, with the company union and the Federal Labor Union on the ballot, was held in September, and amid an atmosphere of fear and intimidation the company union won the election.[46]

The Federal Labor Union refused, however, to call off the strike and maintained token picketing for seven years. The strike ended in April, 1941, when the company, wanting to use union construction workers for plant expansion, asked the WSFL president, Herman Seide, to call off the strike. In return, the company offered jobs to all workers still on strike except for the three principal officers of the FLU, Charles Heymanns, Rudolph Renn, and Otto Janisch.[47]

Later episodes in a second Kohler strike are part of CIO history. The national movement toward industrial unionism led to the formation of the Congress of Industrial Organizations (CIO) in 1935. The Wisconsin State CIO separated from the WSFL in 1936. There were therefore two state labor organizations from 1936 to 1958. The story of the Wisconsin CIO is the subject of the next chapter.

Wisconsin Labor in World War II and the Postwar Years

Figure 2 (page 63) illustrates the growth of union membership during World War II, when government support of collective bargaining and inherent wartime problems such as shortages of labor, long hours, and inexperienced supervisors enabled unions to gain new members

Growth continued at a healthy pace for two years after the war, then slowed perceptibly with passage of the Taft–Hartley Act in 1947, which gave employers tools with which to slow expansion of unionism. Perhaps the most significant part of the Taft–Hartley Act were those sections which freed the employer to participate in union representation elections and to yield every propaganda weapon an employer could muster.

The recession of 1949 also helped to curb union growth. Another spurt then occurred as a result of increased industrial production during the Korean War (1950–1953). Thereafter, growth, although positive, was slow. Causes of the slowdown remain conjectural, but several factors can be singled out. First, most of the big industrial plants in Wisconsin already were organized. Second, the Taft–Hartley Act made it easier for employers to oppose unions. Third, the continued rivalry of the AFL and CIO, competing with each other in efforts to organize new plants, made organization more costly and discouraged membership. That obstacle was removed with the merger of the two national groups in December, 1955, and of the Wisconsin state central bodies in 1958. From then on, there was one state labor organization, the Wisconsin State AFL–CIO. In recent years, union growth in the traditional sectors of manufacturing and crafts has slowed to a crawl. Instead, it is in the public sector that unionism has flourished.

In 1974, Wisconsin ranked fifteenth among the fifty states in the percentage of unionized non-agricultural employees, which then stood at 32 per cent.[48] More recently, the figure has fallen to 27 per cent, because growth in employment has been primarily in the non-unionized sectors of the economy—among service, technical, and clerical workers—rather than in manufacturing, which is highly unionized. The size of individual Wisconsin unions is shown by the following table for the years 1962 and 1972.

WISCONSIN'S LARGEST UNION AFFILIATIONS, 1962 AND 1972

		1962	1972
1.	Auto Workers, Aerospace, & Agricultural Implement Workers, AFL–CIO	47,880	52,470
2.	Wisconsin Education Association Council	NA	43,000
3.	Machinists & Aerospace Workers International Assoc., AFL–CIO	31,260	42,320
4.	United Steelworkers of America, AFL–CIO	22,890	33,050
5.	International Brotherhood of Teamsters, Ind.	26,250	32,020
6.	American Federation of State, County & Municipal Employees, AFL–CIO	16,930	31,300
7.	United Paperworkers International Union, AFL–CIO	NA	23,860
8.	Allied Industrial Workers	12,530	18,620
9.	Carpenters, AFL–CIO	14,320	15,350
10.	International Brotherhood of Electrical Workers, AFL–CIO	15,330	13,340
11.	Laborers, AFL–CIO	9,410	11,400
12.	Boilermakers, Iron Shipbuilders, AFL–CIO	4,800	9,740
13.	Retail Clerks International Assoc., AFL–CIO	6,630	9,720
14.	Meat Cutters & Butcher Workmen, AFL–CIO	10,180	9,030
15.	Operating Engineers, AFL–CIO	6,650	8,510
16.	Communications Workers of America, AFL–CIO	4,010	8,140

Source: Letter from Leo Troy, Professor, Department of Economics, Rutgers University, November 14, 1977, based on union reports to the U.S. Dept. of Labor.

In 1978, a merger of the Retail Clerks and the Meat Cutters and Butcher Workmen created the Food and Commercial Workers Union, moving them up from twelfth and thirteenth places to about eighth. The United Paperworkers was created by a merger of two unions, the Papermakers and the Pulp Sulphite and Paper Mill Workers. If present trends continue, there will be more mergers and thus bigger and fewer unions in the future. By 1980, the top four, according to reports from each union, were the American Federation of State, County, and Municipal (AFSCME), with 49,800 members; the Wisconsin Education Association Council (WEAC), with 45,000; the International Brotherhood of Teamsters (IBT), with 45,000; and the United Auto Workers (UAW), with 40,693.

These figures show that in recent years the largest growth in Wisconsin union membership has been in the government and service sectors. In the depression years of the early 1980's, growth not only stopped, due to an unemployment peak in Wisconsin of 12 per cent, but there were even substantial membership declines, especially in the auto and metal fabricating unions.

Public Employee Unionism

By 1980, one of the largest unions in the country as well as in Wisconsin was the American Federation of State, County and Municipal Employees, AFSCME. A young union, having received an AFL charter in 1936, it pioneered unionism for state and municipal employees. It is the only current national union which was founded in Wisconsin, its birth a natural outgrowth of the progressive character of both Wisconsin's labor movement and the liberal state administration led by the La Follette political movement.

Throughout the 1930's and 1940's, national collective bargaining legislation omitted protection for employees of the state, municipal, and federal governments. The Wagner Act of 1935, the Magna Carta of trade union rights, did not apply to government employees. Strong public feeling concerning the sovereignty of government led to the conclusion that governments could not bargain with their employees. Philip La Follette, governor of Wisconsin in 1932, did not share this aversion to public employee unions. When in the spring of 1932, Henry Ohl, president of the WSFL, and Colonel A. E. Garey, director of the state personnel department, met with La Follette, the governor not only approved the idea of a union for state employees but allowed himself to be quoted to that effect.[49]

The state employees' union formed at that time was unusual in several respects. It began as an organization for the state's department administrators and the clerical, fiscal, and technical employees. Later, it broadened its membership to include all state and municipal employees. The union first was named the Wisconsin State Association of Administrative, Clerical, Fiscal, and Technical Employees, and received an AFL federal labor union charter, No. 18213, on May 16, 1932. Its original purpose was to preserve the state's civil service system, which was threatened by the severe competition for jobs during the Depression. The union members' fears for the system soon proved well grounded.

In September, 1932, Governor La Follette was defeated in the primary election. In November, a Democratic landslide brought in not only a Democratic governor, but also a Democratic State Assembly and a Democratic–Conservative Republican majority in the Senate. When the legislature convened in January, 1933, the Democrats, whose party had not been in state office for almost forty years, moved to dismantle the long-standing (since 1905) state Civil Service Act.

At that time, the union had only about fifty members, among whom the most active was Arnold Zander, the state's senior personnel examiner.

Zander obtained permission to work temporarily on a half-time basis at his state job, while the union paid him $150 per month to lobby against the civil service repeal plan. Zander and his immediate superior, Colonel Garey, teamed up to mobilize labor, farm organizations, veterans, women's organizations, and municipal leaders against Wisconsin Senate Bill S-8, which would have abolished the entire state civil service system.[50] Several state newspapers joined the effort to preserve the civil service. The public outcry orchestrated by Zander saved the system and with it Federal Labor Union No. 18213, which then grew rapidly, having demonstrated its ability to preserve jobs.

To convert one federal labor union into a national union of state and municipal employees took another three years of almost full-time effort by Zander. In October, 1933, he attended the AFL convention in Washington, D.C., and was encouraged by President William Green. Zander kept in touch with two groups: (1) the state and municipal employees' associations in other states, which were not unions but were tied loosely to the national civil service movement; and (2) a much smaller group of AFL-affiliated federal labor unions. These affiliates encouraged Zander to proceed with the organization of a national union covering employees at all levels of government. But by that time, 1935, the AFL had given jurisdiction over state, county, and municipal employees to the American Federation of Government Employees, a union whose actual membership included only federal employees. It took another year to obtain from the AFL a separate national charter for the American Federation of State, County, and Municipal Employees (AFSCME). At its meeting of October 8, 1936, the AFL executive council granted a national charter for AFSCME. Its national headquarters remained in Madison until 1957, when it was moved to Washington, D.C. By 1980, the Wisconsin-born AFSCME had become the nation's fourth largest union, with over one million members.

By 1930 the WSFL and its Socialist leadership had developed a close relationship with the Progressive wing of the Republican party, represented by the La Follettes. Zander, who served as president of AFSCME from its founding in 1936 through 1966, was himself a product of Wisconsin's German, Socialist, and trade union culture. His father, a sawyer in Two Rivers, Wisconsin, was a Socialist and an early trade union activist in the WSFL. Zander held an undergraduate degree in engineering and a doctorate in city planning from the University of Wisconsin. When he needed to set up a retirement system for state employees, he sought assistance—as had Frank Weber and Henry Ohl in past years—from the economics department of the University of Wisconsin.

In 1935, Professor Edwin Witte recommended that a graduate student of his, Roy Kubista, take a position as research assistant with the newly formed AFSCME. Kubista's first task was to get the legislature to establish a retirement system for state employees, achieved in 1943 when the legislature passed the bill and overrode the veto of Governor Walter Goodland. In 1947 the state, with AFSCME's backing, enacted one of the nation's first wage-escalator clauses tied to increases in the Consumer Price Index. Kubista went on to serve as the national secretary–treasurer to the union, and then, from 1936 to 1970, was executive secretary of the Wisconsin State Employees' Association. Even after his official retirement, he continued to serve as a legislative representative for the State Association.

By the end of World War II, AFSCME already was recognized by the city and county governments in Wisconsin's urban centers. But in the small towns and highway departments in rural counties, AFSCME locals were destroyed time and again by dismissals of union leaders. Associations of police and firemen bargained in some cities, but were generally unable to sign contracts. Teachers' associations still were generally dominated by the administrators.

At this juncture there appeared two young lawyers who were to have far-reaching influence in the establishment of collective bargaining for public employees. The first was John Lawton, a staff member in the Dane County District Attorney's office and a member of AFSCME Local 720. At the end of the war, Lawton went into private practice, but had AFSCME Council 40 as one of his clients. It was more than a legal practice. It included organizing, handling grievances, and assisting in collective bargaining. In 1946, the law firm added another young attorney just out of the army, Gaylord Nelson. Nelson assisted the union as Lawton had done, and in addition, was elected state senator representing Madison in 1948.

The public outside of the big cities was not accustomed to unionized public servants, and the growth of AFSCME was extremely slow. The only real hope for the future of public employee unionism in Wisconsin was a law which would protect municipal employees in their rights to join a union, just as the Wagner Act of 1935 had done nationally for workers in private industry. Lawton proved to be a superb lobbyist. Such a law passed the Wisconsin legislature in 1953, but the bill was vetoed by Governor Walter Kohler, Jr. It was six years before a similar bill could be passed.

This time it was signed with enthusiasm by the new governor, Gaylord Nelson.

The 1959 bill protected municipal employees from dismissal or other discrimination for union activities, but the legislature had not been willing to require municipal employers to engage in collective bargaining. AFSCME nevertheless grew moderately under the 1959 act. The public gradually became accustomed to unions among government employees. Two years later, the legislature was ready to take the next step by making collective bargaining mandatory following a determination that the union represented a majority of the employees. The third law was passed in 1962. It granted either the union or the employer the right to call in an outside "fact-finder" who could merely report the facts of the dispute to the public. In 1965, the legislature cautiously extended limited bargaining rights to state employees.

Each of these laws was subject to severe controversy—public employees and the Wisconsin labor movement were in favor of it; small cities and county boards were opposed. Legislators at home on weekends were deluged with visits by the local public employees. On one occasion, a state senator reported that while on his way to Madison he was stopped by a police siren. When he asked the police officer if he had been stopped for speeding, the officer replied that he only wanted to talk to the senator about the collective bargaining bill.

For one hundred years, employees in private industry had been able to legally negotiate union shop agreements. But not until 1972 were Wisconsin municipal employees granted the right to "fair share" agreements, a requirement that employees need not join the union, but must pay a fee, equal to the dues, to the union which bargains for them.

This succession of favorable laws from 1959 through 1972 brought rapid growth of union membership among public employees throughout Wisconsin. Policemen, firemen, teachers, county highway departments, and city employees developed effective unions. However, strikes by the Milwaukee police, the Madison firemen, and the Hortonville teachers threatened the future of municipal collective bargaining. The 1977 legislature offered an alternative to strikes by prohibiting them if either party asked for binding arbitration to resolve collective bargaining impasses. Strikes vanished from the municipal scene. In 1982 the binding arbitration law was renewed for another five years.

These laws made Wisconsin the pioneer state in legislation encouraging unionism among public employees. By 1980, AFSCME had become Wisconsin's largest union. In addition to AFSCME, other large public sector unions in the state included the Wisconsin Education Assocation Council, the Wisconsin Federation of Teachers, the International Union of Firefighters, and the Wisconsin Professional Police Association. Craft unions throughout the state and in municipalities, such as the Carpenters, Plumbers, Electricians, Stationary Engineers, Firemen and Oilers, and Painters have contracts that cover their members when engaged in public building maintenance. It was, in fact, these craft unions which pioneered in collective bargaining with the city of Milwaukee and with the University of Wisconsin before there were laws permitting collective bargaining by municipalities and the state. City and state governments often had accepted the wage rates already stated in contracts in the private construction industry.

The first state teachers' unions to affiliate with the AFL predated the 1932 origin of AFSCME. They were locals of the American Federation of Teachers (AFT), an affiliate of the AFL. These locals were organized in the Milwaukee Teachers College, the Milwaukee Vocational School, and the Milwaukee public schools. The American Federation of Teachers, Local 223, composed of faculty at the University of Wisconsin at Madison, was formed in 1930, although it never has enrolled more than a small proportion of the faculty.

The great majority of Wisconsin's teachers belonged not to an AFT union but to an association, the Wisconsin Education Association (WEA), founded in 1855. From its origin through the 1950's, the WEA was dominated by school administrators even though principals, superintendents, and teachers all attended the local association meetings together and were all eligible for office. The WEA in this period did not carry out formal collective bargaining, although classroom teachers in many local associations met with superintendents and school boards to present requests for changes in salaries and fringe benefits.

Following the 1959 passage of the state law permitting collective bargaining by municipalities, the Wisconsin Federation of Teachers concluded that the act gave teachers the right of collective bargaining. Neither the WFT nor the WEA had been involved in writing the bill or lobbying for its passage. In several of the larger cities in the state, the WEA and the WFT were rivals in determining which of them represented the teachers. The WFT considered that the new law would permit it to petition the Wisconsin Employment Relations Board for a representation election, but that the WEA would not be allowed on the ballot because it failed to meet the law's definition of a "union" insofar as the participation of superintendents and principals made it a "company-dominated organization" and thus not eligible to bargain for employees.

The two organizations locked horns over the issue in the city of West Allis in 1962 and 1963. Hostilities broke out when the West Allis School Board granted the WEA exclusive recognition without an election conducted by the Wisconsin Employment Relations Board, and proceeded to sign a contract with the West Allis–Milwaukee Teachers Association, the WEA affiliate. On complaint by the West Milwaukee–West Allis Federation of Teachers, AFL–CIO, the Employment Relations Board ruled that although the contract between the WEA and the West Allis School Board was illegal, the WEA was not an employer-dominated organization.[51] However, to effectively represent teachers in collective bargaining with school administrators, the WEA restructured itself, expelling administrators from its organization. This transformed it into a union and qualified it to bargain under the provisions of the Wisconsin Labor Relations Act.

The Wisconsin Education Association Council, which always has had the largest membership of the two organizations, now represents the vast majority of Wisconsin teachers in collective bargaining and in political action and lobbying for legislation affecting teachers and the public schools. It is not affiliated with the AFL–CIO. The Wisconsin Federation of Teachers, AFL–CIO, represents teachers of the state's vocational and technical schools, University of Wisconsin faculties on most of the non-Madison campuses, state employees in several departments including the Department of Public Instruction, teachers in some school systems, and employees of hospitals and nursing homes.

CHAPTER 6

The Wisconsin State CIO

WHEN UNIONISM began to grow explosively in 1934 and 1935, one man in particular understood the significance of this development. He was John L. Lewis, president of the United Mine Workers and a member of the executive council of the American Federation of Labor (AFL). Lewis had witnessed the strong growth of the labor movement once before, in 1919 and 1920, but he had also seen it recede and wither under the open-shop offensive of the 1920's, bolstered by a government hostile to unions. From 1920 to 1933, he and other labor leaders had found it impossible to organize. Now, however, the mood of the workers and the attitude of government had changed. The key to successful unionism, Lewis believed, was to organize the mass production industries on an industrial basis, one union per factory.

The AFL system, on the other hand, was to organize each craft in a plant into a separate union, and at the AFL conventions of 1934 and 1935, the craft union leaders blocked Lewis's efforts to set up an organizing drive on an industrial basis. Rebuffed by the craft union majority at the 1935 convention, Lewis convinced six AFL unions to join the United Mine Workers in forming a Committee for Industrial Organization (CIO) to launch a massive organizing drive among those major manufacturing industries which were still non-union: auto, steel, agricultural machinery, rubber, oil and chemical, electrical, maritime, textile, and hard rock mining. In September, 1936, the AFL executive council suspended all the unions which were members of the Committee for Industrial Organization.

In 1935 the Wisconsin State Federation of Labor (WSFL) had become concerned over the impending split in the labor movement. As we have seen in the previous chapter, by means of federal labor unions it had achieved considerable success in organizing many of Wisconsin's mass production factories—including the Nash Motor Company in Kenosha and Racine, Seaman Body in Milwaukee, and the A. O. Smith Steel Works in Milwaukee. Most of the federal unions in Wisconsin were industrial unions, taking into the local all workers except a few skilled maintenance workers and the toolroom machinists.

To head off the impending split, the WSFL drew up a "peace plan" and submitted it to the AFL executive council in August, 1936. The AFL rejected the plan, but the WSFL sent Jacob Friedrick as a delegate to the November, 1936, convention in Tampa, Florida, to push for a vote on the Wisconsin proposal for labor peace. Its terms were as follows: the AFL would support fully the CIO's drive to organize unions in the steel and rubber industries on an industrial basis; the CIO would limit its actions to those industries until the AFL evaluated the effort and took further steps; the president of the AFL would appoint a committee representing international unions, federal labor unions, state federations, and city centrals to study the organization of the labor movement. The WSFL felt that because the city centrals and state federations were closer to the workers in the plants, their judgment would resolve the issue in favor of industrial organization. But the Wisconsin plan never even reached the voting stage at the convention; a point of order maneuver by William Hutcheson, president of the Carpenters, killed it. The convention then went on to expel the CIO unions from the AFL.

The CIO continued full steam ahead, however, organizing new unions and raiding such existing AFL unions as the already sizable Auto Workers. The CIO was now a separate labor organization, renamed the Congress of Industrial Organizations (CIO). It grew beyond all expectations, and so did the AFL. Together they added 10 million members to the labor movement by the end of 1947.

The CIO Captures the Big Metalworking Plants

The CIO's greatest efforts in Wisconsin were carried out by two unions, the United Auto Workers and the United Steelworkers. The UAW sought to enroll automobile workers, automobile parts workers—of which there were many in Wisconsin—and agricultural implement workers. The first big Wisconsin plants to go over to the CIO were those that had been represented by the AFL Auto Workers. In July, 1936, the AFL National Auto Workers Council affiliated with the CIO, which meant that the WSFL lost not only the unions in the big auto plants—Nash as well as General Motors in Janesville—but also the unions in many smaller auto parts manufacturing plants, such as the Modine Radiator Company and the Young Radiator Company, many of which had been affiliated with the WSFL. Among the non-automobile AFL unions that transferred to the CIO was the one at the huge Allis–Chalmers manufacturing plant at West Allis.

Another large union that joined the CIO was that at J. I. Case, the agricultural implement company in Racine. Because it is the oldest manufacturing plant in Wisconsin (founded in 1847), labor relations at J. I. Case chronicle the prolonged struggle of workers for union recognition from the earliest craft unions to today's powerful AFL–CIO unions. The strong Molders Union, Local 131, founded in 1867, had members in the Case foundry from 1867 until the 1880's, when the local disintegrated. Newly organized Molders Local No. 310 also had difficult relations with Case: a strike in 1899, a lockout in 1902, and a prolonged foundry strike which began in February, 1905. It dragged on through 1907 with Molders Union, No. 310, failing to regain recognition by the Case Company.[1] Especially during World War I there were members of the Molders Union working at the Case plant, but management did not recognize nor bargain with them. In 1920, management at J. I. Case established a company-dominated union. Company control of this union was so pervasive that the final step in its grievance procedure was arbitration presided over by a Case vice-president.

In 1933, before the CIO existed, workers at J. I. Case began to organize a plant-wide union under the leadership of a Case worker, Frank Sahorske, who was a member of the Molders Union. These workers did not want their new organization to be a federal labor union affiliated with the AFL, owing in large part to the fact that under AFL rules, an industrial union could be dismembered by the craft unions. For example, the Molders Union could have had all Case Company Molders transferred from the plant-wide union to the Molders Union.

In 1934, therefore, the Case workers, assisted by a Racine attorney, Harold Cranefield, took the unusual step of incorporating the Wisconsin Industrial Union, Local 1, even collecting the money for a $100 incorporation fee. Within a short time Local 1 had enrolled a majority of the workers and had written a letter to management requesting a meeting to bargain over wages, hours, and working conditions. But Case, which was more than normally reluctant to accept unionism and collective bargaining, ignored the letter. To get management's attention, the local's members sat down at their workplaces for two days, stating they would start work when collective bargaining negotiations began. At eleven o'clock on the third day, the sheriff arrived and ordered the workers to work or leave the plant. They marched out and began picketing, transforming the sit-down into a normal strike. It lasted four months, from October, 1934, to February, 1935, when the Case Company entered into collective bargaining relations and an agreement was reached concerning union recognition, wages, hours, and working conditions.[2]

During the strike, Racine workers demonstrated a strong sense of solidarity. No one crossed the picket line of Local 1, even though within the plant there were 100 members of AFL Federal Labor Union, No. 20009, and a company union. FLU, No. 20009, joined Local 1, which in 1936 affiliated with the CIO as UAW, Local 180. Sahorske, president of Local 1, became the president of Local 180, and Harvey Kitzman, president of FLU, No. 20009, became vice-president. Sahorske described what occurred when J. I. Case was asked by letter to recognize this union:[3]

> The result of this letter to the company was that instead of agreeing to recognize Local 180 of the United Automobile Workers, 79 of us, that is the officers and stewards, were discharged for not living up to the company policy. . . . After considerable discussion, membership wanted to strike the company but I and the other officers and stewards who had been discharged believed that the management of the J. I. Case Company would recognize their mistake and would change their position about our discharges, return us back to work and agree to recognize Local 180 UAW. Therefore we felt it was best to carry on and not strike at that time. After more discussion it was decided that I as president appoint members to take our places in the plant. I asked for volunteers and practically every member volunteered to act in our place. I then proceeded to appoint 79 members to act in our capacity in the shop and take the place of the 79 who had been discharged. . . . Just as soon as the company management found out who the 79 workers were who had been appointed to take our places in the plant, the company fired those 79 workers. We then held another membership meeting and I not only appointed another 79 other workers to take the place of the 79 workers who had been discharged, but also appointed 79 more so that if the company fired the first 79 workers, there would be 79 others to take their place. . . . After the company had discharged . . . 1,250 workers, about 600 workers remained in the plants of the J. I. Case Company. We, Local 180 UAW, then held a membership meeting and after considerable discussion took a strike vote and notified the company that if they did not return us, the discharged workers, to our jobs and negotiate an agreement with us, we would strike the plant. After waiting 3 days and receiving no reply from the company, we struck the plant. The strike lasted approximately 4 months. Toward the end of the strike the company agreed to meet and negotiate an agreement. The strike ended with an agreement between J. I. Case Company and Local 180 UAW.

The assistance which Racine merchants gave Local 180 members and their families during the 1936–1937 strike is a very moving story, as told in Sahorske's words:[4]

About two weeks before Christmas, J. I. Case Company ran an ad in the Racine daily paper offering all workers that were on strike, other than the first 79 they had discharged, their jobs if they returned to work by December 21, and in addition to their jobs the company offered a $100.00 Christmas bonus. When we, the officers of Local 180 UAW, saw this ad in the Racine daily paper, we became quite concerned. . . .

We decided to give a Christmas basket to every striking member of Local 180 UAW. I was instructed to appoint a committee of 3 including myself to contact the merchants for fruit-filled Christmas baskets. Mind you, we had no money. We were broke. The first merchant we contacted was Mr. Joe Domanik, who operated a wholesale grocery establishment and also an agency for the Pabst Brewery.

After informing him why we were meeting with him, we also informed him that we were broke, and had no money, and that if we won a strike, he would be paid. If we lost the strike, we just didn't know how he would get paid and in all probability not at all. After listening to us and thinking this last statement over, he made the following remark: "Look, if you fellows have nerve enough to come to me and tell me what you have just told me, I have enough faith in you to go along." . . .

The day before Christmas, December 24, Harvey Kitzman, our vice president, was Santa Claus and handed out the baskets. No family went hungry no matter how large. I remember one family that had 9 children, making a total of 11 in the family. This family got the biggest basket, which included 6 chickens.

After the strike ended and we had won, we started paying Mr. Domanik what we owed him in monthly installments of approximately $1,000.00 per month until the bill was paid.

In 1937, inspired by the United Auto Workers victory against General Motors in the sitdown strikes at Flint, Michigan, workers from dozens of Wisconsin plants asked for unionization. The new CIO United Auto Workers opened a district office in Milwaukee. Larry Carlstrom from UAW, Local 82, at the Modine plant in Racine, and George Kiebler, a welder from the Seaman Body plant in Milwaukee (UAW, Local 75), became secretary and president, respectively, of the new UAW District Office.

According to Carlstrom, worker interest in unionism was so strong that most organizing was done by plant volunteers. Self-appointed worker committees would call at the UAW District Office, receive union membership cards, and, with little or no help from the full-time organizers, proceed to sign up the entire plant.[5] For example, in early 1937, Carl Griepentrog, a worker at the Line Material Company in Milwaukee, called on George Kiebler at the District Office and took away with him a batch of application cards. Workers quickly and eagerly signed them. The company recognized the union after receiving assurance from Father Francis J. Haas, a Wisconsin Labor Relations Board official, that a majority of the employees had indeed signed the UAW membership authorization cards.[6] In this instance there was no delay for a labor board election.

One of the worker committees which came to the UAW district office was from Briggs & Stratton, a large Milwaukee manufacturer of auto parts and small engines. Union "fever" had broken out in 1934, when fifteen Briggs & Stratton workers met with two organizers from the Milwaukee Federated Trades Council. The next day, fourteen of the fifteen were fired. This effectively cooled interest in a union for a time, but after formation of the CIO, it revived. In December, 1936, several Briggs & Stratton employees called on George Kiebler at the UAW District Office. He not only gave them the application cards but set up a special meeting at which Homer Martin, UAW–CIO president, spoke. Several hundred attended. Martin, an ex-Baptist preacher, had a tremendous impact on his audience. Within three weeks, all 1,300 Briggs & Stratton employees had joined the union. The company granted recognition without asking for an election.

The first agreement gave the union exclusive bargaining rights; a 20 per cent wage increase, half of which replaced a former bonus; a grievance procedure; and seniority on layoffs and recalls. At the contract ratification meeting, members overwhelmingly passed the motion for acceptance. Then a member arose and asked, "What about vacations?" The union president, Clifford Matchey, went back to the company to try to get a week's vacation. Briggs & Stratton agreed to shut down during the week of the Fourth of July, with pay.[7] For the first few months, relations between the company and the union were informal and harmonious; only later would they deteriorate. During the union boom in the summer of 1937, the workers at Harley–Davidson, Globe Union, and Trostel Tannery in Milwaukee, West Bend Aluminum and Highway Trailer in Edgerton, and the Oshkosh Truck Company, among others, also started UAW–CIO locals.

In 1939, United Auto Workers President Homer Martin left the CIO and set up the UAW–AFL. Only a minority of the UAW–CIO locals and leaders followed him. One who did so was George Kiebler, but Larry Carlstrom stayed with the UAW–CIO. Carl Griepentrog, along with the union he had organized at Line Material, followed Kiebler into the UAW–AFL. In 1944, Griepentrog became regional director of the UAW–AFL, and in 1957, its national president. Following the merger of AFL and CIO in 1955, the UAW–AFL was renamed the Allied Industrial Workers.

Compared to the UAW–CIO, which was able to start rapidly and successfully in Wisconsin merely by bringing in the already formed AFL auto unions, the Steelworkers Organizing Committee (after May, 1942, the United States Steelworkers of America) had a late and difficult beginning in Wisconsin. The Steelworkers' primary aim was to organize basic steel plants, of which there were none in Wisconsin. It was only secondarily interested in organizing Wisconsin's numerous metal fabricating plants. However, just as the startling victory of the sitdown strike at Flint, Michigan, had sent auto workers flocking to the UAW, so the United Steelworkers' amazing feat of organizing all of United States Steel without a strike inspired the workers in Wisconsin's fabricating plants. John L. Lewis became their hero.

The Steelworkers' 1936 organizing staff in Wisconsin at first consisted of only one man, Meyer Adelman, formerly a pastry cook in Chicago, who was given the impressive title of Director of District 32. Adelman was a dynamo. At first using volunteer help, he distributed leaflets in every large metal fabricating plant, from Fairbanks Morse on the Illinois border to National Presto in Eau Claire. However, it took more than leaflets to win union recognition from Wisconsin's large metal fabricators. In the late 1930's and early 1940's, the anti-union attitude of these manufacturers equaled their workers' enthusiasm for unions. Most of the Milwaukee companies were members of the Milwaukee Metal Trades Association, an employers' organization with thirty-five years' experience in opposing unions, beginning with the Machinists' and Molders' strikes of 1901 and 1906. The contest at the big Harnischfeger plant in West Allis was typical of the resistance put up by these Milwaukee industrialists. It took two years and two strikes for the Steelworkers to gain a written contract with Harnischfeger.

Conditions in 1937 at Harnischfeger were typical of the period: no paid vacations; no seniority in layoffs, recalls, or promotions; no contractual pensions; and no workers' grievance committee. The first strike occurred in April, 1937, and lasted a little over a week. The settlement granted workers limited paid vacations, but the union victory was clouded: management refused to sign an agreement, merely calling the settlement a statement of company policy. During the next year, the company fired the union president and two other officers and then precipitated a strike in 1938 when it announced a 15 per cent wage cut. As the strike dragged on, the company made several unsuccessful attempts to open the plant with the co-operation of a company union. The National Labor Relations Board ordered the reinstatement of the Steelworkers' officers, and finally, after two and a half months, the strike ended with an agreement; the workers had to accept a 10 per cent wage reduction, but the union received full recognition, a signed contract, and arbitration as the final step in the grievance procedure.[8]

Adelman masterminded the organizing and collective bargaining at Harnischfeger from beginning to end. Under his skillful leadership the Steelworkers eventually won recognition at many of the other major metal fabricating plants in Wisconsin: in the Milwaukee area, Heil, Nordberg, George Meyer, Chain Belt (now Rexnord), and Bucyrus-Erie; in Eau Claire, National Presto; in Ripon, Barlow and Seelig Manufacturing Company (now Speed Queen); and in Beloit, Fairbanks–Morse.

Adelman added several workers from these new Steelworkers' locals to the Staff of District 32. One of these was Walter Burke, who was to become the secretary–treasurer of the United Steelworkers of America. Burke had graduated from high school in 1930 and, after four years of only sporadic employment, landed a more permanent job with a Fond du Lac refrigerator company. This company had a slack season every June, and the workers had no assurance of being recalled. A union contract could guarantee that layoffs and recalls would be made in accordance with years of service, and, according to Burke, workers desired this security as much as they desired wage increases.[9] When Burke saw in 1937 that the United Steelworkers had gained a contract with U.S. Steel and, closer to home, with the Barlow Seelig washing machine company in Ripon, he wrote to the Steelworkers' District office in Milwaukee asking for help in forming a union at the Fond du Lac refrigerator company. The workers quickly enrolled in the union; Burke was elected president, but was fired in a management effort to break the organization. The National Labor Relations Board ordered him reinstated, and he received back pay.[10]

Burke became secretary–treasurer of the state CIO in 1938, and then, upon the death of Meyer Adelman in 1947, director of District 32. In 1965, after a fierce election battle, he became secretary–treasurer of the national organization.

The CIO thus experienced spectacular growth in its early years, 1937–1941, justifying the theory that the way to organize factories was to do so on an industrial basis instead of splitting a plant into separate craft unions. When Rudolph Faupl, one of the WSFL organizers during the late 1930's, was asked by the author why the AFL had not organized such plants as Harnischfeger, Bucyrus–Erie, Heil, Chain Belt, and Speed Queen, he replied that it was because the AFL would not permit the State Federation to organize the unions on a purely industrial basis.[11]

In the competition between the AFL and CIO to organize new unions, the CIO often attempted to win over unions already chartered by the AFL. The Wisconsin plants involved in that process were A. O. Smith, International Harvester, and Briggs & Stratton in Milwaukee; Allis–Chalmers in Milwaukee and in La Crosse; Highway Trailer in Edgerton; and Simmons in Kenosha. In Kenosha and Racine, after the first few years, local union leaders significantly muted the AFL–CIO rivalry. A unifying force in each of those cities was both the AFL and CIO unions' support of a single labor paper, the Kenosha *Labor Press*. The extent of the rivalry can be seen in a comment made by its publisher, Harold Newton: "Yes, we maintained both AFL and CIO support for our labor paper, but with every issue I literally had to use a ruler to see that each side received exactly equal coverage."[12]

Divisions Within the CIO

After its brilliant organizing successes of 1937 and 1938, the CIO in Wisconsin began to run into difficulties. Several of the new, young leaders in the state were so left-wing in their ideology and in their public relations and political activities that they brought on ten years of internecine warfare within the state organization. In newspapers and during legislative hearings, certain state CIO leaders began to be labeled Communists. Worst of all, in 1938, Fred Wolter, president of the CIO United Electrical Workers local at the Allen–Bradley plant, wrote a letter to the Milwaukee *Sentinel* charging Communist leadership of the CIO: "The fight going on in the UAW is a struggle to retire Communists from active leadership in the CIO . . . . The Communistic element which is being ousted from leadership and control in the Allis–Chalmers Local is also in control of the State and County CIO and this is the main reason why the majority of the CIO Unions in the state refuse to affiliate."[13]

So serious was the situation that in 1939 the leadership of the state CIO decided to improve its image by having the two "tainted" incumbent chief officers, President Emil Costello and Secretary–Treasurer Gunnar Mickelsen, each refuse to run for re-election and agree to nominate as his successor a member from outside the left-wing faction. Following an impassioned plea for unity, Costello nominated as his successor Harvey Kitzman, who had become head of UAW, Local 180, at the Case Company in Racine. Mickelsen nominated as his successor Walter Burke, now a Steelworker staff representative. Both were elected unanimously, inspiring Larry Carlstrom, still an official at the UAW Regional Office, to hail Kitzman's nomination as "a new birth of freedom."[14]

The new freedom did not last; the old executive board was unchanged. Divisive issues not settled by the change of officers included the policy of contributing to allegedly Communist-dominated organizations, sending CIO delegates to those organizations, and, especially, passing foreign policy resolutions that followed each zigzag of the foreign policy of the USSR. At the 1940 state convention, after hours of rancorous debate, a resolution was passed urging complete neutrality in the European war. At this time, France had fallen and the Nazi air blitz of London was in full force. Emil Costello argued for the neutrality resolution: "If we are going to aid organized labor in Great Britain, the best thing American labor can do is to stop this bloody conquest that is going on, by refusing to aid one side or the other."[15] The policy of neutrality urged by Costello was a reversal of the "collective security" policy which the state CIO had advocated prior to the Nazi–Soviet pact of August, 1939, in which Germany and Russia agreed to divide Poland. Russia not only remained neutral while Hitler attacked Britain and France, but urged Communist parties around the world to recommend neutrality for their countries.

The two state officers elected in 1939, Kitzman and Burke, were ineffective against the left-wing executive board. Kitzman was an isolationist, as was Wisconsin Senator Robert La Follette, Jr., and therefore found himself in agreement with a policy of neutrality for the United States during the period of the Stalin–Hitler Pact, August, 1939, to June, 1941, when Hitler attacked Russia. Walter Burke's boss was Meyer Adelman, district director for the Steelworkers. Adelman was a member of the executive board of the state CIO and an active supporter of the pro-Soviet foreign policy of the state CIO executive board. Not surprisingly, Burke maintained silence on foreign policy issues and occupied himself with the organizing programs and the finances of the CIO.

The 1941 convention experienced the same abrasive divisions as had the conventions of 1939 and 1940, but in a different way. It met in Milwaukee from October 30 to November 1. By that time, the Nazis had driven through Russian-occupied Poland and put the Russian armies in full retreat. The convention's foreign policy resolutions reflected a dramatic turnabout from those of the previous convention: "Resolved . . . that we urge the greatest and swiftest mobilization of aid to Britain, the Soviet Union, China, and all other peoples fighting Hitlerism; and that we call for the immediate repeal of the Neutrality Act . . . we stand ready and eager . . . [to send] an expeditionary force."[16]

In a speech urging passage of the resolution, Emil Costello, reversing his 1940 course, stated: "Surely there is no one in this hall who cannot agree that Hitler today is the greatest threat, not only to American democracy but to Democracy over the entire world. We have seen what has happened to France, and with the fall of France we have seen what has happened to the French Federation of Labor. . . . The defense of Moscow and Leningrad means the defense of Washington, New York and San Francisco."[17]

There were, however, delegates who dissented. One was Paul Steffes, from UAW, Local 75, in Milwaukee:[18]

> I will not go along with such a resolution . . . signifying your intention that you are willing again to send an army of boys to fight a battle in Europe. That's a long and far position from the one taken about twelve or fourteen months ago. . . . I will say that I am a citizen of this country, and . . . that I have not been a patriot since June 22 only, when Hitler invaded Russia. These are the remarks of an American citizen born and raised here.

Another was Roy Speth, from the same union: "I know that there were many of us last year in the minority on that particular question [foreign policy]. . . . I hate to see the delegates here and the council itself become the laughing stock."

Other foreign policy resolutions split the membership. Most important was an attack on nine of Wisconsin's ten congressmen and on both of the state's U.S. senators, Robert La Follette, Jr., and Alexander Wiley, for their isolationist votes. The one congressman who escaped censure was Milwaukee's Fourth District representative, Thaddeus Wasielewski, whose Polish constituency led him to vote for lend–lease and other measures which might save Poland. (Ironically, Wasielewski was to be defeated in the Democratic primary five years later by the left-wing CIO leadership, who opposed him because he objected to the Soviet-dominated government in Poland.)

The resolution passed at the 1941 convention read: "Be It Resolved: That we protest the action of these 9 congressmen and senators . . . in giving a bad name to the State of Wisconsin causing it to be regarded as an 'appeasement' state and causing questions to be raised throughout the country as to the loyalty of Wisconsin and its readiness to defend our country."[19] The resolution aroused complaints from many supporters of La Follette, who had a strong pro-labor record, and recently had led a Senate investigation of Wagner Act violations. The new CIO unions were major beneficiaries of the senator's efforts.

The tension between these factions meant that debates not related to foreign policy also became battlegrounds. The anti-leftists wanted to have roll call votes recorded so that they could hold the delegates accountable for their particular votes, and they wanted to elect all executive board members at large instead of apportioning delegates by unions. The left wing won both of these votes. Another battle took place over the method of selecting the delegate to the national CIO convention. Before the state convention, the executive board had elected as the state delegate Harold Christoffel, a leftist and president of UAW, Local 248, at Allis–Chalmers. Anti-leftists fought hard but unsuccessfully to block Christoffel's selection.

For all of these reasons the state CIO conventions in this period were contentious and acrimonious; boos as well as applause were heard frequently. In 1940, President Kitzman at one point announced that "any delegate [who] spends his local union's money for no other reason than to 'boo' is a damn poor sport and ought to be run out of this convention. (Applause) As long as I am chairman . . . there is not going to be any booing and if you don't think so just try it."[20]

The outbursts were indicative of the extremely tense feelings over the basic issue, control of the state CIO by left-wing leaders. Those not in this group felt strongly that they represented a majority of the workers in the plants, but that the left wing had command of the administrative machinery and managed, through superior organization, to dominate the state conventions. At the conclusion of the 1941 convention, President Kitzman refused to accept renomination. Later he declared that he was fed up with being a "front" man for the Communists.[21]

From 1942 through 1945, the internal conflict in the Wisconsin state CIO seemed to wind down as all groups concentrated on winning the war. The state leadership in 1942 strongly supported a second front to assist Russia, which was reeling from the German attack. When World War II ended, however, dissension reappeared, and with increased intensity.

Defeat of the Left Wing

Both the Milwaukee County Industrial Union Council (IUC), which was the CIO city central body, and the Wisconsin CIO (whose official name was the Wisconsin Industrial Union Council) were at this time controlled by executive boards which consistently had followed the Communist line in support of the Soviet Union. The revolt against their leadership began in the summer of 1946.

The leftist views expressed in the Wisconsin edition of the *CIO News* had been a continuing irritant to many workers and local union officers. In July, 1946, United Steelworkers, Local 1114, at the Harnischfeger plant in West Allis passed a resolution condemning the *News* for "its attempt to inoculate the rank and file members with ideologies that are Un-American and which are contrary to the desires and beliefs of the vast majority of CIO members."[22] Local unions were further outraged by the Milwaukee IUC's Political Action Committee, which endorsed a candidate opposing Congressman Thaddeus F. Wasielewski in the state's Fourth Congressional District. The plan of the anti-leftists was to call for a special Milwaukee IUC meeting to readmit the many locals which had not been paying the per capita tax because of their opposition to the leadership of the County IUC, thus augmenting the number of votes against the officers in the regular election on October 16.

The special meeting, scheduled for October 13, almost did not take place, because the left-wing IUC secretary–treasurer failed to send out the notices. Informal notification occurred, however, and at the meeting eight new locals, including the huge Local 9 of the Brewery Workers, were affiliated and their delegates seated. At the regular October 16 meeting, the IUC secretary–treasurer attempted to sabotage the election by refusing to provide a list of the delegates. The election was held nevertheless, and the anti-leftist slate was elected overwhelmingly. Feelings of the factions ran so high that police officers had been needed to keep unauthorized persons out of the room during the counting of the 370 ballots, which was not completed until 8:50 the next morning. The ballot boxes then were placed in a safety deposit box at the First Wisconsin National Bank.

The deposed leaders appealed the election to the national CIO, which sent two officers to Milwaukee to look into the situation. They exonerated those newly elected, but deferred their installation pending a final decision. Meanwhile, they appointed a temporary administrator to look into the records and books of the IUC. The audit and final report of November stated that for a number of years the IUC had made substantial contributions to organizations not endorsed by the national CIO, and that the IUC had issued statements and taken stands on international and national events not approved by the CIO. The IUC finances were found to be in disarray. However, the National CIO officers' report ruled that some locals had not been eligible to vote in the October 13 election and therefore ordered a new election. For the new election it broadened the eligibility. The new election was held on December 4, 1946, and resulted in a complete purge of the left wing.[23]

The ouster of this faction from the Milwaukee County IUC was a forerunner of the more important and dramatic battle for control of the state CIO at the December, 1946, convention in Wausau. Since its formation in 1937, the state CIO executive board had had a left-leaning majority.

Before 1946, opponents of the state leadership, as we have seen, had tried a number of tactics. From 1937 through 1939 they expressed opposition by withholding dues from the state CIO. After some concessions were made by the state CIO in 1939, more United Auto Workers locals paid their dues. In 1940 and 1941 the opposition fought hard but unsuccessfully to block the pro-Soviet foreign policy resolutions at the state conventions.

In 1946, however, the opposing faction had a leader, a United Auto Worker representative from Milwaukee, Walter Cappel, who brought together in one convention caucus most of the anti-leftist unions in the state CIO. For some time, Cappel had been an outspoken critic of leftist elements in the CIO. The core of the incumbent left-wing leadership came from the huge UAW, Local 248, at Allis–Chalmers, which sent seventy-nine delegates and alternates to the convention, almost three times as many as the next largest local. The state president, Robert Buse, was from Local 248. The secretary of the state CIO, Mel Heinritz of the United Public Workers, was the chief strategist for the leftists. A power behind the scene was Harold Christoffel, the founder and for many years president of Local 248. At this convention he held the important post of chairman of the rules committee.[24]

As the convention began, it looked as though the anti-leftist group carried slightly more credentials (votes apportioned according to the size of the union), but the left wing had more delegates actually present and thus, on voice votes, carried the motions. The Milwaukee *Journal* reported that this was "perhaps due to their reputed packing of the hall with non-delegate supporters, as alleged by Cappel."[25] On roll call votes, the anti-Communists probably could have predominated, but when they asked for roll calls, the chair refused on grounds that the credentials committee had not reported on who officially could vote.

In fact, although the convention began on Thursday, the credentials committee did not report until Sunday noon, just in time for the election of new officers. All of the committees at the convention were ruled by a left-wing majority, and the anti-leftist resolutions submitted to the resolutions committee promptly died there. The major argument in the credentials committee was whether it was to follow the rules of the state constitution, which stated that voting credentials were to be based on average per capita payments over the past twelve months, or the rules of the national CIO, which stated that credentials were based on per capita payments over the past three months. The newly admitted anti-leftist Brewery Workers, with 7,000 members, would be eligible to vote under the rules of the national CIO but ineligible under those of the state.[26]

Tension among delegates mounted as anti-leftists began to fear that, despite their majority, the credentials committee would rule them ineligible and delay a report until late Sunday, when many delegates would have returned home. But on Friday night, the midwest regional director of the CIO, F. J. Michel, arrived and specified that the rules of the national CIO must be followed. His ruling was a large step toward an anti-leftist victory, but by then important out-of-state officials had begun to appear who were intent on salvaging some of the left wing.

R. J. Thomas, a CIO vice-president, arrived in Wausau and quietly met with several members of Cappel's coalition in an effort to win them over to his goal, a compromise according to which the incumbent state president, Buse, would withdraw, and the left would support Herman Steffes for president. In return, the anti-leftists would support the incumbent Mel Heinritz as secretary–treasurer. Herbert March, vice-president of the United Packinghouse Workers, Ernest DeMaio of the United Electrical Workers Union, and other strong supporters of the left wing came from the national CIO to promote this plan. The regional director of the United Auto Workers, Joseph Mattson, a bitter enemy of Cappel, sent in six UAW staff representatives to try to save the left-wing majority.[27]

On Saturday the credentials committee still had not reported. Despite Michel's insistence that national rules be followed, Heinritz and Buse declared that such rules could not be applied retroactively. On Saturday night, however, Allan Haywood, national vice-president in charge of state and county central bodies, arrived and reaffirmed the national CIO credential and election procedures. To ensure compliance, he stayed through the election on Sunday and at noon the credentials committee finally reported in support of the national rules. The Brewery Workers could vote.

President Buse withdrew his own nomination in favor of anti-leftist Herman Steffes. The leftists then hoped to pick up enough votes to save Heinritz as secretary–treasurer. Concerted lobbying against Walter Cappel by the national representatives had an effect. Certain anti-leftist locals let it be known that they would not support Cappel as secretary–treasurer, but neither would they support Heinritz. When the nominations were finally made on Sunday, after the long-delayed credentials report, these locals nominated a third candidate for secretary–treasurer, John Sorenson, an anti-leftist Steelworker. In a dramatic speech, Cappel withdrew his own nomination and supported Sorenson, who won narrowly over Heinritz, 37,595 to 35,134.

Because of the delayed election, the convention conducted no other business. When on Sunday afternoon those opposed to the left wing tried to change the constitution so the executive board could be elected by the entire membership instead of by delegates from certain unions, too many of their supporters had already left for home. This reform had to be delayed until 1947, when it resulted in the election of a completely anti-leftist slate.

How could it happen that the 512 delegates to the 1946 Wisconsin state CIO convention could succeed in splitting the votes of the entire convention almost evenly over the question of support for a union leadership which for ten years had consistently followed the Soviet foreign policy line? When the first CIO unions were being organized in 1936, 1937, and 1938, members of the left wing achieved leadership positions in some of the most important unions. The same thing, of course, happened in other states. The background of these particular labor leaders understandably led them to the left. Several had been members of the state Socialist party.

In the 1920's and early 1930's, the Soviet government was regarded by many liberal Americans as a noble experiment, attempting to build a society which placed the welfare of common people above that of private wealth. The Great Depression and a consequent unemployment rate of 25 per cent in 1932–1933 caused many Americans to become bitterly critical of capitalism.

No doubt a few of these CIO leaders actually joined the Communist party and union members merely followed their leaders, unaware of their political affiliation. Particularly visible was the foreign policy advocated by American Communists, which followed the twists and turns of Soviet foreign policy. Since we have no way of knowing which CIO leaders may have joined the Communist party and which merely supported Soviet foreign policy, I have used the term "left-wing" to cover both categories. Although only a handful of leaders were "left-wing," they had great influence on the administration of many local unions and on the votes of local union delegates to state CIO conventions.

One leader who had considerable influence was Meyer Adelman, district director of the United Steelworkers, whom we have described earlier as a courageous and excellent organizer and a master of collective bargaining strategy. For some years, the Steelworker locals tolerated his foreign policy stands and his support of the state CIO leadership because of his outstanding trade union qualities. But in 1946, Steelworker locals took an active part in expelling leftist leaders from both the Milwaukee IUC and the state CIO. In the 1946 state executive board election, Adelman, who had been a member since 1937, was replaced with another candidate by the Steelworkers caucus.

The 1946 purge of both the Milwaukee County IUC and the state CIO was a precursor of the expulsions in 1949 and 1950 of ten Communist-dominated international unions from the national CIO, paving the way for the later merger of the AFL and CIO.

The dual role, providing both strength and divisiveness, that left-wingers played within the Wisconsin labor movement cannot be overlooked. They arrived on the scene at a propitious time when workers, fed up with unemployment and unfair treatment by employers, were willing to risk their jobs to form a union. These leaders were outstanding organizers, courageous, imaginative, and willing to work around the clock at low pay in the interest of unionism. Yet their dogged adherence to Soviet foreign policy had decidedly negative effects. It alienated them from their membership; it increased employer resistance to unions; it lowered labor's standing with the public; and it seriously weakened labor's political influence. The 1946 and 1947 purges unified the CIO and made possible the slow rebuilding of labor's public image and political influence.

CIO Growth After World War II

Figure 2 in the preceding chapter reflects accurate figures on the Wisconsin state CIO membership from 1946 to merger in 1957, but data are very sketchy for the 1930's and early 1940's. The first state CIO convention was held in 1938 in Milwaukee, and no membership figures were published. Because of the bitter political battle within the Wisconsin CIO unions, many locals refused to pay their per capita dues. Not until 1946 do the state CIO convention proceedings give reasonably accurate data on paid-up membership.

In the postwar period, the CIO grew not only by organizing new unions but also by affiliating with previously non-CIO unions, the biggest of which was the National Federation of Telephone Workers, a group that in 1949 affiliated with the CIO as the Communications Workers of America. These workers were employees of the nation's telephone companies and manufacturers of communications equipment.

As early as 1921, the Bell Telephone System management nationally had organized a company union, which, by 1934, had done little or nothing to raise employee wages. In that year telephone management, realizing workers' dissatisfaction with this company union, established a Plant Employees' Association in an effort to pacify the more militant workers. The association was reorganized in December, 1935, to end company payment of its expenses, a step necessary to bring it into compliance with the National Labor Relations Act (Wagner Act) of 1935. The new association remained, however, at least psychologically linked to the company. Its officers in Wisconsin therefore set up still another organization, the Telephone Guild of Wisconsin, an independent federation affiliated with the National Federation of Telephone Workers (NFTW). The guild negotiated annual contracts through 1947.

In view of the long history of company unions in the Bell System, there remained some suspicion, at least on the part of outsiders, that the NFTW was also company-dominated. The fact that it was not affiliated with either the AFL or CIO increased these suspicions, but they were put to rest when, in 1947, the NFTW conducted a nationwide strike against the Bell System. In Wisconsin, support for the strike was overwhelming. Small Wisconsin cities, which never had experienced a strike, now faced the unusual situation of seeing their telephone exchanges picketed by female operators. Two years later, the Communications Workers of America (CWA), the new name adopted by the NFTW, voted to affiliate with the CIO, adding several thousand members to the Wisconsin State CIO.

A second national union that affiliated with the CIO was the Brewery Workers, which joined the CIO in 1946 and in Wisconsin, as we have seen, played a role in the credentials fight in the state convention that year. Most of Wisconsin's CIO members belonged to unions that were formed in the 1930's in the mass production industries—the United Auto Workers, the United Steelworkers, and the United Electrical Workers—but the Brewery Workers were an exception. Their union was first heard of in the great eight-hour-day strikes in May, 1886, when the Milwaukee Brewery Workers belonged to the Knights of Labor. Subsequently, Brewery Workers Local 9 became one of the most powerful unions in the Milwaukee Federated Trades Council and in the Wisconsin State Federation of Labor. The Brewery Workers International Union was not one of the ten AFL unions that joined the CIO in 1936. But, due to prolonged jurisdictional rivalry with the Teamsters in which the AFL sided with the Teamsters, it joined the CIO in 1946. Its large membership in Wisconsin gave it considerable influence in the state CIO.

In 1953 Local 9 proposed to the joint employers' bargaining committee a reduction in hours from 40 to 35 per week, a wage increase of 25 cents per hour, improvements in health and pension plans, and additional holidays. The local's proposals were designed to catch up with pay and hours at East and West Coast breweries and were put forth when the contract expired on May 1. With no agreement in sight, what was to be an eleven-week strike began on May 15. All of Milwaukee's breweries were struck— Schlitz, Pabst, Miller, Blatz, and Gettleman. Although brewery employers in Milwaukee offered Local 9 no reduction in weekly hours, on June 1, the Schlitz Company proposed to the workers at its Brooklyn plant a weekly cut in hours, from 37.5 to 35, and a wage increase of 66 cents above the Milwaukee base rate of $2.00.[28] These tactics only increased worker solidarity.

The strike dragged on into a hot summer. On June 26, members of Local 9 turned down an offer of 15 cents more per hour, voting 6,274 to 348. Although the companies were losing their summer business, they appeared as adamant as the workers. In reality, the situation varied among companies. Schlitz and Pabst had large breweries in other cities, while Miller, Blatz, and Gettleman had plants only in Milwaukee; the financial losses to employers were therefore uneven. In late July, the Blatz Company broke from the employers' bargaining committee, made a substantially more costly offer directly to Local 9, and reached a settlement. The other employers then asked the local to negotiate, which it did. With Blatz ready to start up production, the other companies hastened to accept the terms of the Blatz agreement and granted gains of 63 cents an hour, including a thirty-minute paid lunch; improvements in the pension program and in life insurance; two more holidays; higher shift premiums; and call-in pay (a minimum payment for reporting for work).[29]

Other Postwar Strikes Among Wisconsin CIO Unions

For better understanding of these years of unionism, it is helpful to put them in historical perspective. Richard Lester, a specialist in industrial relations, has described his view of the historical progression of management's relations with labor as encompassing four stages.[30] The first is that of complete rejection of unionism, a typical management policy up to the New Deal labor legislation of the 1930's. The second is arm's-length bargaining, which characterizes the first three or four years after the initial signing of a contract. In many cases this stage lasted through World War II and up to 1950. The third stage is that of management acceptance of unions and usually is characterized by union shop agreements. This period has lasted for the past twenty-five or thirty years. The fourth period, as described by Lester, is one of genuine co-operation between labor and management. By 1982 only a few companies had entered the fourth period.

The Wisconsin paper industry reached the third stage by 1943, but the transition from stage to stage in other industries, particularly in metal fabricating, was more halting. The 1930's was a time of frequent strikes as the firms fought to retain their traditional non-union status. By 1955, though, most companies had arrived at Lester's third stage.

Strikes were not permitted during World War II. But the war's end brought a resurgence of strike action, especially in metal fabricating. The strikes were due, in part, to workers' pent-up frustration over the slow resolution of grievances and wage settlements during the war years, but to a greater extent, they centered on wages or production standards. Some of these strikes resulted from management's withdrawal of the union security which the War Labor Board had enforced for the duration of the war; this marked a backward step from "acceptance" to "arm's-length bargaining." Two companies which regressed in this fashion were J. I. Case, the scene of strikes in the 1930's, as described earlier in this chapter, and Allis–Chalmers, the huge manufacturing company located at West Allis.

The postwar strikes at these companies were of unusual duration: fourteen months at Case, eleven months at Allis–Chalmers. United Auto Workers, Local 180, at Case and UAW, Local 248, at Allis–Chalmers narrowly survived the strikes, which drew national attention. Both plants produced the agricultural machinery that was in short supply after the war. For this reason, President Harry Truman threatened to seize the plants and settle the strikes, but he did not carry out the threat.

The Case strike was conducted against a management which, despite the labor legislation of the New Deal and the union–management peace of World War II, appeared not to have accepted unionism. During the war, the War Labor Board had abrogated the provisions of a 1937 Case Company letter tying Local 180 to an open shop in perpetuity, and pressured the company into a one-year agreement that included a maintenance-of-membership clause, requiring everyone who joined the union to continue to pay dues for the duration of the contract. At the end of the war Case refused to renew any form of union security or to arbitrate grievances, citing the letter of 1937 as a reason for not bargaining over union security.

In 1946 the National Labor Relations Board, followed the next year by the Wisconsin Supreme Court, declared the letter insufficient reason to refuse to bargain. Case nevertheless refused to grant any form of union security, and the strike struggled on into its second year. After fourteen months, the intervention of the U.S. Undersecretary of Labor brought a settlement. Case granted a substantial wage increase, but made no concessions on union security. Local 180 had lost the strike in that it had failed to win a union shop; it had won in the sense that it had survived. The way was open for another strike as soon as the union regained its strength. Harvey

Kitzman, soon to be elected UAW regional director, had led the union during this long strike.

The next strike at Case did not come until 1960. It was over the same issue of union security and lasted six months. The company's new president, William J. Grede, went on television to express the Case philosophy: "Compulsory union membership was 'un-American and un-Christian.'"[31] A settlement eventually was reached, after the governor of Wisconsin appointed a panel of three university professors, headed by Nathan Feinsinger of the University of Wisconsin Law School, to mediate. Again, the settlement failed to grant union security, although the union did gain arbitration as the final step of the grievance procedure.

The president of Local 180 during the 1960 strike was Tony Valeo, who kept the union going even though there was almost no chance of victory. But, unlike Frank Sahorske in 1934–1935, or Harvey Kitzman in 1936–1937 and 1945–1947, Valeo had a chance to participate in a new relationship with Case. By 1961 the company was approaching bankruptcy. A new president, Merritt D. Hill, began to reverse Case's sixty-year anti-union position. In 1962 the company granted a check-off of union dues. This 1962 contract contained a special clause entitled "Mutual Interests" which spelled out the desire of both parties for "more harmonious relations."[32] The next contract, in 1963, conceded a full union shop and established a co-operative relationship with the union. Much of the credit for this change must go to Valeo, who, despite the bitterness of two prolonged strikes, was able to respond co-operatively and constructively when the new management accepted the union as a permanent institution.

The dispute between Allis–Chalmers and UAW, Local 248, began in 1946, when a new contract was to be negotiated. The company did not want to grant the union security clause—the requirement that employees maintain their membership in the union—which the War Labor Board had compelled the company to grant in 1943. This, plus disagreements over wages and grievance procedures, precipitated a strike which received substantially more publicity than the strike at Case. Allis–Chalmers was a much larger company, but an additional reason for publicity was that for several years the management had been collecting information on the local's principal officers, allegedly showing that they were Communists or Communist sympathizers. Milwaukee newspapers gave ample space to these charges. A congressional committee came to Milwaukee and held hearings on the accusations.

The length of the strike, eleven months, plus the accusations of Communism, demoralized the workers, and Local 248 called off the strike in

March, 1947. Employees returned to work without a union contract. The UAW executive board in Detroit suspended the accused officers of the local and appointed an administrator. Within two years, new officers had negotiated a contract that finally granted maintenance of union membership. In December, 1947, at the State CIO Convention in Milwaukee Walter Reuther, president of the UAW International, declared of the long strike: "We lost because there were people in positions of leadership in that local who put their loyalties outside of their union, outside of the rank and file and outside of their country. . . . We are never going to permit the membership of any local union to be betrayed in that situation."[33]

By 1950, unions were firmly established in the state's various metalworking industries, in the huge papermaking industry, and in such trades as meat packing, printing, construction, and brewing. Management had come to accept unionism, and periodic labor agreements were negotiated regularly, most of them containing effective union security clauses. Strikes were infrequent and were usually of short duration. Specified grievance procedures, including binding arbitration as a final step, brought generally peaceful labor relations during the term of a contract.

There was, however, an exception. During the 1950's, one particular labor dispute dwarfed all others and made the village of Kohler the focus of national and congressional attention. Despite its prolonged labor problems during the years 1934 to 1941, the Kohler Company in the postwar period continued to support the company union, the Kohler Workers Association. The KWA had no strike fund and no right to resort to arbitration if grievances could not be resolved; in fact, decisions on wage changes and the rates for particular jobs normally were made unilaterally by the company.[34]

In 1946 the Wisconsin State Federation of Labor petitioned the National Labor Relations Board for a union representation election at Kohler and was defeated 1,561 to 916, with the KWA actively opposing the WSFL. By 1950, however, some of the younger Kohler employees wanted a union that would better represent their interests. The United Auto Workers were approached. Regional director Harvey Kitzman offered to help, sending in organizers to get authorization cards for a National Labor Relations Board election. The election was scheduled for March 27, 1951. During the campaign, the Kohler Company boosted the KWA through advertisements in the Sheboygan paper and radio broadcasts. The UAW lost the election—the results were 2,064 for the KWA, 1,575 for the UAW, and 76 for no union—but received substantially more votes than had the WSFL in 1946.

This relatively good showing encouraged the UAW to continue organizing. For the first time, Kohler workers openly began to protest bad working conditions. For example, in the enameling department, which was always hot, the company shut off the fans in April, 1952, to reduce the amount of dust. Some of the workers, growing sick and dizzy from the heat, went to the medical department. A few were given permission to go home, but the most active UAW supporters were told to go back to work. When they refused they were fired.[35]

The officers of the KWA grew more demanding in bargaining with the company. The company, in turn, criticized Egbert H. Kolhagen, editor of the KWA paper, for the paper's militant tone. In a surprise move at the end of April, 1952, the officers of the KWA recommended affiliation with the UAW. A referendum among KWA members favored UAW affiliation by 2,248 votes to 1,129. A National Labor Relations Board election was held in June, and the UAW won, even though the race had become three-cornered when the Milwaukee-based UAW–AFL entered.

Following the election victory, I asked Kolhagen how it had happened that he, who had stood with the Kohler Company and against unionism for eighteen years, turned against the Kohler Company and joined the UAW. "The last straw," he replied, "was when the Company took away our dignity. During the last KWA negotiations, Herbert Kohler pointed his finger at me and told me to 'Sit down.'"[36]

Despite expectations that a strike might develop, the UAW and Kohler reached agreement on a one-year contract in February, 1953. The major achievement was gaining arbitration as the final step of the grievance procedure. The 1953 contract marked the first time in this century that the Kohler Company had dealt with any body other than a company-dominated union. The agreement brought a relaxation of tension, which had mounted when, during negotiations, the company, as it had done in 1934, installed searchlights on the roofs of the plant; brought in cots, food, and cooking equipment in preparation for a siege; and armed its guards, purchasing shotguns, tear gas, revolvers, and thousands of rounds of ammunition.[37]

As the term of the contract neared its end in the spring of 1954, the Kohler Company repeated these strike preparations. No agreement was reached, and on April 3, 1954—approximately twenty years after the beginning of the prewar strike—the second Kohler strike began. It was to last even longer than the first, ending officially in September, 1960. The company offered reinstatement to approximately 1,400 strikers. Settlement of the strike came after a decision by the National Labor Relations

Board that the Kohler company was guilty of refusal to bargain. The company agreed to 4.5 million dollars in back pay and pension credits to illegally discharged strikers, who were rehired. But not until December, 1965, eleven years after the strike began, was a new contract between UAW Local 833 and the Kohler Company signed.

The protracted period of strike action engaged national attention in the press and on television. In 1958 a U.S. Senate committee, the McClellan Committee, held five weeks of hearings in Washington, D.C. There were several unique features in this conflict. When the strike was two months old, the company resumed production with replacement workers. The UAW then conducted a national boycott of Kohler plumbing fixtures which resulted in controversies in many local communities from San Francisco to New York, among government officials, unions, architects, and contractors over the merits of supporting Kohler workers or their employer.

But the strike was fought most bitterly on the streets of Sheboygan and in the town of Kohler. At the beginning, masses of workers gathered before the gates of the huge plant in "belly-to-back" picketing. Court appeals by the company brought injunctions limiting union picketing. As is true of all strikes, there was bitterness among the strikers, those who continued to work, and those who took new jobs at Kohler. The company reported 836 cases of vandalism against persons working during the strike, including the dynamiting of automobiles. The union reported thirty-six cases of vandalism against union members.[38]

Even after the strike was called off in 1960, the company spent another five years in court appeals. The UAW international union had spent 14 million dollars to support the strike, most of it in benefits for the striking Kohler workers.[39] Despite the suffering and bitterness of the long strike, the years since 1965 have seen the Kohler Company reverse its policy of "union exclusion" and move rapidly into "acceptance of unions."

The Impact of the CIO

When the new CIO succeeded in winning 10,000 Wisconsin auto workers away from the AFL and the WSFL in 1936, there was, of course, great concern expressed by the WSFL leadership. The subsequent rapid growth of the state CIO to approximately 60,000 members by 1946 resulted, however, mostly from affiliation of newly organized workers who had not previously belonged to any union. Over the same period, the WSFL grew from 40,000 in 1936 to 130,000 in 1945. The formation of the CIO in Wisconsin brought to the fore new cadres of organizers, mostly young and enthusiastic. These men and women inspired thousands of Wisconsin workers to make a new assault on the anti-union policies of employers. With the help of the Wagner Act of 1935, they succeeded in establishing collective bargaining in hundreds of Wisconsin factories which had previously excluded unions.

The CIO's emphasis on industrial organization, instead of organization by craft, provided representation for the semi-skilled and the unskilled, who previously had been unrepresented in collective bargaining. The CIO generally put greater stress on labor's participation in community services for the poor and the disadvantaged. The National AFL–CIO merger of 1955 recognized this contribution by making a place in the merged organization for the CIO administrative structure for community services.

In regard to political action, the CIO, by the 1950's, had demonstrated a special ability to mobilize many of its members for volunteer political legwork—distributing political leaflets, registering its members to vote, and contributing money to union-endorsed candiates. Above all, the CIO's contribution to the Wisconsin labor movement was the addition of 80,000 members and a large body of full-time leaders.

CHAPTER 7

Leadership

C HAPTER 4 DESCRIBED the first leadership competition in the Wisconsin State Federation of Labor (WSFL), which ended in a Socialist victory at the WSFL convention of 1900: Frederick Brockhausen was elected secretary–treasurer and Frank Weber, a Populist before he became a Socialist, was elected general organizer (equivalent to president). Socialist control lasted for forty years, a period during which there were no leadership contests.

The WSFL officers were outstanding, and transitions in the leadership were smooth, largely because the Socialists groomed younger members to replace older officers. This was particularly true of two young Milwaukee trade unionists, John J. Handley, business agent of Machinists Lodge 66, and Henry Ohl, Jr., of the Typographical Local 23. When the Socialists won control of Milwaukee government in 1910, they had both the city government and the labor movement in which to train their protégés. Handley was given a job in the Department of Public Works and Ohl, leader of Local 23's successful strike for the eight-hour day in 1907, was made deputy city health commissioner. When Frederick Brockhausen retired in 1912, Handley was elected without opposition to succeed him as WSFL secretary–treasurer.

Destined to become president, Ohl received further grooming. In 1914 he was hired by the WSFL as an organizer at a salary of $100 a month plus expenses to travel the state and persuade existing unions to affiliate with the federation. He was extraordinarily successful in increasing WSFL membership. In 1916, under the direction of Frank Weber, he worked as an organizer and strike leader in Marinette when the city experienced what came close to a general strike. When Weber resigned as general organizer, Ohl was elected unanimously to that post. (In 1923 the title "general organizer" was changed to president.) Weber continued to be the principal leader of the Milwaukee Federated Trades Council (FTC) until 1934. Thus both organizations had solid and continuous Socialist leadership. At this time it was not unusual to have Socialists in the labor movement, but rarely did they control a state federation. What were the consequences of this control? For one, these Socialist leaders had their differences with the more traditional leaders of the national AFL. As we shall see in Chapter 8, they especially took issue with AFL President Samuel Gompers' insistence on the endorsement of pro-labor candidates from the Republican and Democratic parties instead of from the Socialist party.

The most profound difference between the Wisconsin Socialist leadership and the AFL was over the entry of the United States into World War I. In 1916 the WSFL passed a resolution opposing U.S. participation in the war,[1] and at its 1917 convention in St. Louis, the Socialist party voted to oppose the war effort. Samuel Gompers, a strong supporter of U.S. war participation, advocated American aid for France and Great Britain even before the United States formally declared war.

For the leaders of the WSFL this difference between the two groups must have presented a painful dilemma. Once the war effort began, however, they reversed their position and led the WSFL in active support. Frederick Brockhausen was appointed to the Wisconsin State Council of Defense. At the WSFL's 1918 convention, Ohl presented a long resolution pledging to stand "unflinchingly behind the government in every effort to crush plutocracy" and commended the "efforts of the United States Department of Labor, the Shipbuilding Labor Adjustment Board, and the Federal War Labor Board."[2]

The war and postwar years were marked by hysteria directed against those who opposed the war, and then, after the Russian revolution, against radicals, suspected radicals, and labor leaders. Wisconsin U.S. Senator Robert M. La Follette, Sr., voted against entry into the war, for which he was castigated throughout the state and even was burned in effigy on the University of Wisconsin campus in Madison.

Businessmen who feared the spread of communism tended to see every effort of American labor to organize and bargain collectively as a step toward revolution. During the 1919 national steel strike, many local communities under the control of the steel corporations refused to allow union meetings. In Wisconsin, International Harvester, which had a big plant in Milwaukee, set up a company union whose membership was restricted to United States citizens. Kimberly–Clark, the large Wisconsin paper manufacturer, established a company union whose purpose was "to stop Bolshevism, IWWism, Socialism, and Sovietism."[3]

The U.S. Department of Justice was a participant in the hysteria, deporting aliens and prosecuting, under the terms of various wartime laws, citizens it considered to be dangerous radicals. Victor Berger was a victim of this persecution. In 1918, one week before he was elected to Congress, he was indicted for violation of the 1917 Espionage Act. He was convicted, chiefly on the basis of editorials in his newspaper, the Milwaukee *Leader*, and sentenced to twenty years in prison. The House of Representatives then voted, with only one dissent, to deny him his seat. He won by a large margin the special election that was called to fill the vacancy. Again, the House of Representatives denied him his seat. Two years later, the Supreme Court reversed Berger's conviction.[4]

The WSFL and the Milwaukee FTC were outspoken critics of this public intolerance and the violations of civil liberties. At its 1920 convention the federation passed a resolution presented by Jacob Friedrick, representing Machinists Lodge 66, which demanded the release of all political prisoners and conscientious objectors, the quashing of all cases still pending under the provisions of the Espionage Act, the repeal of that law, and the restoration of the rights of free speech, free press, and peaceable assemblage.[5] The following year, in the face of anti-communist hysteria, the convention's Resolution No. 27 stated that because the Russian government was a workers' government and supported United States union-made goods, "the WSFL demands the immediate recognition of the Russian Soviet Republic and resumption of trade relations."[6]

The Milwaukee Federated Trades Council also stood firm against public sentiment during this period. It invited La Follette to speak at its meeting of January, 1918, which took place at the height of the anti-La Follette demonstrations. Similarly, on both occasions when the House of Representatives refused to seat Victor Berger, the FTC passed resolutions condemning that action.[7]

It is an interesting sidelight to note that, in contrast with this strong support of civil liberties, there were also labor resolutions opposing importation of "coolie labor." In 1917 a WSFL resolution had displayed flagrant racism by referring to the goal of preserving "the purity of the Caucasian race and their standards of livelihood."[8]

When the Socialist leaders of the WSFL had had to choose between the opposing Socialist and trade union positions on World War I, they had chosen the latter's. In doing so, however, they had not deserted their commitment to civil liberties. Their pragmatic support of unionism and their firm belief in civil and social justice were to characterize the leadership of the WSFL during the next two decades.

Leadership in the 1920's and 1930's

Besides the postwar anti-communist activity, much of which was directed against unions, labor had to face a new open-shop drive by industrialists who were determined to rid themselves of the unions that had grown during the war. Unable to organize amid this climate, Ohl and Handley directed their efforts toward legislation, particularly for unemployment compensation, and toward labor education, both topics of the next chapters.

In the 1930's, the coming of the New Deal and its enactment of many of the reforms which Socialists had been advocating for so many years gradually moved Ohl and Handley from their strict adherence to Socialist party doctrine and candidates to cooperation with the liberal Wisconsin Progressives (discussed in Chapter 8). In 1937 they gave up their Socialist party membership, the immediate reason being that the Socialist party's national convention adopted a resolution favoring the newly formed CIO. Although it was not anti-labor, it took sides against that faction of the labor movement, the AFL, to which Ohl and Handley had devoted their lives. As leaders of the WSFL, Ohl and Handley remained, philosophically, socialists, and the WSFL continued to pass socialist resolutions at each state convention.

The key WSFL staff members hired in the 1930's frequently were Socialist party members. They were the organizers who, in the great New Deal boom in unionism, went out into the state, formed new unions, and assisted locals in collective bargaining and handling of grievances. An extremely able group, most were successful local union officers. They included Rudolph Faupl, president of Local 19340, one of the newly formed federal labor unions at the Geuder, Paeschke, and Frey plant in Milwaukee; Andrew Biemiller, education director of the Socialist party in Milwaukee, assistant to the Socialist mayor, Daniel Hoan, and a state assemblyman; John Strobel, who held among other offices that of recreation director of the WSFL—a post created by President Ohl to counteract the paternalism of employers who financed athletic teams among their employees. Non-Socialist staff representatives were David Sigman, a La Follette Republican assemblyman from Two Rivers; and Charles Heymanns, a former Kohler Company worker who had shown outstanding leadership during the first Kohler strike, beginning in 1934. Sigman was elected to the WSFL executive board and later, on Ohl's recommendation, was made the AFL regional director.

The End of Socialist Leadership

Despite forty years of successful leadership, in three short years, 1940–1943, the entrenched socialist leaders were displaced completely by a more conservative, less politically oriented group of men. The principal reason for the changeover was the enormous growth of the labor movement. In 1933 the WSFL had 17,537 members, according to per capita dues payment; in 1937 the membership was 66,161; by 1940, 94,957.[9] And of course this growth was paralleled by that of the Wisconsin State CIO.

Ironically, it was this unprecedented growth in both the WSFL and in the CIO which undermined the socialist leadership of the WSFL. As previously described, several of the large federal labor unions, which the WSFL leaders had helped to organize and whose support they had enjoyed, defected to the CIO. Even a WSFL executive board member, Emil Costello, president of Federal Labor Union, No. 18456, at the Simmons Company plant in Kenosha and a top political leader for the WSFL, moved to the CIO. The Simmons local itself voted, in a state-supervised election, to remain with the WSFL, and Costello refused to resign his WSFL board seat. For the only time in its history, the federation held a trial and expelled one of its members. Because many newly organized industrial unions flocked to the CIO, the WSFL gained a lesser share of this new growth.

At the same time, the WSFL membership in the building trades, trucking, and service industries was increasing, and from this growth sector new leaders were rising. Most were not Socialists; all were young and ambitious, and all wanted a greater voice in the State Federation. A key member of the new group was Peter T. Schoemann, a plumber who headed the Milwaukee Building Trades Council. A very capable leader, he was on his way to the national presidency of the Plumbers Union. A second figure among these leaders was William Nagorsne, president of the Milwaukee Joint Council of Teamsters. A third was a strong anti-Socialist, William H. Cooper of the Building Service Union, soon to become its national secretary–treasurer.

These challengers made their first move at the 1939 WSFL convention, where they raised the number of building trades representatives on the executive board from three to seven out of a total of thirteen. It was not possible to challenge President Ohl or Secretary Handley directly because of the immense prestige stemming from their universally recognized ability and their long-time contributions to the labor movement. At the 1940 convention, however, the opposition strengthened its hold on the executive board by defeating an Ohl loyalist, David Sigman, and it almost defeated board member and socialist heir apparent for the WSFL presidency, Jacob Friedrick.

In October, 1940, Henry Ohl died of a heart attack while conducting federation business in Washington, D.C. The executive board convened to pick a successor. The two candidates were Herman Seide of the Carpenters Union, who had been secretary of the Milwaukee FTC for the past seven years, and Jacob Friedrick, who was an organizer for the FTC under Seide. Both had been longtime Socialists. Friedrick had been a business agent for the Machinists as far back as World War I. He had been on the staff of either the Milwaukee Federated Trades Council, the WSFL, or the Milwaukee *Leader* continuously since 1921. He had been associated closely with Ohl and Handley for two decades and was the WSFL's expert on both workers' compensation and unemployment compensation. He had represented the WSFL on the board of the University of Wisconsin's School for Workers since 1931. Most recently, from 1935 through 1938 when Ohl and Handley were deeply involved in political and legislative activity through the Farmer–Labor Progressive Federation, Friedrick invariably turned up as chairman of the key committees. The board's vote was seven for Seide and five for Friedrick. Seide's election was a substantial victory for the insurgent leaders.

In 1941, a year and a day after the death of Henry Ohl, Jack Handley, secretary–treasurer of the federation since 1912, died. Friedrick and William Nagorsne were the candidates in the election to replace him. Even before the executive board convened, informal caucusing indicated that Nagorsne had the votes to win,[10] and Friedrick was defeated a second time. Nagorsne was an important Teamster leader, yet compared to Friedrick, he was a virtual newcomer. His victory was another rejection of the old Socialist leadership.

In May of 1943, after only eighteen months in office, President Seide died. The executive board convened for the third time in less than two years to select a principal officer. On the first ballot, George Haberman, a part-time staff representative of the WSFL who, during Seide's illness, had assisted him on a full-time basis, received seven votes; George Hall, a building tradesman from La Crosse and a member of the WSFL executive board to which he was first elected in 1939, and Arthur Olsen, a member of the WSFL executive board, and Jacob Friedrick each received one vote; one ballot was blank. Friedrick and Hall withdrew. On the next ballot, Haberman received ten votes, Olsen one.

George Haberman formerly had been a Milwaukee city building inspector and a member of the American Federation of State, County and

Municipal Employees. Earlier, he had been an Iron Worker. As a federation staff member, he was a part of the Ohl–Handley machine and even had belonged, for a short time, to the Socialist party. Nevertheless the executive board's selection of him was definitely a break with the old guard, because, again, his experience and length of service were substantially less than those of Jacob Friedrick.

This shift from the Socialist leadership of Ohl and Handley to the more conservative building and service trades leadership of Haberman and Nagorsne had not been ratified yet by the delegates at a statewide convention. The next WSFL convention was to take place at Eau Claire in late August, 1943. Would the new leadership have to face a delegate challenge? If so, it would be the first since 1900, when Frederick Brockhausen defeated Martin Jesko for the office of secretary–treasurer. Paul J. Smith, a close associate of AFL president William Green, and a regional director of the AFL, expressed in a letter his hopes that there would be no challenge:[11]

> It was my privilege while in Milwaukee to have a long dinner conference with President Haberman . . . at which we went into . . . the internal affairs of the Labor Movement in Wisconsin.
> I certainly was delighted by the election [by the executive board] of our mutual friend George Haberman, and I am truly hopeful that he will not encounter any opposition for re-election at the convention. The way it looked when I was in Wisconsin my hopes will be realized because I understand Schoemann and the gang are h--l bent on such a program.

Nevertheless, at the convention a challenger was nominated for the presidency. He was Rudolph Faupl, president of Fabricated Metal Workers, Local 19340, and also a staff organizer for the WSFL. In 1943 he was serving as the Wisconsin labor representative on the War Labor Board in Chicago. Then only thirty-five, he had been selected six years earlier by Ohl to be the first full-time organizer for the WSFL. Through his years as an organizer, Faupl became well-known, especially among the state's federal labor unions, many of which he had helped to organize. As a favorite of Ohl's and a Socialist, however, he was anathema to the Haberman supporters. The delegates at the Eau Claire convention were sharply divided: the vote was 600 for Haberman and 507 for Faupl.

Faupl's opposition clearly came from the coalition of the building trades, teamsters, and service trades that had taken control of the executive board away from the Socialists and industrial unionists. The 1943 nominating speeches do not reveal the real issues which separated Haberman and Faupl, and no campaign documents have survived, if, in fact, any were issued. In 1976 the author asked Faupl why he had run against Haberman. He answered that he wanted a president committed to carrying on the traditions and ideals of men such as Frank Weber, Henry Ohl, and Jack Handley. His first choice had been Jacob Friedrick; when Friedrick would not run, Faupl did so.[12]

A letter from Paul Smith, written a month after the election, expressed his strong feelings against Faupl: "Hitler, Bonaparte, Mussolini and John Lewis are not the only people who were born with an excessive amount of self-reliance and lust for power." Then, referring to Faupl's birth in Hungary, he wrote: "Some people would have been a heck of a long time in Hungary, at least longer than fifteen years, before they would ever have had the privilege or the opportunity to try to lead a state-wide Labor Movement."[13]

Faupl went on to leading positions in the labor movement. At the end of 1945 he became a grand lodge representative with the International Association of Machinists. Shortly thereafter he became head of the Machinists' International Department, representing them in the International Metalworkers Union. Later, on the recommendation of George Meany, president of the AFL, the U.S. Department of Labor appointed him a delegate to the International Labour Organization, located in Geneva, Switzerland. Even though his work took him abroad, he maintained close ties with the Wisconsin labor movement and each year spent some time in the state visiting his early trade union associates.

At the 1944 WSFL convention, the challenge to the Haberman presidency continued, that year from Jacob Friedrick. This time the issues were put forth in campaign documents, although Friedrick himself never campaigned and never asked anyone to support him. To one person who had urged him to do a little "horsetrading" when the executive board was replacing Handley in 1941, he had responded that he had been around a long time, that everybody knew what he stood for, and if they wanted him, they would vote for him.[14]

In the 1944 campaign, a letter by the Friedrick supporters stated that since 1939 a small group, composed primarily of building trades union leaders, had wanted to "control the election of officers and Executive Board members of the Federation."[15] Most of the Friedrick supporters were industrial unionists. John Cudahy, president of the large federal labor union at International Harvester's Milwaukee plant, was a key leader in the federal labor union groups which made up 22 per cent of the WSFL membership in 1943.[16] Other unions supporting Friedrick were the Pulp, Sulphite, and Paper Mill Workers; the International Brotherhood of Papermakers; the Machinists; and the United Auto Workers–AFL. The principal nominating speech for Friedrick, given by Faupl, tied Friedrick closely to the distinguished WSFL officers of the past: Weber, Ohl, Handley, and Seide.

The Haberman supporters published a campaign leaflet deriding the Friedrick backers for holding caucuses in advance of the convention, an action which it labeled "dual unionism." It asked: "Is this business of holding secret meetings part of the old world way of running a labor movement?"[17] The phrase "old world way" referred to the fact that Friedrick was born in Hungary and had emigrated to America when he was twelve years old. The anti-foreigner tactic was similar to that used to defeat Faupl the previous year. Most of the thirty-five names listed as signers of the Haberman campaign leaflet were building and service trades leaders. The largest single group was the Teamsters, who were allies of the building trades.

Among Haberman's supporters, anti-socialism was also a strong ideological issue. When at the 1944 convention a Milwaukee *Journal* reporter asked Haberman about the election, he stated that his opposition was made up of former Socialists, now Progressives, who looked to the WSFL to save the Progressive party, and that he had refused to allow the State Federation to get involved in partisan politics. When the reporter asked Friedrick to list his objections to the Haberman administration, he declined to do so—not surprisingly, since at that time union leaders were usually reluctant to discuss union infighting with the press, which was generally considered to be unfriendly to labor.[18]

Haberman defeated Friedrick 722 to 579, a greater margin than his victory over Faupl the year before. The WSFL's increase from 1943 to 1944 resulted from a split among delegates from the large Federal Labor Union, No. 19806, at the A. O. Smith plant in Milwaukee. According to Haberman's opponents, two delegates, each of whom carried several hundred proxies from No. 19806 and who presumably voted for Haberman, subsequently were offered positions as staff representative on the state and AFL national staffs respectively.[19]

In spite of these defeats, Jacob Friedrick continued to play an important role in the Wisconsin labor movement. In 1945 he was appointed AFL regional director for Wisconsin. In 1951, when Frank Ranney resigned the secretaryship of the Milwaukee Federated Trades Council, Friedrick ran for that office and was elected over Werner Schaefer, an operating engineer who had strong building trades support. Friedrick was reelected regularly by the FTC until his retirement in 1969 at the age of seventy-seven. He served for nine years on the Board of Regents of the University of Wisconsin, including two years as its president in 1961 and 1962. In 1955 he received a unique honor for a labor leader when the University of Wisconsin awarded him an honorary degree, Doctorate of Laws.

No WSFL convention was held in 1945 owing, it was explained, to the government's wartime restrictions on unnecessary travel. However, Carl Griepentrog, then regional director of the UAW–AFL, thought cancellation of the convention was a subterfuge and instituted a lawsuit against President Haberman to force the calling of a convention in accordance with the WSFL constitution. The suit went to court, where it was ruled that the membership must vote. The WSFL then held an election by mail, in which Haberman's presidency was confirmed. He was not challenged again for eighteen years. At the 1946 WSFL convention four anti-Haberman executive board members were defeated.[20]

In looking over these six years of contention for the leadership of the WSFL, there seem to be two main differences between the old-guard faction and the insurgents: one a straightforward trade union difference, craft vs. industrial unionism; the other a less clear-cut political division, Socialist vs. non-Socialist leadership. We have seen that these differences were roughly paired: Socialist leadership and industrial unionism vs. non-Socialist leadership and craft unionism.

One might wonder why the industrial union candidates, Faupl in 1943 and Friedrick in 1944, did not ride to victory on the crest of the wave of industrial unionism, which had been building so strongly since 1933. One important reason was that the wave had washed away industrial union support of the WSFL. As we saw in Chapter 6, many of the WSFL's industrial unions went over to the CIO in 1936 and 1937, and the subsequent growth in industrial unionism in Wisconsin went to the State CIO, not the WSFL.

The issue of Socialism was generally not overt in the campaigns for federation offices. When in 1939 the insurgents from the building trades began their campaign to gain control of the executive board, Ohl and Handley had already resigned from the Socialist party. When Friedrick was a candidate to succeed Ohl in 1940, he was still a member of the party, but formally resigned in 1941, the year the Wisconsin Socialist party withdrew from the Farmer–Labor Progressive Federation. Also in that year, the Socialist party required a loyalty oath, which Friedrick refused to give.[21] However, for all practical purposes Friedrick had withdrawn from the Socialist party in 1935 when the Farmer–Labor Progressive Federation was formed. Faupl was still a member of the Socialist party when he opposed Haberman for the WSFL presidency in 1943, but the issue of Socialism was hardly mentioned in that campaign, possibly because, according to George Hall, Faupl's membership in the party was not generally known.[22] On the other hand, several Haberman supporters were Socialists: Anthony J. (Tony) King of the Plumbers Union, Arthur Urbanek of the American Federation of State, County, and Municipal Employees, and Gilbert Fiebrink of the Laundry Workers.[23]

Yet in the minds of some of those who were leaders among the insurgents, the question of Socialist power in the WSFL was very much an issue; to some it was the whole issue. George Hall, a member of the WSFL executive board from 1939 to 1970 and secretary–treasurer of the organization from 1951 to 1970, believed Socialist control was one of the issues. In an interview he said: "Yes, I helped houseclean the Socialists. I never liked the Socialists." He also cited non-ideological factors, however. Even though he was a member of the building trades he did not give them credit for Haberman's election. He said they did not vote as one block, but were split. His impression was that Haberman's followers formed a sort of social club. Friedrick, on the other hand, was "a loner, not good socially" but a "brilliant speaker."[24]

In a 1951 interview William Cooper, who had nominated George Haberman at both the 1943 and 1944 conventions, spoke bitterly of the Socialists, who he said had monopolized the WSFL and the Milwaukee FTC for many years. A membership card in the Socialist party had been a criterion for obtaining a job with the WSFL. He was proud of his role in joining with the building trades and others to break what he believed was the Socialist monopoly of the leadership of the WSFL.[25]

It was during the convention debates on resolutions that the issue was openly debated. Chapter 4 described the adoption of the 1894 resolution calling for "collective ownership of all means of production and distribution." After the Socialists' victory at the 1900 convention, other resolutions were added successively until, by 1907, the Preamble and Platform read:[26]

> 8. The municipal ownership of all public utilities. (This means the co-operation of the citizens in public concerns and the abolition of private monopoly of public necessities, by which the few are enriched at the expense of the many.)
>
> 9. The nationalization of telegraphs, telephones, railroads and mines. (These are natural monopolies and should be owned and operated without favor, at cost, in the interest of the whole people. In the hands of private citizens these interests are in jeopardy.)

10. The collective ownership by the people of all means of production and distribution. (By this is meant that when an industry becomes so centralized as to assume the form of a trust or monopoly and hence a menace to the best interest of the people, such industry should be assumed by the government. This is true protection to the weak, those least represented in legislation.)

These planks were only an annual reaffirmation of early leadership's socialist creed since there was never the slightest possibility of their enactment.

With the deaths of Ohl and Handley, the anti-socialist leaders felt strong enough to attack these sacrosanct planks. Opposition to them came from two sources. The first was the International Brotherhood of Electrical Workers (IBEW), which had organized the privately owned utilities in the state. It knew that wages were higher under privately owned utilities than in municipally owned plants. Moreover, Wisconsin law did not require municipalities to recognize a union for collective bargaining. The second source of opposition was the insurgents who were capturing leadership from the socialists. At the 1942 convention, a resolution by an IBEW local to cut out the plank on municipal ownership was referred to the executive board. At the 1943 and 1944 conventions the Faupl and Friedrick election challenges to Haberman precluded an attack on the socialist planks. There was no convention in 1945. At the 1946 convention, however, the Haberman forces were in complete control and all three socialist planks were eliminated without so much as a floor fight. The pro-socialist, anti-Haberman faction subsequently claimed that the vote for removal of the planks took place late in the afternoon when the delegates were attending a tour of the city provided by the Superior Trades Council.

At the 1947 convention, three resolutions calling for restoration of the planks were introduced by leaders of the anti-Haberman faction. A full-dress debate took place. Those speakers opposing the planks pointed to the collective bargaining advantages of dealing with private employers. These views were presented ably by leaders in the Haberman faction: Peter T. Schoemann, president of the Milwaukee Building Trades Council; Frank Ranney, secretary of the Milwaukee Federated Trades; and William H. Cooper of the Building Service Employees Union.

Three of the speakers favoring the socialist resolutions were leaders of federal labor unions. A fourth was Carl Griepentrog, regional director of the UAW–AFL. They maintained that the removal of the planks by the 1946 convention had been "flat, outright appeasement" and that "the rivers, mines, and resources are here for all of us, and should be given to all of us at minimum cost through public ownership."[27] The most influential argument for restoring the public ownership planks came, however, from delegate John Plokowski of Fire Fighters, Local 215:[28]

> Brother Cudahy has reminded you of that great labor leader [Frank Weber] whom we have cherished all through the years of the life of the Wisconsin State Federation of Labor. . . . I refer you to the 1923 session of the Wisconsin State legislature of which I had the honor of serving with Frank Weber. I remember the day when "Old Pop" . . . guided us through the session. We young students were very glad to listen to his teachings because of his great experience. I am going to remind you of what "Pop" told me and some of us younger members of the 1923 legislature. He said, "Boys I am getting old—I'm 75—I'm not going to be here very long. It is for you younger men to carry on." Members of this convention, if "Pop" were here today and saw that the one great thing that he has cherished, that is part of the preamble of this constitution . . . [has been removed], "Pop" would turn over in his casket.

This presentation so moved the delegates that the Haberman leadership beat a strategic retreat. A compromise restored plank 8, favoring municipal ownership of utilities, and plank 9, favoring nationalization of the means of communication, transportation and natural resources. Plank 10, calling for collective ownership of the means of production and distribution, was dropped.[29]

The two planks remained in the preamble until the WSFL's merger in 1958 with the CIO. The more radical CIO had never had socialistic planks of this nature in its constitution, and the new preamble followed a national pattern adopted by the AFL–CIO, which, of course, did not take into account Wisconsin's unique past.

The New Leadership

By 1946 the new leaders were firmly in control of the WSFL. George Haberman was able to provide the type of leadership favored by his diverse supporters who did not want the strong presidency of someone like Henry Ohl. The anti-Haberman movement fell apart; the block of federal labor unions, a dominant part of this faction, disintegrated. At the end of World War II the federal labor unions entertained a vague hope that the AFL might give them a national organization in place of their traditional status as local unions affiliated directly with the AFL. Haberman made peace with some of his federal labor union opponents by recommending this change to the AFL and by appointing one of the FLU activists to a position on the WSFL staff. The AFL denied his request. Instead, in accordance with AFL policy, some of the FLU's voted to join such existing national unions as the Boilermakers, the Machinists, and the UAW–AFL.

As a result, they were no longer separate unions tending to vote as a bloc in WSFL elections, but locals of national unions, each tending to vote as did its respective national organization. Federal labor unions had commanded 22 per cent of the votes at the WSFL's 1943 convention; by 1956, just before the merger of the WSFL and the state CIO, their membership had fallen to 11 per cent.[30] With their candidates Faupl and Friedrick engaged elsewhere and their power base destroyed, former Haberman opponents gained election to the WSFL executive board as Haberman supporters.

Haberman's years in office, 1943–1958, were not easy ones. Rivalry with the CIO eroded the prestige and influence of the president of the WSFL. Before 1938 he was clearly the most influential union official in the state; thereafter, he was rivaled not only by the president of the State CIO, but also by several new layers of leaders in the regional offices of the rapidly growing national unions—the regional directors of the United Auto Workers–CIO, the United Auto Workers–AFL, and the United Steelworkers. These regional offices each had a full-time staff that was three to four times larger than the staffs of four or five people directed by the president of the WSFL or the state CIO. The rise of regional directors with full-time staffs, a depth of leadership unknown in the days of Weber and Ohl, generally enhanced the labor movement's influence, however, since it signified the influx of thousands of union members. When the merger of the WSFL and the state CIO occurred in 1958, much of the luster returned to the head of the new organization, the Wisconsin State AFL–CIO.

The national AFL and CIO merged in 1955 and the new body required state and city labor bodies to merge in the near future. The rules for these mergers designated that the president of the merged body would be from the larger of the old bodies, the vice-president from the smaller. In the Wisconsin AFL–CIO the president would come from the WSFL, with 180,000 members, while the executive vice-president would come from the 80,000-member State CIO.

Although Haberman thus could expect to be the first president, the prospect of merger may have disturbed his peace of mind. If, after merger, the CIO industrial unionists were to combine with the AFL industrial unionists, his coalition of building trades and service industries might be outnumbered. Moreover, the CIO leadership was chiefly in the hands of two men: Walter Burke, district director of the Steelworkers, and Harvey Kitzman, regional director of the United Auto Workers. Although neither of these men would want the presidency of the merged body, they would serve on the executive board and might prove hard taskmasters.

Charles Schultz, a much younger man, had been president of the Wisconsin Industrial Union Council (State CIO) since 1952. A UAW member at the Allis–Chalmers plant in West Allis, he had been elected president of UAW, Local 248, after the ouster of the left-wing leadership in 1947. In his large local Schultz had displayed the ability to mobilize sizable groups of workers and had gained a reputation as a tough collective bargainer. He had been able to put together very quickly a coalition of other ambitious young leaders which in 1952 toppled the incumbent State CIO officers and elected him president. As such, he was aggressive in collective bargaining and in raising money for political action.

Both Schultz and Haberman were self-willed—decidedly not complementary personalities. Since neither one looked forward to merger, they delayed it as long as possible. Nevertheless, when it came in 1958 the new state executive board was a model of harmony. The old issues—industrial unionism and jurisdiction—that had divided the AFL and the CIO, had been settled at the national level. The issue of left-wing ideology had been removed by both the state CIO at its convention of 1946 and by the national CIO in 1949 and 1950, when it expelled ten left-wing CIO unions. The principal job of the AFL and CIO state merger committees was to create new positions for the incumbent officers of both bodies, and this was accomplished smoothly. Without an election contest and in accordance with AFL–CIO directives, Haberman became president of the new State AFL–CIO, George Hall secretary–treasurer, and Charles Schultz executive vice-president.

The State AFL–CIO, 1966–1983

At the first post-merger convention in 1960, by agreement there was no contest for the presidency. However, Schultz had resigned as vice-president and an election was held to fill his post. The candidates were two very able ex-CIO union officials: John Schmitt, recording secretary of Brewery Workers, Local 9, in Milwaukee, and Howard Pellant, a staff representative of the United Auto Workers and a state assemblyman. The contest was over personal qualifications rather than issues, and Schmitt won by 125,209 votes to 64,878. There were no contests in 1962, but in 1964, Haberman, now within two years of retirement, was challenged by John Heidenreich, the Directing Business Representative of the large Machinist District 10, centered in Milwaukee.

If the old WSFL industrial unions that had opposed Haberman in the mid-1940's had joined with the CIO's industrial union membership, Heidenreich would have won handily, especially since the Teamsters Union, so crucial to Haberman's earlier WSFL victories, had been expelled from the AFL–CIO in 1957. But the first nominating speech made it clear that the old coalition of industrial unions versus the building and service trades had holes in it. Haberman's lead nominator was Walter Burke, whose union beginnings were described in Chapter 6. Since 1947 he had been district director of the United Steelworkers, a former CIO union. Burke's speech, a masterful eulogy, included the following excerpts:[31]

> This man whom I have known and respected for many years is a mature man, a man of vast experience and demonstrated leadership qualities. He stands as a mighty oak tree, tall and strong against the sky. Here is a man who knows the meaning of toil. Here is a man who knows from experience the struggles and heartbreaks which went into the crucible from which emerged the American labor movement. Once weak, ineffective and scorned, but now strong, respected and powerful, this movement is today united under the banner of AFL–CIO. . . .
>
> As Chairman of the CIO merger negotiating committee, I came to know this man whom I am about to nominate for the Presidency of this organization on a close, personal basis. During these long and at times difficult negotiations, numerous problems arose, and at times tempers and patience ran short. He persevered and we persevered, and merger was finally achieved.
>
> As we meet here today in this great convention with the former AF of L craftsmen harmoniously intermingled with former CIO industrial union members, one must certainly conclude that our merger in Wisconsin has been an outstanding success.

The election was very close: Haberman received 106,068 votes, Heidenrich 92,698. The results made it clear that the contest concerned personal qualities and, to a certain extent, places on the executive board. No ideological issues were apparent, nor was there any division by former AFL or CIO membership. The Wisconsin State AFL–CIO now seemed to be a truly united labor movement.

In 1966 Haberman retired as president of the Wisconsin AFL–CIO. At the state convention that year there was only one candidate to replace him, John Schmitt, executive vice-president since 1960. The fact that Schmitt, a member of a former CIO union, could replace Haberman in an uncontested election is additional evidence of the healing of the internecine quarrels of the period 1936–1955.

After serving in World War II, Schmitt had returned to Milwaukee and taken a job at the Pabst Brewery. He became a union activist and by 1952 was recording secretary of the huge Local 9 of the Brewery Workers. The older leaders of Local 9, who then were being replaced, were the last of the German-speaking Socialists who had been staunch supporters of Victor

Berger, Frank Weber, and Henry Ohl. New leaders such as Schmitt were neither Socialist nor anti-Socialist. The transition in the Local 9 leadership was based more on age than ideology.

Schmitt led Local 9 in the Milwaukee brewery strike during the "long hot summer" of 1953. The outstanding gains of the contract that ended this strike entrenched Schmitt's leadership of Local 9 and gave him state-wide recognition within the CIO. In 1952 he had supported the winning candidate, Schultz, for president of the State CIO against Herman Steffes. The issues in the ideological fight against the CIO left wing, which had brought Steffes to the helm in 1946, had evaporated by then. The significance of the Schultz election was merely that a younger, ambitious leader was supported by other rising leaders, among them John Schmitt.

The labor movement over which Schmitt presided differed in several significant ways from the earlier state labor bodies. This was due chiefly to the increased size of the movement. Prior to the Wagner Act (1935) the membership of the WSFL was not only small, but was also subject to sharp declines. After 1935, union membership increased annually so that by 1978 the State AFL–CIO had 276,000 members.

One of the differences from the past, resulting from this growth, was reflected in the salaries paid to union officials. Significant financial sacrifices were required of labor leadership in the early years, around the turn of the century. Frank Weber received only five dollars for each day he spent on WSFL business. In 1919 Henry Ohl received $2,400 per annum. During the Great Depression, WSFL officers and staff gave up half of their salaries because of the federation's reduced income. In the CIO, early organizers for the UAW and Steelworkers often went without any salary. The situation of local union members and union activists was even worse, since they often were fired and blacklisted when strikes were lost and local unions destroyed. The early CIO state presidents were paid only their factory worker's wages: Steffes in 1947 received one dollar per hour, the exact rate he was getting as an assembler at Nash Motor's Milwaukee plant; Schultz received $8,500 in 1952. George Haberman's salary, despite his long tenure in office, was always modest, $5,500 in 1944, $12,000 in 1956, and even, as head of the merged labor movement, $15,000 in 1964.[32] In his last two years in office, however, he did have some outside earnings. The Milwaukee *Journal,* noting that the car he was driving was registered to an Illinois heating and plumbing company, learned from Haberman that he was chairman of the board of directors of the firm as well as a director of Milwaukee's West Side bank.[33]

Today, full-time labor leadership is an attractive career, and there are an estimated 400 full-time union officials in Wisconsin. In 1982 the Wisconsin AFL–CIO president, John Schmitt, had a salary of $52,000.[34] Regional directors of industrial unions and the heads of very large local unions or joint councils may receive salaries of $40,000 to $55,000. Full-time building trades officers frequently receive a salary from their local unions for every working day in the year equal to the top hourly rate of its members. Union staff representatives of industrial, professional, or service unions generally receive $32,000 to $45,000, which is somewhat higher than the average wage of their union members.

There are even some perquisites for officers of the local unions. In many industrial unions the steward has highest seniority, meaning that in times of layoffs he or she will be the last worker laid off in the department. The top officers of local plant unions are frequently able to perform much of their work, such as grievance handling, on company time, paid either by the company or the union. The contract negotiating committee usually is reimbursed by the union for time missed from work. Local officers who do not hold full-time positions in the union still, however, are not paid for the enormous amount of time spent in administering their unions. Officers of local unions now are recognized as leaders in their communities and often are appointed to local government and community service committees.

If one were to compare union leaders' salaries with the value of the wages and fringe benefits which the members have gained through collective bargaining and the economic value to union members of the legislation which has resulted from labor's political activity, their salaries are modest, and fall far below those of their counterparts in management.

Perhaps the most significant difference between today's Wisconsin AFL–CIO and the earlier state labor bodies is in the work that it does. When the WSFL was formed, one of its primary functions was to organize local unions and negotiate contracts in communities around the state. We have seen that it helped to organize federal labor unions in heavy industry in the years 1933 to 1941. In the 1950's, however, organizing was taken over almost completely by the big international unions. In 1934, for example, the WSFL directed the organizing of Federal Labor Union, No. 19845, at the Kohler Company, and President Ohl participated in the collective bargaining and in the prolonged strike that ensued. It was WSFL President Herman Seide who made the decision to end the Kohler strike in 1943. In contrast, it was the United Auto Workers–CIO which in 1952 sent a large staff of organizers to Kohler and paid for the daily radio broadcasts and full-page newspaper ads which helped to bring a union election victory. Only a large union like the UAW, with the resources of dues-paying members numbering over a million, could have supplied benefits during the strike that lasted from 1954 to 1960. These expenses, totaling $13 million, far surpassed the resources of either the Wisconsin State CIO or the WSFL.[35]

Since the 1950's the chief job of the Wisconsin AFL–CIO has been to lead the state labor movement in selecting and achieving its political and legislative goals. To these ends it carries on political and union education and public relations, endorses candidates, raises political campaign funds, and lobbies in the state legislature.

By 1983 Schmitt had led the Wisconsin AFL-CIO for seventeen years, with no opposition to his presidency. The State CIO had no such continuous leadership. Emil Costello served two years as president, 1937–1939; Harvey Kitzman two years, 1939–1941; Thomas White three years, 1941–1944; Robert Buse two years, 1945–1946; Herman Steffes five years, 1946–1951; and Charles Schultz six years, 1952–1958. One must go back to the WSFL administrations of Weber, twenty-four years, 1893–1917, and Ohl, twenty-three years, 1917–1940, to find such unchallenged tenure.

To appreciate the length and stability of Schmitt's leadership one must understand the organization of central labor bodies. The presidents of central bodies in the American labor movement have no structural authority over their affiliated unions. This is true of the heads of city centrals, state federations, and even the president of the national AFL–CIO, Lane Kirkland. In other words, being the president of a labor central body is similar to being president of the United States under the Articles of Confederation, under which each state was sovereign.

Each local affiliate of the Wisconsin State AFL–CIO is under the control of its own national union. The State organization can use persuasion only to obtain the support of local unions for its statewide endeavors. To bring about 100 per cent agreement among all Wisconsin unions on such matters as political endorsements and legislative priorities is an impossibility.

Concerted labor action is even more difficult to obtain because some of the state's largest unions are not affiliated with the Wisconsin AFL–CIO. The Wisconsin Education Association never has been affiliated and the Teamsters, not since 1957. The United Auto Workers withdrew from the AFL–CIO in 1968. Although it returned to the AFL–CIO in 1982, as of 1983 it had not re-entered the Wisconsin AFL–CIO. Nevertheless, on about 95 per cent of the major issues which have come before the Wisconsin labor movement during Schmitt's tenure, a labor position has been arrived at and supported by the Wisconsin AFL–CIO executive board and by a large majority of the affiliated locals, some supporting the position actively, others nominally. The legislative influence of the State AFL–CIO from the mid-1960's through 1977 has been rivaled only by the legislative influence of the WSFL under Ohl in 1932 and 1937–1939. The specific legislative gains of this period are given in the next chapter.

The Wisconsin Labor Movement's Contributions to National Labor Leadership

A description of leadership in the Wisconsin labor movement should not be restricted to leaders of the WSFL, the State CIO, and the Wisconsin State AFL–CIO. Many talented workers rise to leadership in their local unions and never leave their home communities. Others move from the local to full-time staff positions in their international union. In some cases their work would be servicing local unions within a hundred miles of their home. In other cases the staff job would require moving to the union's national headquarters in Washington, D.C., in Detroit, or in Pittsburgh. A few local officers or staff representatives will become regional directors of their national unions. Such offices for this area are in Milwaukee, Chicago, or Minneapolis. These elected regional officials usually direct the work of their unions over several states. Their salaries are above those paid to the State AFL–CIO officers. A very few of these regional officials become top officers of their national unions. Although not a populous state in regard to union membership, Wisconsin has contributed many distinguished national union leaders. A listing of some of them is found in the Appendix (page 247).

CHAPTER 8

Political Action

I N 1867 WISCONSIN labor's primary political objective was state legislation to limit the workday to eight hours. Although defeated in this effort, labor leaders learned that other groups, particularly business, were better organized and had more money to spend on influencing voters and legislators. One of the major purposes of the formation of the Wisconsin State Federation of Labor in 1893 was to exert greater influence on the state and national legislatures. As we have seen, today the chief functions of the state central body are lobbying, political endorsement, political action, public relations, and education.

Goals and Strategy

At the first convention of the WSFL, in 1893, and at every convention since then, resolutions have called for political action, often in the form of specific legislation. The resolutions have been of several types. Until 1946, there was always one that reflected the socialist background of the leadership—the call for government ownership of all means of production and distribution. These were idealistic goals and, lacking public and sometimes even labor support, they generally could not be pushed through the legislature. In 1894, other resolutions reflected a populist orientation: universal suffrage; free compulsory public education; freedom for Eugene Debs, the railway union leader who had been jailed following the Pullman Strike; and a state income tax, twenty years before it became a reality.

The third class of resolutions concerned those dealing with the practical problems faced by labor. These were twenty to forty years ahead of their time. They included abolition of child labor (1893), enactment of safety and sanitation laws in mills, mines, and railways (1893), the eight-hour day (1893), worker compensation (1894), government work relief for the unemployed (1894), wages in cash (1896), and abolition of the company store (1896).

123

During the period of Socialist leadership, 1900–1940, the political program of the WSFL differed noticeably from that of other state federations. In other states, political action by labor movements commonly meant reaching a series of political bargains by which the labor movement pledged support to any Republican, Democratic, or independent candidate who promised to support labor reforms, such as compensation for injured workers, an income tax, or an anti-injunction bill. This was the policy of Samuel Gompers, president of the American Federation of Labor (AFL), which could be phrased as "Reward your friends and punish your enemies," a policy that the WSFL specifically attacked in a 1904 convention resolution.

In 1908, for example, Gompers undertook to oppose certain anti-labor congressmen, especially the committee chairmen who prevented bills favorable to labor from reaching the House floor. One of Gompers' targets in 1908 was John J. Jenkins, the Republican congressman from Wisconsin's northernmost district, who was chairman of the House Judiciary Committee. In the primary election the labor federations of Superior and Ashland threw their support behind Jenkins's opponent, a Progressive Republican assemblyman, Irvine Lenroot, who had an excellent labor record in the State Assembly and who specifically opposed labor injunctions, the chief campaign issue. But Brockhausen turned down Lenroot's requests to the WSFL for help on the grounds that the Federation would aid only Socialist candidates. Gompers himself was slow to lend support, but finally wrote an anti-Jenkins editorial in the AFL journal, *American Federationist*. The brotherhoods of railroad workers actively supported Lenroot, who won handily by 17,284 to 11,035 votes in a victory of national significance to labor. He had done so without the support of the WSFL.[1]

Under its Socialist leadership the WSFL continued this policy until the 1930's. The one exception was the federation's support of Robert M. La Follette, Sr.'s presidential campaign in 1924, which the AFL also supported.

Workers' Compensation

From 1900 to 1936 the WSFL worked hard in support of candidates of the Socialist party. Within the city of Milwaukee the results were phenomenal. For most of that period, 1910–1912 and 1916–1940, Milwaukee had a Socialist city administration, although Socialists seldom controlled the city council. It was of enormous help to the labor movement to have a mayor, a city attorney, and often a sheriff who did not use the police and sheriff's deputies against union pickets. In fact, the city administration made it difficult for employers to operate factories during strikes or to import strikebreakers and private detectives.

On the state level, labor's political efforts were handicapped by the fact that only from Milwaukee could it elect Socialists to the legislature. Five Socialist legislators, including WSFL officers, were first elected in 1905. Their number peaked in 1919–1920, with sixteen members in the Assembly and four in the State Senate.

State legislators' salaries were too low to live on, so the WSFL paid a monthly subsidy to those who were both union officials and Socialists; prior to the 1930's, non-Socialist legislators were not eligible for this subsidy. David Sigman and Andrew Biemiller came into the labor movement by this legislative route. In the 1930's they were key, pro-labor legislators. The WSFL hired them as staff members so that it would be financially possible for them to continue serving in the legislature.

In 1911 the Socialists had fourteen seats—twelve in the Assembly and two in the Senate. In that year Wisconsin labor won its first major legislative achievement: passage of the Workmens' Compensation Act. The 1911 state legislature also passed other labor legislation: regulation of safety standards, a ten-hour day for women, a child labor law, and a law making it illegal for advertisers to make false representations about working conditions, wages, or the existence of a strike.[2] Labor's success in the 1911 session, however, was due as much or more to the support of progressive Republican Governor Francis McGovern and his followers as to the support of the fourteen Socialist legislators from Milwaukee.

In 1905, when WSFL Secretary–Treasurer Frederick Brockhausen, an Assembly member, introduced the first workers' compensation bill in the Wisconsin legislature, the need for such legislation was long overdue. Each year thousands of workers were killed or maimed on the job without compensation from the employer. Common law recognized three principles that served to exonerate the employer. The first was that of "contributory negligence," under which, for example, an employee who had lost an arm would have to convince the court that he had not been negligent to any degree in order to recover such damages as medical and hospital care, lost wages, and financial damages for permanent injury or death. The second principle was "assumption of risks": if an injured employee had known that a piece of machinery was dangerous and in need of repair, he was denied damages—and if the worker had protested the unsafe condition to the foreman, this was evidence that he had knowledge of the unsafe condition and voluntarily had assumed the risks of the job. The third principle was the "fellow servant doctrine," which meant that an injured worker could not receive damages from the employer if the employer could blame any part of the accident on a fellow employee. For example, if a foundry worker's failure to properly plug a furnace containing molten metal resulted in the death of workers on the succeeding shift, the employer under common law was blameless.

Although the WSFL had advocated workers' compensation in its convention resolutions since 1894, the legislature took no notice until labor leaders were elected to the State Assembly and introduced their own bills. In 1904, workers' compensation was put at the top of the agenda at the WSFL state convention. In each biennium thereafter, 1905, 1907, and 1909, Brockhausen introduced the federation's bills to provide compensation. The legislation was expertly drafted by the eminent Charles McCarthy, head of the state's Legislative Reference Library.

By 1909 public sentiment regarding workers' compensation was catching up with the position of the State Federation. A great deal of the credit for selling workers' compensation to business and to the public must go to John R. Commons, a distinguished member of the Department of Economics at the University of Wisconsin. For several years he had worked closely with State Federation officers Weber and Brockhausen. Commons urged the members of the powerful Milwaukee Merchants and Manufacturers Association to support workers' compensation. Addressing their meeting in December, 1908, he told the packed house that a proper bill "would place the relations of capital and labor in this state on a more harmonious basis than any state in the Union can boast of."[3]

There was as yet no agreement on the specific terms of the bill. There was no functioning workers' compensation law anywhere in the country and hence no model to draw upon. The 1909 legislature, therefore, appointed a joint interim Committee on Industrial Insurance to study the components of such a bill and report back to the 1911 legislature. Representatives of the WSFL and of the Wisconsin Manufacturers Association assisted the committee. Representative Wallace Ingalls from Racine, a member of the legislative committee, made a trip to Germany and England where workers' compensation had been in operation for many years. In Wisconsin, the employers generally wanted workers to contribute one-third or one-half of the cost of the insurance; the WSFL insisted that employers bear all the costs. The employers wanted a voluntary system, under which each employer could elect to offer workers' compensation or to remain under the old system. The WSFL fought for compulsory enrollment of all employers, but also wanted to permit an injured worker to choose between accepting the modest compensation payments specified in the law or suing in the courts for damages under the old system.[4]

The Workmen's Compensation Act, passed in 1911, was a compromise. Labor gained in that the employers were obligated to pay full costs, but employers gained the voluntary provisions, although, if they opted to remain in the old system, they had to give up the principle of "assumption of risks" and the "fellow servant doctrine." Labor agreed to a provision allowing the worker to choose, at the time of hiring, whether to be covered under workers' compensation insurance or to retain the right to sue the employer for damages. Most workers and large employers enrolled under the compensation act. In 1931, workers' compensation finally became compulsory for employers and employees.

Although the Wisconsin labor movement can take credit for being the first to advocate a workers' compensation bill in Wisconsin, by 1911 a number of the state's largest manufacturing firms supported the idea of workers' compensation, although it is not clear how much support these manufacturers gave this specific bill. Years later, Governor McGovern reported that when the bill finally reached his desk, he did not hear affirmatively from any employer.[5]

Since its enactment, the law has undergone constant surveillance by labor and management advisory committees, and the need for changes in the law is reviewed periodically. John Commons's prediction in 1908 that workers' compensation would bring a more harmonious relationship between capital and labor in Wisconsin than in any other state cannot be verified, but it certainly has established an area of long-term labor–management co-operation.

Minimum Wages for Women

Two pieces of legislation in this period concerned women workers. In 1911 the Wisconsin legislature passed a WSFL-supported bill limiting the hours of work for women to ten hours a day and fifty-five hours a week for daytime work; night hours were limited to eight hours a night and forty-eight hours a week. Two years later the law was weakened by allowing the Wisconsin Industrial Commission, which had responsibility for its administration, to permit longer hours of work; the commission allowed longer hours at the pea canneries and later, in the 1920's, in other seasonal industries. In 1913 the legislature passed a law giving the Industrial Commission the power to establish minimum wages for women. The Milwaukee Merchants and Manufacturers Association opposed the bill. Its president stated that hundreds of girls would be fired because their employers would not consider their work worth the specified minimum wages.[6] The Socialist legislators supported both the maximum hours law and the minimum wage law for women, but, surprisingly, Weber broke with the Socialists and opposed the 1913 minimum wage law for women. He explained his opposition at the WSFL convention in 1913: "A minimum wage law no doubt would weaken or destroy the unions of women workers, which they maintain for their protection as well as the regulation of wages and hours. I am in favor of a minimum wage and maximum hours of labor, but I want both established by the workers themselves through their trade unions."[7]

The groups that favored passage of the hours and wage laws for women included the Wisconsin Consumers League, the National Consumers League, and the Milwaukee Federation of Churches. The Wisconsin Consumers League was composed of social workers, college professors and graduate students, and administrators of social legislation. The wage law was passed by the Wisconsin Senate, 12 to 8, and by the Assembly, 57 to 7. It was supported by Progressive Republicans, the Socialists, and some of the Democrats.

The WSFL's opposition to setting minimum wages for women by law was short-lived. In 1914 and in 1918 it joined the Wisconsin Consumers League and the Milwaukee County Council of Social Agencies in petitioning the Industrial Commission, as required by law, to make a determination of a "living wage" for women. In 1919 the commission set the minimum wage at 22 cents an hour for experienced women. For telephone operators, this minimum resulted in a 33 1/3 per cent increase in their average pay.[8] When the federal Wage and Hours Act was passed in 1938, the Wisconsin law lost its importance for working women engaged in interstate commerce. It continued to be useful in intrastate industries, especially the service industries. In the 1960's and 1970's the law lost significance because by then women's wages generally were above a minimum "living wage." Also some of the women's rights groups considered it sexist and discriminatory.

Changes in Political Policy

We have noted that under the leadership of Henry Ohl and John Handley the WSFL moderated its socialist ideology by supporting United States participation in World War I and then, after the war, by actively seeking to co-operate with farmers and other progressive groups. It even considered the establishment of a new non-Socialist political party. What were the reasons for this change in policy? Although labor's support of

Socialists had been remarkably successful in Milwaukee, it was a failure in the rest of the state, where the Socialists had little support.

Unions affiliated with the WSFL, meanwhile, were increasingly successful in working for pro-labor candidates within the Wisconsin Republican party, where the Progressive wing, led by the La Follettes, had considerable power. In Outagamie County, for example, a Farmer–Labor League successfully supported candidates on the Republican ticket. In 1922 George A. Schneider, vice-president of the Papermakers Union and member of the WSFL executive board, won election to Congress from the Seventh District (Appleton) on the Republican ticket, having defeated, in this case, a La Follette-endorsed candidate in the primary.

In the early 1920's the WSFL joined the strong Midwestern movement to create a farmer–labor alliance, which in Wisconsin hoped to amalgamate the Milwaukee Socialists, the La Follette Progressive Republicans, and farm and labor organizations. This effort failed because the Socialists in Milwaukee would not give up their party affiliation, and the La Follette Republicans would not share control with organized labor or other groups.

Nevertheless, the results of the 1922 elections were unusually favorable, from labor's viewpoint. John Blaine, a Progressive Republican, was elected governor. Senator Robert La Follette was re-elected by an enormous majority. Victor Berger, the Milwaukee Socialist, was again sent to Congress, and twenty-five labor-endorsed candidates went to the state legislature, thirteen of them Socialists. However, this was not enough to achieve the WSFL's prime legislative goal, the establishment of a system of unemployment compensation. That had to wait until 1932.

The Nation's First Unemployment Compensation Law

Addressing the 1898 WSFL convention, general organizer Frank Weber declared that labor was in the vanguard of every great reform. This was certainly true of unemployment compensation. The Wisconsin labor movement first asked for assistance for the unemployed in 1910. In July, 1918, the State Federation highlighted the need for unemployment insurance as part of a postwar social program which also included old age and health benefits. In the summer of 1920, with the postwar depression already beginning, the federation looked again at unemployment insurance. Professor John R. Commons, with whom the WSFL had co-operated in passing workers' compensation in 1911, addressed the annual convention at La Crosse, where he advocated unemployment insurance, among other forms of social insurance. The State Federation created a special committee composed of President Ohl, Secretary Handley, and Jacob F. Friedrick to meet with Commons for the purpose of drafting an unemployment insurance bill to be introduced in the 1921 legislative session. The bill that Commons and his university students drew up proposed that employers, workers, and the government each contribute one-third of the cost, as was done in Europe. But Handley converted Commons to the idea that if the employers paid the entire cost, there would be more incentive for them to prevent unemployment.[9]

In 1921, fourteen years before Congress passed enabling legislation for unemployment compensation, the Wisconsin legislature considered a compulsory unemployment compensation bill under which employers would pay the full cost. Introduced by State Senator Henry Huber, a prominent Progressive Republican, the bill was narrowly defeated in the Senate, 14 to 11. Its principal support came from organized labor, reinforced by vigorous lobbying efforts from John Commons and his graduate students.[10] Not surprisingly, the main opposition to unemployment compensation came from Wisconsin manufacturers. Another strong attempt was made to pass the Huber Bill in 1923. It failed when the Manufacturers Association proposed that there be an interim study of the bill, then reversed its position and opposed even that study bill, which was killed by a vote of 17 to 16.[11] It is interesting to note that the State Federation's vigorous support for unemployment compensation was carried on despite the fact that the American Federation of Labor consistently opposed any form of compulsory unemployment insurance.

In 1929, just before Wisconsin and the rest of the nation began to slide into the throes of the worst economic depression in American history, the WSFL revived the issue of unemployment compensation by having its own bill introduced by Assemblyman Robert Nixon. John Commons' work was now turned over to his graduate students, Paul Raushenbush and Elizabeth Brandeis, and to Harold Groves, who had become an assemblyman and a La Follette activist. Groves had introduced his own bill, which was more palatable to employers because it allowed each firm to have its own reserve account, unlike the Nixon bill, which pooled all reserve funds. Two crucial items were necessary for passage: agreement on one bill, and the support of the farm groups, which had the votes to kill the bill if they joined the manufacturers, as had happened in 1921 and 1923.

The State Federation settled its differences with Groves, and his bill was presented to the 1932 legislature. At hearings throughout the state, organized farm groups supported the legislation, which did not affect their economic interests since farmers as employers were excluded from coverage.

The Wisconsin Manufacturers Association bitterly fought it. This time management used different tactics since outright opposition in the face of heavy unemployment would not be politically feasible. The association also feared the bill might pass because Governor Philip La Follette was a supporter of the bill and worked closely with the State Federation of Labor and with Raushenbush and Groves. The Manufacturers Association therefore sought to modify the bill with a voluntary plan in place of the compulsory terms of the Groves bill.

At this point Governor La Follette offered what looked like a major concession to the employers, stating that the employers had expressed willingness to set up voluntary plans, and if they did so, covering 139,000 workers within a year, there would be no need for a compulsory plan. This provision defused the hard core opposition and the unemployment compensation bill sailed through the Senate 19 to 13, and 65 to 15 in the Assembly. Governor La Follette signed it on January 28, 1932. Among those present at the signing was Henry Ohl.

The voluntary plans never materialized despite great urging by the Wisconsin Manufacturers Association. The death of the voluntary effort was assured when, at a big meeting of manufacturers in Milwaukee, Paul Raushenbush, now the administrator of the law for the Industrial Commission, pointed out to the assembled employers that if enough of them adopted voluntary plans, the compulsory feature would lapse and thus all their competitors who had not established voluntary plans would never be required to do so.

Only fourteen voluntary plans were submitted, covering about 5,000 workers. The compulsory feature then went into effect.[12] Because of the severity of the depression, the beginning date was set forward to 1934; nevertheless, it was the first unemployment insurance act in the nation. In 1935 the federal government passed enabling legislation as an incentive for other states to follow Wisconsin's lead.[13]

Enactment of the Unemployment Compensation Act was a more difficult achievement for the State Federation than was enactment of the Workmens' Compensation Bill of 1911, in view of the fact that employers almost unanimously opposed unemployment compensation, whereas some of them, particularly those with large firms, had supported workers' compensation.

The early 1930's saw the enactment of a series of unprecedented labor laws in Wisconsin. The action began in 1929, when a bill was passed making "yellow-dog contracts"—in which employers required workers to stay out of unions for the term of the contract—unenforceable. (Earlier, in

1887, an anti-yellow-dog law had been passed, but it was declared unconstitutional in 1902.) Labor in 1929 was politically weak, especially because an anti-union industrialist, Walter J. Kohler, sat in the governor's chair. But, by adding an amendment that made illegal creamery contracts prohibiting farmers from joining cooperatives, the bill's supporters picked up enough farm votes to pass it. Under the first administration of Governor Philip F. La Follette, 1930–1932, other labor bills were approved. In 1931 a labor code was passed; it severely limited the issuance of injunctions by Wisconsin courts and declared it was public policy to promote collective bargaining.[14]

Despite the success of the State Federation's political program during Philip La Follette's administration, the WSFL leaders were not ready to break with the Socialist party and become La Follette Progressives. In the September, 1932, primary election Walter Kohler defeated La Follette. The WSFL leadership maintained its tradition of supporting the Socialist party not only in the 1932 election, in which the Socialists expected to make large gains due to heavy unemployment, but through the 1934 election as well. In 1934 Franklin Roosevelt's New Deal was getting under way, but unemployment was still high and the unemployed were becoming militant. Excerpts from a radio address by Jacob Friedrick illustrate how doctrinaire the WSFL leaders still were in the 1934 election. Friedrick, at that time, was a member of the WSFL executive board and also was recording secretary of the Milwaukee Federated Trades Council.[15]

> I want to urge all workers, organized as well as unorganized to support the complete Socialist Party ticket in Tuesday's election.
>
> I urge the election of the Socialist candidates not so much on the basis of the fact that they are part of us workers, not even on their splendid past records. I urge it mainly on the basis that they are a part of an organized group that has a sane, concrete, definite plan for an economic and social adjustment that will eliminate the present exploitation of the many by the few, and will substitute a system of production and distribution to meet the needs of all instead of the profits of the few.
>
> Members of the trade union movement have through bitter experience learned the need of solidarity and organization, that is why they are members of the organized labor movement. . . . in voting the straight Socialist ticket you will be voting for an organized political movement of the working class . . . this political organization works as a unit, just as your union works as a unit.
>
> Such a vote will leave you with not regrets but will give you the consciousness that you have performed your duty to the working class as an organized worker in an organized manner.

Yet the 1934 election returns indicated that the continued support of Socialists was divisive, weakening labor's ability to exercise statewide political power. In fact, 1934 was the last year that the WSFL and the Milwaukee FTC supported a Socialist ticket for state offices.

The Farmer–Labor Progressive Federation

In 1934 Henry Ohl judged that the time was again propitious for a farmer–labor party. The farm depression in Wisconsin had radicalized the farm organizations. By 1932 farm incomes had fallen to only 45 per cent of their 1929 level.[16] As described in Chapter 5, farmer discontent even had reached the point of a milk strike which the governor had used the National Guard to break. This acute farm distress was a lever which Ohl might use to make farm organizations more receptive to cooperation with labor. Ohl was also aware that Thomas Amlie, a First District congressman, had established a political organization called the Progressive League which was agitating for a third party among both farm and labor groups.

By the spring of 1934 the sentiment for a farmer–labor party had become so compelling that Philip and Robert La Follette, Jr., quickly moved to head off this new party, which they would not control, by beginning a third party of their own. They issued a call for a conference to be held at Fond du Lac on May 19, 1934. This conference set up the Progressive party of Wisconsin which was completely under the control of the La Follette brothers and their political followers who had formerly run on the Republican ticket.

Ohl felt that the La Follettes had stolen the third party which labor had nursed and groomed. In addition, he was unhappy with the party itself. Labor, farm, and other liberal organizations were excluded from its leadership, and its platform omitted any significant modification of capitalism toward socialism, which Ohl believed was essential to create jobs for the millions of unemployed.[17]

The new Progressive party did win major offices in the November, 1934, elections. Philip La Follette was elected governor a second time and Robert retained his U.S. Senate seat. It did not win a majority in either house of the state legislature. Although the WSFL had not endorsed Governor La Follette, it worked closely with him in the legislative session as it had in the 1931–1932 session.

In the 1935 session labor, with the governor's blessing, introduced a "Little Wagner Act" bill which would give Wisconsin workers not engaged in interstate commerce the protections which the national Wagner

Act gave to workers engaged in such commerce. A second major bill which labor supported was a $209 million jobs bill that Governor La Follette proposed. But a coalition of Republicans and conservative Democrats in the state Senate killed both bills and all other legislation in which labor was interested. This same conservative Senate coalition also killed major farm legislation, primarily a bill to slow down farm foreclosures.

The 1934 election and the 1935 legislative session had made clear that when the liberal vote was split between Socialist and Progressive candidates, candidates with a name like "La Follette" could win statewide races, but conservative Democrats and Republicans would win enough legislative seats to defeat legislation wanted by labor, by farmers, and by the unemployed.

The WSFL therefore, in October and November of 1935, called a series of conferences to form its type of third party, the Farmer–Labor Progressive Federation. It included the following nine economic and political groups: the WSFL; the Wisconsin Workers Alliance (an organization of unemployed); three farm organizations—the Wisconsin Milk Pool, the Farm Holiday Association, and the Farmers Union; the Railway Brotherhoods; the Progressive League (a liberal organization headed by Tom Amlie, a left-of-center Progressive); the Socialist party of Wisconsin; and the Progressive party.[18] The CIO, which was not yet established in Wisconsin, joined the party a year later.

As the FLPF took shape, in preparation for the 1936 elections Ohl chaired every conference, knocking heads together to establish a unified program among these diverse groups, each of which wanted to push its own interests within the FLPF. For example, the Socialists, a large and crucial group, demanded that the platform contain a plank calling for "production for use" instead of for profit, that the FLPF make a pre-primary election endorsement of one candidate for each office, that it only endorse candidates who were members of the FLPF, and that some of the candidates endorsed by the FLPF run under the Socialist party label.

The Progressive party, in order to gain majorities in the Assembly and the Senate, desperately needed urban votes. They hoped they could get them by enlisting the support of the WSFL and the Milwaukee Socialists. At the same time the Progressives, who were strong in rural Wisconsin, did not not wish to share this rural influence with anyone else, and hoped that the FLPF would restrict its organizing to a few urban counties. They stood by the traditional La Follette view of an open primary. The Progressives also demanded that the FLPF support Philip La Follette for governor even though he refused to join the organization. The Progressive party did not want any class-conscious proposals, such as "production for use," in the FLPF platform. In fact, it felt that the use of "Farmer–Labor" in the name evoked too strong a sense of class consciousness.

The Progressive party appointed Governor La Follette's secretary, Thomas Duncan, as a board member of the FLPF. A former Socialist and former secretary to Socialist Mayor Daniel Hoan of Milwaukee, Duncan was well equipped to contribute leadership and promote Progressive party interests in the FLPF. The farm organizations were interested chiefly in planks to help the farmers, such as one preventing foreclosures of farms which were in default on mortgage payments.[19]

Miraculously, Ohl succeeded in maintaining unity in the FLPF through the November, 1936, election and well into the 1937 legislative session. His success was due, in part, to the fact he was president of the WSFL, the largest organization in the FLPF with the exception of the amorphous Progressive party. Also, Ohl could draw on the labor movement for many of the experienced people needed by the FLPF. For instance, when the Federation needed an organizer to build up membership, Ohl produced an able candidate, Henry Rutz, who headed an eleven-state Workers' Education Program for the federal Works Progress Administration. Rutz, a union printer and member of the Socialist party, worked skillfully even though the Federation never provided his promised two-hundred-dollar monthly salary. Ohl had additional expertise in Jacob Friedrick, executive board member of the WSFL and an organizer for the Milwaukee FTC; the FLPF borrowed him full time. At FLPF conferences Friedrick served as chairman of the Federation's constitutional committee and as chairman of the resolutions committees, where his skill at drafting did much to maintain the unity of the diverse groups.

Although each of the groups within the FLPF pushed for its own particular interests, the important thing was the concessions which each group was willing to, or induced to, make for the sake of presenting one united, liberal slate to the voters. Heretofore the two main political groups within the FLPF, the Socialists and the Progressives, each had presented a full slate of candidates. The Socialists in 1936 agreed to no longer put Socialist party candidates on the ballot as they had been doing since 1898. This left the FLPF one slate, that of the Progressive party, upon which to concentrate its resources.

The Progressives, in turn, agreed that in some of the districts in which Socialist and Progressive party candidates had formerly fought each other, particularly in certain Milwaukee state Assembly and Senate districts, the Socialists would choose one of their own members to run for that seat, albeit under the Progressive party label. The Socialists agreed that in certain other districts no Socialist would run against the Progressive party's candidate in the primary election.

The Socialists also agreed to give up their "production for use" plank in the FLPF platform. These agreements and concessions by the Socialists were crucial to the success of the FLPF, because the Socialists had 50,000 votes in the Milwaukee area, without which the Progressives could not win control of the state legislature. Daniel Hoan, the mayor of Milwaukee, was a key figure in achieving these agreements. Also, the fact that the leaders of the FLPF, Ohl, Handley, Rutz, and Friedrick, were party members helped immensely in gaining this Socialist party action.

The three farm organization leaders, Kenneth Hones of the Farmers Union, Harry Jack of the Milk Pool, and Charles Goldamer of the Farm Holiday Association, stood with Ohl on all critical FLPF controversies.

Ohl was a hard-liner on excluding all Communist organizations and, for the first year, many individual Communists, from the FLPF. Undoubtedly Ohl was well aware that the collapse of the farmer–labor political movement of 1920–1923, in which he was interested, was due, in part, to the Communist takeover of the movement at its Chicago convention in July, 1923.[20]

Excluding Communists was a difficult task. The Communist party of Milwaukee insisted on endorsing all of the FLPF candidates in Milwaukee. Its endorsement damaged the FLPF by alienating its rural membership and the more conservative Progressives. When the leadership of the Wisconsin Workers' Alliance, an organization of unemployed workers affiliated with the FLPF, fell to the Communists, and when the CIO joined the FLPF, it became impossible to screen membership to exclude Communists. Eugene Dennis, head of the Wisconsin Communist party, further embarrassed the FLPF on the eve of the 1936 election by publicly boasting that five of the FLPF's endorsed assembly and county office candidates were card-carrying Communists.[21]

Although the nine-group Farmer–Labor Progressive Federation was in many respects a creaky machine, the November, 1936, election justified all the effort which labor had put into it.

Labor at the Summit: The "Little Wagner Act"

The state election of November, 1936, gave Wisconsin labor a degree of power it never had held before. Governor Philip La Follette was re-elected with a majority of 200,000 as compared to 13,000 two years earlier. The Progressive party gained control of both houses of the legislature, even though it had only 48 of the 100 seats in the Assembly and 16 of 33 in the Senate. Governor La Follette's persuasiveness (as well as patronage) convinced several conservative legislators to vote with the Progressives on organizing the two houses and on major bills.

The credit for the election victory of 1936 goes only partially to the FLPF. Franklin Roosevelt's landslide carried in liberal majorities nationally and in Wisconsin. But the FLPF deserves much credit for encouraging those liberal voters who favored the Democratic candidate for president to ignore the other Democratic contenders and vote instead for the Progressive party candidates.[22] In the Assembly, a Progressive and FLPF member, Paul R. Alfonsi, was elected speaker by a vote of 50 to 49. Andrew Biemiller, a Socialist and organizer for the WSFL, was elected majority leader. In the Senate, Walter Rush, who was a Progressive member of the FPLF, became the speaker. Labor's bills were at the top of the agenda, and a grateful governor gave complete support.

The most important and most controversial bill was the "Little Wagner Act," a WSFL bill also backed by the newly formed Wisconsin State CIO. Ohl and Handley insisted that the long and complicated bill be enacted "as is," with no amendments. The opposition at the legislative hearings was impressive. The Wisconsin State Chamber of Commerce labeled it "discriminatory." The big manufacturing firms wanted it killed. Harold W. Storey, representing Allis–Chalmers, said he was an outlaw among employers because he only wanted the bill amended, not killed. The Wisconsin Council of Agriculture demanded an amendment exempting all farmer-owned co-operatives. Ohl and Handley brought in a stream of labor leaders to testify for the bill. Just as with Workers' Compensation and Unemployment Compensation many years earlier, University of Wisconsin professors of law and economics urged its passage. The Assembly, without permitting any amendments, passed the bill by a vote of 63 to 24.[23]

The real battle for the Little Wagner Act took place in the Senate. Here the farm legislators began to gag on the no-amendment edict. Ohl, still insisting on no amendments, was near defeat. At this point Governor La Follette intervened, fearing that if labor's key bill was defeated, the FLPF might turn down all of the his bills. La Follette convinced Ohl that he must accept two minor amendments or else all was lost. One amendment established an advisory labor–management commission; the other required the registration of unions by the state.

The Little Wagner Act come to the Senate floor on April 1, 1937. No senator was allowed to leave the floor. Sixty amendments and thirty motions for a recess were defeated. There were a hundred roll call votes, each decided by a majority of one or two votes. Twelve hours later the bill was passed.[24]

The act, formally titled Wisconsin Labor Relations Act of 1937, prohibited specific employer practices: discrimination against workers for union membership and union activity, blacklisting, spying on workers, establishment or support of a company-dominated union, and interference with workers' rights to organize. Like the Wagner Act, the state law set up a board that ruled on charges of violations and which administered secret elections to determine if workers wanted a union. If a union won the election, the employer was compelled to engage in collective bargaining with it. Unlike the Wagner Act, the Wisconsin law permitted an employer to grant a closed shop without direct evidence that the employees favored it.

Altogether, labor had introduced about forty bills in the 1937 session and almost all of those dealing with labor problems were passed. The one near-exception was a farmer-instigated bill for licensing all labor organizers, portent of a rural revolt against labor. It passed the Assembly 46 to 37. By a parliamentary ruse Biemiller was able to bring up the bill again for reconsideration, whereupon, on the last day of the session, it was filibustered to death by Sigman, Biemiller, and John Grobschmidt.

Labor was also high on the list of gubernatorial appointments. Henry Rutz was appointed the state's emergency relief administrator. Raymond Richards of Wisconsin Rapids, a staff representative of the Pulp, Sulphite, and Paper Mill Workers, and Edward Brown of Milwaukee, business agent of Local 494 of the International Brotherhood of Electrical Workers, became the first two labor leaders to be appointed to the University of Wisconsin Board of Regents. Ohl and Handley would not accept any positions for themselves; the only reward they would accept personally for their support of the governor was legislation for their members.

The Collapse of Labor's Political Power

The farmers' uneasiness with their labor alliance, which had begun to surface during the 1937 legislative session, changed to open hostility and then to outright fighting against labor when, in the following year, unions began to organize some of the agricultural processing plants—a creamery, a canning factory, and ten Milwaukee poultry and egg firms.[25]

The workers in a farmer-owned co-operative creamery in Richland Center joined the union and asked the manager to sit down and bargain over the union's proposals. Instead, the manager fired two foremen who had joined the union. Then several hundred farmers descended on the plant to bring in new employees to replace the plant's unionized workers. The union, which had not struck, took its case to the National Labor Relations Board, which required the management to rehire the union members and pay their lost wages.

There was a strike of several weeks' duration at the Frank Pure Food Company, a canning company, in Franksville. It occurred when the company asked the workers to accept a wage cut, and was settled by federal and state mediators.

The Milwaukee *Journal* reported on this strike with front page articles, the headlines of which seemed deliberately worded to increase the farmers' ire—for example, "Dollars Are Plowed under as Strike Uproots Hopes of Spinach Farmers." The *Journal* then vividly described a $1,200 loss incurred by a farmer, Leo Lichter, when he could not sell his spinach to the cannery because of the strike:[26]

> It isn't everyday that a farmer or anybody else for that matter, loses that much money. Lichter might as well have been running his disc over 1,200 dollar bills. The muscles contracted along his jaw. His hands tightened on the steering wheel of his tractor. Then he squinted into the sun and ripped into the even rows of dark green leaves—six acres of them.

After pointing out that more than one hundred other Franksville farmers would do the same, the *Journal* quoted Lichter at length:

> We're throwing our crop to the winds because the unions are irresponsible. . . . I'm not blaming the strikers so much as their leaders who are thriving by racketeering. When the workers voted to strike, they looked like they were at a funeral. . . . We're going to take the farmer out of the Farmer–Labor party and see how we can get along by ourselves for a while.

In this and other news stories, the *Journal* gave no remotely comparable report on the causes of the strike and the feelings and problems of the workers.[27]

Reporting of this nature lends credence to a conclusion drawn by one extensive study of the FLPF—that the Milwaukee *Journal* and many other newspapers in the state wrote stories which were designed to pit farmer against worker, worker against union leader, and Socialist against Progressive, in a deliberate attempt to break up the FLPF's effective amalgamation of the farmer, labor, Socialist, and Progressive votes.[28]

Two of the three farm organizations affiliated with the FLPF broke with the Federation. Kenneth Hones, the Farmers Union member active in the FLPF, continued to support labor's right to organize agricultural processing plants. The Wisconsin Council of Agriculture, which with

80,000 members was the most powerful farm organization in Wisconsin, declared "political war" against labor and the Little Wagner Act. Leaders of the Farm Holiday Association announced their support for Republican candidates.[29]

This desertion by the farm leaders who had helped him to organize the FLPF was a great disappointment to Ohl. Since 1935 he had supported their legislation even when it resulted in higher food costs for the workers, as, for example, the 15 cent tax on colored oleomargarine passed by the 1935 legislature.

Other cracks were appearing within the FLPF. By mid-1937 the newly formed Wisconsin State CIO was locked in an organizing and raiding battle with the state's AFL unions, which substantially dissipated the resources of both groups as well as their desire for joint political action. Inevitably it spilled over to the FLPF, where the CIO attempted to wrest control from the WSFL. At the request of the CIO, the FLPF held a special conference in January, 1938, to consider the CIO's request to enroll its entire claimed membership of 80,000. Until then, membership had been up to the individual. The peak FLPF dues-paying membership had been about 5,000, and was considerably less in January, 1938. Ohl stated that the WSFL was constitutionally forbidden from delivering its membership to any political body and that if the CIO plan of group membership was adopted, the WSFL would withdraw from the FLPF. The vote was 27 to 26 against the CIO proposal.[30]

With the farm organizations bolting toward the Republicans, Ohl and Handley vainly tried to mobilize local unions behind the FLPF. In April they sent out letters to 1,200 affiliated locals asking them to have their members join at a cost of one dollar per member. Nine unions responded—but only to ask further questions. Belatedly, in August, 1938, realizing the possibility of an election defeat, the WSFL and the state CIO contributed $500 each to the FLPF, but it was too little and far too late.[31]

The election of November, 1938, was a monumental disaster for Wisconsin labor. La Follette was overwhelmed by a conservative Milwaukee industrialist, Julius P. Heil. Republicans also captured all other state executive offices, the U.S. Senate seat, eight of the ten congressional seats, a large majority in the Assembly and, together with conservative Democrats, a majority in the State Senate.

What are the probable reasons that the overwhelming victory of the Progressive ticket and its FLPF supporters in 1936 was followed so quickly by this equally great defeat? First, it should be recognized that the conservative resurgence was a national phenomenon. Almost always, a presidential landslide such as that of 1936 has been followed by a resurgence of the losing party, in this case the Republicans, in the next congressional elections. The steep recession, which began in late 1937 and brought falling farm prices in 1938, no doubt helped the Republican comeback. Also, well-publicized strikes, such as the sitdown strikes by Michigan auto workers, caused a reaction against unions and the legislators who supported them. In Wisconsin this reaction was fueled by an increase in the number of strikes from fifty in 1936 to 190 in 1937.[32] And as we have seen, the effectiveness of the FLPF was destroyed by the farmer–labor and CIO–AFL conflicts.

Finally, Governor Philip La Follette chose the spring of 1938 to suddenly launch a national third party. This he did on his own, without consulting the FLPF. He did not even privately consult Ohl, Handley, and Rutz; the state CIO leaders, Costello and Mickelsen; or the farm leaders.[33] Because of La Follette's national party effort, it was not even known until July if he would run again for the governorship, too late for effective campaigning by either himself or another FLPF candidate. The state and national response to La Follette's new party, which had chosen for its symbol an insignia resembling the Nazi swastika, was decidedly negative. Labor was less than enthusiastic because La Follette, in announcing his new party, had severely attacked President Roosevelt, to whom labor was firmly wedded because of his very significant pro-labor legislation. Philip La Follette's monumental folly not only decisively ended his own political career, but also contributed to the 1938 defeat of the FLPF.

To the conservative governor and legislature inaugurated in January, 1939, labor was the main target. The Little Wagner Act and most of the other labor laws were repealed quickly. Most damaging to labor was the enactment of a comprehensive anti-labor act called the Wisconsin Employment Peace Act, which severely restricted union activity. This law prohibited new union security agreements unless approved by three-fourths of the employees in secret-ballot elections conducted by the newly created Wisconsin Employment Relations Board. Union dues and assessments could not be deducted from a paycheck unless duly authorized in writing by the employee. A long list of unfair labor practices by unions was included. For strikes involving harvesting or the processing of farm or dairy products, a ten-day notice was required. Strikes could be called only if authorized by a majority of the employees voting in a secret-ballot election. Secondary boycotts and mass picketing were forbidden. The Employment Peace Act was a precursor of the federal Taft–Hartley Act of

1947. Thus Wisconsin, noted for its progressive and pro-labor legislation, became for a time a national leader in anti-labor legislation.

During the successes of the FLPF, Ohl and Handley had had the unquestioned backing of the WSFL leadership. At the conclusion of the 1937 state legislative session and its passage of the Little Wagner Act, Ohl and Handley were heroes. Dave Sigman, one of the assemblymen who filibustered against an anti-labor bill, was rewarded by election to the WSFL executive board. But no sooner had the failure of the Ohl–Handley political program become evident with passage of the anti-labor Wisconsin Employment Peace Act by the 1939 legislature than revolt surfaced at the conventions of the WSFL.

At the August, 1939, WSFL convention, Ohl's enemies were planning a resolution to break with the FLPF and return to the Gompers political policy of supporting labor's friends of any party. Ohl cut down this opposition in his opening address by calling attention to the pro-labor legislative record of the FLPF legislators compared to that of the Republicans and Democrats.[34] But at the 1940 WSFL convention Ohl faced a resolution, now pushed by leading labor leaders in Milwaukee and elsewhere, to "divorce" the WSFL from any and all political parties.

In the committee chaired by Jacob Friedrick the word "divorce" was removed, but the resolution included Gompers' policy, which always had been anathema to Socialist leaders of the WSFL: "It is recognized that the principle of 'reward your friends and defeat your enemies' calls for supporting such friends on any ticket."[35] At the same convention two of Ohl's close associates on the WSFL executive board were targeted for removal. David Sigman was defeated and Jacob Friedrick, Ohl's closest associate, dropped from first to last place in the number of votes received among those elected to the executive board. By the time of the FLPF convention of June, 1940, neither Ohl, Handley, nor Friedrick were even in attendance.

It is tempting to attribute the collapse of the great Ohl–Handley farmer-labor political coalition to a series of unforeseen causes. Yet Ohl himself made some serious miscalculations. Looking at politics through Socialist-tinted glasses, he had become overly enamored with government by class, specifically a farmer–labor coalition. He thus failed to recognize how ephemeral was the farmer's attachment to that concept. His Socialist ideology blinded him to the profound economic and social changes being wrought by Franklin Roosevelt, who had assembled a much broader coalition behind the Democratic party. Instead of joining this movement, as had the labor movement across the nation, the Wisconsin leadership led its members into a third-party dead end.

Despite its political mistakes the Wisconsin labor movement, including both the WSFL and the State CIO, grew in numbers. Collective bargaining brought economic gains to its members, and yet for its political mistakes it was to wander for twenty years in the political wilderness until the election of Gaylord Nelson as governor in 1958.

McCarthy Defeats La Follette

In 1940 both the WSFL and the state CIO withdrew their support from the now moribund Farmer–Labor Progressive Federation. Not one union made a contribution to it in the summer of 1940.[36] At its annual convention in August, the WSFL turned to the traditional AFL policy, which the Socialist-minded WSFL never had followed, of supporting pro-labor candidates regardless of their party affiliation.[37] But neither the WSFL or the state CIO made any political endorsements for president, for U.S. senator, or for the governorship in the 1940 general elections. An ad hoc Milwaukee Labor Committee, composed of the presidents of the Building Trades Council, the Teamsters, and the CIO Amalgamated Clothing Workers Union, supported Roosevelt and two Wisconsin Progressives—Robert M. La Follette, Jr., for U.S. senator, and Orland Loomis for governor.

For the next six years the WSFL took little part in state elections. Its new president, George Haberman, faced election challenges of his own in the WSFL in 1943 and 1944, so internal politics rather than state and national politics received the WSFL's attention. The state CIO was politically active in 1942 and 1944, when it enthusiastically endorsed a second front in Europe. This unusual expression of political action was due to the desire of the CIO's left-wing leadership to assist Soviet Russia.

The 1946 national election gave a clear focus to the political programs of both the WSFL and the state CIO. The most important post in that election was the U.S. Senate seat of the incumbent, Robert La Follette, Jr., the brother of Philip. A great friend of labor, he had been elected in 1928 as a Republican and in 1934 and 1940 as a Progressive. After much debate he returned in 1946 to the Republican party, the party of his famous father, "Fighting Bob." His decision presented many union leaders with a real dilemma, because after fourteen years of the New Deal, a number of them had developed a strong loyalty to the Democratic party. Union leaders in the lakeshore cities of Milwaukee, Racine, and Kenosha were active in building a liberal Wisconsin Democratic party.

When in March, 1946, the remnants of the Progressive party assembled at Portage to learn which party primary La Follette would enter, the only active labor group there was the Racine–Kenosha delegation, composed of both AFL and CIO local leaders, who strongly urged La Follette to enter the Democratic party or forfeit their support.[38] Ignoring their advice, La Follette chose to run in the Republican primary and narrowly lost to an unknown, Joseph McCarthy, by some 5,000 votes. La Follette did badly in the labor wards of Kenosha and Racine, where labor had endorsed Howard McMurray for the Senate on the Democratic ticket, and in Milwaukee, where the CIO had endorsed Edmund Bobrowicz on the Democratic ticket for the Fourth District congressional race. In his book, *Senator Joseph McCarthy and the American Labor Movement,* David Oshinsky makes the case that it was the low vote for La Follette in the labor wards of Milwaukee, Racine, and Kenosha which enabled McCarthy to win.[39]

The WSFL appears to have done nothing to help La Follette in the 1946 primary. The Milwaukee *Labor Press,* organ of the Milwaukee Federated Trades Council, urged its readers to vote, but made no endorsement itself. The president of the Milwaukee Building Trades Council, Peter Schoemann, stated that he did not believe that labor should endorse anyone in the primary.[40] Almost the only labor support for La Follette was given by the Milwaukee AFL Committee for the Re-Election of Robert M. La Follette, a group of twenty-nine prominent WSFL leaders, including Secretary Nagorsne, but not President Haberman. The committee raised only $175.[41]

If the WSFL was indifferent toward La Follette during the 1946 primary, the state CIO was definitely hostile. La Follette had been critical of the Soviet authoritarian regime, and the Wisconsin edition of the *CIO News* attacked him several times during 1945. The state CIO did not endorse any senatorial candidate, but it did endorse and give aggressive support to Edmund Bobrowicz, a staff member of the left-wing Fur and Leather Workers Union but a political unknown, who ran against and defeated incumbent Congressman Thaddeus Wasielewski in the Democratic primary. Wasielewski, like La Follette, had been critical of Soviet Russia. By endorsing Bobrowicz in the Democratic primary the state CIO was perhaps attempting to kill two anti-Soviet birds with one stone. In Wisconsin's primary elections, voters had to choose a party ballot, and to vote for Bobrowicz meant choosing the Democratic party primary ballot. Having done so, the voter could not support La Follette, who was on the Republican party primary ballot. To the extent that the state CIO's aggressive campaign for Bobrowicz helped to defeat Wasielewski, it also helped to defeat La Follette. Bobrowicz's 12,000 votes were more than enough to have defeated La Follette, who lost to McCarthy by only 5,400 votes statewide.[42]

One would have expected the CIO–United Auto Workers and the United Steelworkers–CIO to have given strong support to Robert La Follette. In 1937, when the UAW was fighting for its life in sitdown strikes and the Steelworkers were striking four major steel companies, investigators for the Civil Liberties Committee of the U.S. Senate, chaired by La Follette, repeatedly presented crucial information on the illegal anti-labor activities of both the big auto companies and the major steel companies. Yet in 1946 neither the UAW nor the United Steelworkers in Wisconsin supported him.

Robert La Follette's defeat by Joseph McCarthy in the Republican primary shocked both the WSFL and the state CIO into joint action. They formed a United Labor Committee to support the Democratic candidate, Howard McMurray, but there was very little grass-roots support for him. In the general election the Republican slate won by a two-to-one margin. The Republicans who gained office were generally not from the Progressive wing of the party, but from the conservative, pro-business wing which had passed the Employment Peace Act of 1939. In 1947 they passed a law prohibiting strikes by employees of public utility companies. The political influence of Wisconsin labor had fallen to a low ebb, and its recovery was to be a slow process.

After the 1946 debacle, union members seemed too stunned to fight back. The state CIO was in disarray owing to the struggle among its leaders. Although the left-wing faction had been expelled from leadership, the prolonged quarrel and the newspaper publicity given it destroyed the membership's confidence in their leaders' political judgment for some years.

The State Federation of Labor was also politically ineffective in these years, although for different reasons. Because the Haberman administration was not structured for participation in grass roots party activity, the State Federation did not exercise the political leadership that had characterized Henry Ohl's and Jack Handley's administrations. It generally limited its activity to rather perfunctory endorsements of candidates shortly before an election. Furthermore, between 1946 and 1952 the WSFL found no election contests which aroused it to action. The only political alternative to the business-oriented Republican party was the state's new Democratic party. Haberman and the Democratic leaders did not seem to be compatible. From Haberman's point of view, the leaders were young, brash, too intellectual, and more important, they were not in office.

In 1958, at the merger convention, a delegate asked Haberman to comment on a Milwaukee *Journal* article which reported that he had attended the recent state Republican party convention and had urged a Republican, Roland Steinle, to run for the State Supreme Court, and that he generally had been fraternizing with Republican leaders. Haberman's answer is important because it outlines his political philosophy:[43]

> I want to tell you here and now, it is a damnable lie . . . I have never in my life voted in a Republican party. I have never fraternized with Republicans until I got on this job, and I know that for the interest of all of labor in this state, I am not going to be stupid enough to fraternize with any one particular party; when the opposition party is in power, (applause) I am going to fraternize with them to get legislation for you. (Applause)
>
> I am not a Democrat. I am not a Republican. I never was a Progressive, and was for a short time a Socialist. . . . I belong to no party . . . I am not going to lay the eggs of the Federation in one basket.

A Return to Effective Political Activity

The first election to arouse Wisconsin labor from its post-1946 stupor was Senator McCarthy's bid for re-election in 1952. He was now a national figure. His anti-labor votes and, at least to some extent, his "Red-baiting," had made him a target of the national labor movement. Strong pressure and financial contributions from national unions brought increased action by Wisconsin labor, and both the state CIO and the State Federation endorsed Thomas Fairchild, McCarthy's Democratic opponent. According to Edwin Bayley, then a Milwaukee *Journal* political reporter, there was an attempt to oppose McCarthy in the Republican primary by inducing Republican Governor Walter J. Kohler to enter that race, and this effort had labor support.[44] Kohler declined to enter.

In preparation for the November election, Wisconsin labor began to engage in anti-McCarthy publicity. The Milwaukee *Labor Press* did an aggressive job of attacking McCarthy's voting record on labor issues, and the state *CIO News* was vigorous in its criticism. But for tactical reasons both papers limited their criticism of McCarthy to his vote for the Taft–Hartley Act and other anti-labor measures and refrained from countering his attacks on U.S. foreign policy. Special efforts were made to register union members, and on election day unions paid workers to canvass working-class precincts and get workers to the polls. McCarthy defeated

Fairchild but trailed the Republican ticket, which included Eisenhower for president and Kohler for governor.

Labor's efforts in the 1952 campaign were greater than any since the 1930's, especially in the metropolitan centers of Kenosha, Racine, Madison, Eau Claire, Milwaukee, and Superior. But it seemed unable to get its message to the outlying industrial centers—in the Fox River Valley, the Wisconsin River Valley, La Crosse and Rock counties, and the Lake Michigan shore north of Sheboygan.

For several years after 1952 the Republican party did not face a serious threat in Wisconsin politics. There was one exception, however. In 1954 the Democratic candidate for governor, William Proxmire, received 49 per cent of the votes; labor had supplied 55 per cent of his campaign contributions.[45] The Republicans took notice. Mark Catlin, Republican floor leader in the State Assembly, introduced and guided to passage a bill which prohibited any political contribution by a labor union, in cash or in kind, whose source was membership dues. Known as the Catlin Act, the law severely reduced labor's contribution to candidates of its choice and deprived the struggling Democrats of a major source of revenue.

Proxmire won a special election held in 1957 to fill the U.S. Senate seat of the deceased McCarthy. A year later Gaylord Nelson, endorsed by labor, was elected governor, and the Democrats won a majority in the State Assembly. This break in Republican control was manifested by the repeal of the Catlin Act in 1959.

The 1960's and 1970's were a period of slow but steady growth for the Wisconsin labor movement. The Wisconsin AFL–CIO membership increased from 260,000 at merger in 1958 to 276,000 in 1978. Political activity increased commensurably in both financial expenditures and sophistication. Today, a Wisconsin candidate for state or federal office, as well as for major municipal posts, who receives the endorsement of the appropriate labor body is eligible for a modest campaign contribution from Wisconsin unions. In crucial contests, especially for congressional seats, funds are sent into the state by international unions to supplement money raised locally.

In the 1977–1978 biennium, labor unions' contributions to candidates for state and local office and to political party committees were approximately $448,000. Of this, $61,637 came from the State AFL–CIO. Labor's contributions in that biennium were 40 per cent of political action contributions from interest groups, but they were only 7.5 per cent of the $6,000,000 spent by all state candidates.[46] Most of labor's money went to Democrats.

David Adamany, a political scientist, put in perspective the importance of labor's financial contributions to the Wisconsin Democratic party. In the early 1950's, when Wisconsin Democrats were out of office and had spent years trailing the Republicans, contributions were few and far between. Then, labor's financial support, although substantially less than in the 1970's, was exceedingly important. In 1976, when the Democrats had considerable influence in state government and the congressional delegation, many individuals and organizations found it worth their while to contribute to Democratic election campaigns. Labor's increased financial support, while very important, was therefore less crucial. Compared to the early 1950's, labor's political expenditures in Wisconsin today are, in fact, smaller in proportion to the total spent by all Wisconsin Democratic candidates.[47]

However one tallies labor's financial contributions, it tends to understate the true value of labor support. Other important political contributions, in addition to financial contributions made to candidates, include endorsements of particular candidates headlined in union publications and leaflets, voter registration drives, phone calls on election day to remind union members to vote, introduction of candidates at plant gates, and the appearances of endorsed candidates at union meetings. A number of labor councils in the industrial counties have convinced local unions to turn over names and addresses of all their members to a central union registration committee, which checks the names against voter registration lists and then notifies unions of members who are not registered. Candidates for major offices have received such assistance as a volunteer union chauffeur (now included as a candidate contribution), as was the case in Proxmire's senatorial campaign of 1957. In state legislative races, labor regularly has endorsed and supported financially incumbents whose voting records are favorable toward its interests. This has proved an invaluable aid to the incumbent candidates in Milwaukee County, who are often challenged in primaries.

In addition, the unions, like other organized groups, put a great deal of effort into lobbying. Early in each biennial legislative session the State AFL–CIO holds a legislative conference in Madison, attended by delegates from most local unions in the state. Here, legislative priorities are voted upon. The task of daily lobbying belongs to the secretary–treasurer of the state body, who, since 1970, has been Jack Reihl. He and a full-time assistant follow every labor bill from committee to committee and through both houses of the legislature. They have ready access to key legislators who have received labor's endorsements, publicity, and financial help dur-

Workers' march, Milwaukee, during the Great Depression.

Milwaukee Journal Photo, SHSW

WHi(X3)25245

Police and strikebreakers clash with striking workers at the J.I. Case plant, Racine, May, 1935.

Confrontation at the Allis-Chalmers plant, Milwaukee, 1932.

Jubilant UAW sitdown strikers leave the General Motors plant at Janesville, January, 1937.

Oshkosh B'Gosh garment workers proudly fulfilled a U.S. government order for camouflage overalls (left) during World War II.

Workers' march in support of veterans' rights, Milwaukee, 1945.

AFL President William Green visits the new WSFL leadership, 1943. Standing, left to right: George Hall, Leonard Pilerson, Frank Ranney, Ernest Terry, Arthur Olsen. Seated, left to right: George Haberman, Mathew Woll, William Green, William Nagorsne.

Henry J. Ohl, Jr.

Al Hayes of the International Association of Machinists.

Kathryn Hartman Lichter of the Fur and Leather Workers, 1943.

John L. Lewis meets with Wisconsin CIO leaders in Pittsburgh, 1938. Left to right: Emil Costello, Harold Christoffel, Meyer Adelman, John L. Lewis, Gunnar Mickelsen, James DeWitt.

Catherine Conroy of the Communication Workers, 1983.

trikers from UAW Local 180 at the J.I. Case lant in Racine, 1960.

Frank H. Ranney of the Teamsters.

Arnold Zander of AFSCME.

Herman Seide.

Jacob F. Friedrick.

Steelworkers District #32 Director Bertram McNamara (left) congratulates Walter Burke on the occasion of Burke's elevation to Secretary-Treasurer of the International in Pittsburgh, c. 1969.

Milwaukee Journal Photo, SHSW

United Auto Workers Local 75 members cast their votes on a proposed contract in a voting booth outside the American Motors factory, Milwaukee, December, 1964.

University of Wisconsin School for Workers in session, c. 1940.

School for Workers photo

George A. Haberman, President of the WSFL (1943–1958) and of the Wisconsin State AFL-CIO (1958–1966).

John Schmitt, President of the Wisconsin State AFL-C from 1966.

Collective bargaining, c. 1960, between Allied Industrial Workers Local 323 and representatives of the Baso Products Company, Milwaukee.

ing campaigns. In lobbying on important bills, the state president joins the secretary–treasurer. Either official may testify before legislative committees, but the most effective persuasion is done in personal contacts with legislators.

Many of the state's unions have their own lobbyists. Delegations of local unions frequently come to Madison to talk to their assemblyman or senator, and most of the central bodies as well as many local union committees regularly meet with their legislators in home towns. On special occasions rallies are held on the steps of the capitol.

Of course, given the combination of factors which affect Wisconsin elections—national voting trends, economic conditions, candidates' personalities, and so on—it is impossible to say what part labor's increased political effort, directed in the 1960's and 1970's mainly toward Wisconsin Democratic party candidates, has played in the success of the Democratic party over those two decades. The only demonstrable fact is that by 1977 the Democrats had gained a two-thirds majority in both state legislative branches, held all of the statewide offices, both United States senatorial seats, seven of Wisconsin's nine seats in the House of Representatives, and that all of these successful candidates had received labor's endorsement and financial support.

Similarly, many factors determine what bills are passed by a legislature, but, as noted in the previous chapter, the period from the mid-1960's through 1977 was one of the high points of labor's influence in the Wisconsin legislature, and its legislative gains were correspondingly impressive. Substantial improvements were made in unemployment compensation and workers' compensation laws. Unemployment compensation was liberalized considerably in 1960, when weekly payments were tied to a percentage of the average weekly wages up to a certain maximum. This made unnecessary the previous periodic wrangling between labor and management over the unemployment benefit level. And in 1977 the one-week waiting period required before becoming eligible for unemployment benefits was eliminated. The Wisconsin Employment Peace Act was modified to require a favorable vote by only a simply majority of the employees to implement a maintenance-of-membership contract. Major laws were passed giving municipal employees, including teachers, and state employees the collective bargaining rights which had been granted to employees in private industry by the Wagner Act in 1935.

Labor's influence also could be seen in the greater number of appointments of union members to state governing boards and advisory commissions. Since 1960 five union officials—Jacob Friedrick; Bertram McNamara, director of District 32 of the United Steelworkers of America; Raymond Majerus, director of Region 9 of the United Auto Workers; James Jesinski, president of Teamsters Local 200; and Catherine Conroy, retired CWA staff member—have served on the Board of Regents of the University of Wisconsin. Friedrick and McNamara both became presidents of the board. Hugh Henderson, a Steelworker staff representative, was a member of Governor Lee Dreyfus' cabinet from 1979 to 1982, serving as head of the Department of Employment Relations. He was appointed subsequently to the Labor and Industry Review Commission in the Department of Industry, Labor and Human Relations. John Schmitt sits on more public and private boards and committees than has any previous union official. Of equal importance is the number of appointees to governmental boards for whom his recommendation is important.

As is usually the case, the Wisconsin labor movement has not achieved all of its legislative goals; there is as much bargaining and compromise, as many victories and defeats, in this area as in contract negotiations. But during these two decades, Wisconsin labor has come to have a political status equal to that of business, agricultural, environmental, and other such groups in Wisconsin.

The history of the past three decades may make it seem that the Wisconsin labor movement is wedded to the Democratic party. Yet, unlike the early leaders of the WSFL who were philosophically tied to the Socialist party, today's leaders belong to no particular party, but choose candidates according to Samuel Gompers' principle—reward your friends, punish your enemies. The reason that more Democrats than Republicans have received labor endorsements and support in Wisconsin during this period is that more Democrats have voted for labor-supported bills. Over the years, labor and the Democrats have tended to build a somewhat symbiotic relationship, each needing and nourishing the other. But times change, and political relationships also change.

CHAPTER 9

Education and Social Issues

THE WISCONSIN LABOR movement has displayed a strong faith in education. Its early leaders actively supported the establishment in 1910 of a statewide system of vocational and adult education, which was and is tax-supported, and until recently was virtually tuition-free. In 1926 the WSFL held a statewide conference devoted exclusively to education. The speakers touched on all phases of education, from elementary to university levels, and from vocational to labor courses. One hundred eighty unionists and speakers participated.

From Labor Colleges to School for Workers

The Ohl–Handley leadership further advanced the cause of labor education in the 1920's by setting up special "labor colleges" which continued to function into the 1930's and then evolved into the School for Workers at the University of Wisconsin

The 1920 WSFL convention urged city central labor bodies to establish labor colleges to provide education for workers in the area of trade union administration. Twelve of these "colleges," whose faculty members were labor leaders and sympathetic academics, were established in different cities beginning in 1921. Because of the depression of 1921–1922 and the postwar decline of the labor movement, resources were strained to maintain them. The Milwaukee Labor College was the most successful, conducting classes from 1921 through 1936. Jacob Friedrick taught there for many years, as did Maud McCreery, reporter for the Socialist paper, the Milwaukee *Leader*.[1] Harold Groves, of the University of Wisconsin's Department of Economics, taught at the Madison Labor College. Selig Perlman, of the same department, offered to travel to Milwaukee to teach, but there is no evidence that he did so.

The Green Bay labor college did not get started until 1928. At the meeting of the Green Bay Federated Trades Council on November 22, 1927, Henry Ohl urged the formation of a labor college. Congressman George

A. Schneider also spoke in support, and a five-man committee was appointed to establish the school, its course to be "taught by an instructor thoroughly familiar with Labor Economics." Held in the Green Bay Vocational and Adult School, the eight-week course began early in 1928. Tuition was two dollars, paid by the local unions. A teacher from Green Bay's East High School conducted the course and was paid fifty dollars. Fifteen students came regularly. The Labor College Committee, in an effort to help women, secured a woman volunteer instructor who, in accordance with what the male committee deemed appropriate, was to conduct afternoon classes in home management and related subjects. When the subject matter was proposed to the prospective women students, they made it clear that they preferred to learn parliamentary law. Thus rebuffed, the Labor College Committee invited the women to attend the men's sessions.[2]

The labor colleges created a tradition of education for union members and thus laid the groundwork for strong labor support of the School for Workers. Even in the Depression year of 1932 the Green Bay Council collected and appropriated money ($125.00) to send a union member to the six-week School for Workers summer institute in Madison. A year later the council voted to donate $30.00 toward a scholarship to the school, "providing we have a choice of selecting a male scholar from the ranks of labor. If this privilege is not granted we only donate $10.00 to this cause." Nevertheless, a woman was selected, Rose Burkhardt, a member of the Pulp and Sulphite Workers Union.[3]

The Superior Trades and Labor Council had undertaken labor education long before it set up its Labor College in 1927. In 1913 it sponsored a public lecture given by the nation's most famous labor lawyer, Clarence Darrow. An advertisement in the Superior *Evening Telegram* invited the public to attend at a cost of fifty cents, twenty-five cents for youths. A teacher from the Superior Normal School introduced the speaker, and four Trades Council leaders sat on the stage. Darrow presented arguments for the closed shop, and on political action advised: "The worker should do as the banker does, and the manufacturer, vote solely in the interest of his own class."[4] Three hundred and forty people attended, but the council lost $51.00, as expenses exceeded the income.[5]

Although Henry Ohl felt that labor colleges run by the local trades councils were not very successful and needed the help of the state university, the Western Paper Manufacturers Association, an anti-union arm of Wisconsin's paper company employers, thought that these colleges were effective enough to warrant surveillance by its spies. One of the association's spies, number 15, on December 1, 1927, reported to the association that the Appleton Labor College had fifty enrollees, but when it met that evening it was "poorly attended." He further reported that a G. W. Campbell of Oshkosh was in charge of both the Oshkosh and Appleton labor colleges.[6]

In 1924, when several of the colleges were being forced to close owing to lack of funds, Ohl submitted a special request to John R. Commons at the University of Wisconsin, asking if the university, which offered training to the professions and to business, could provide instructors for trade unions. In 1925, at the instigation of Industrial Department of the YWCA, the University of Wisconsin established a six-week summer school for female factory workers, which became the Summer School for Women Workers in Industry.

In its early years 1925–1931, the School recruited about forty young factory women per year for a six-week resident program at the University of Wisconsin in Madison. The goal of the program was to provide self-improvement, leadership, and culture to young women whose factory employment had deprived them of some of the finer things in life. The curriculum did include an acquaintance with trade unions.

The university paid the salary of a full-time director, Alice Schoemaker, a former YWCA staff member. A university faculty committee did much of the teaching and raised scholarships for the students.

Since the University of Wisconsin did not have the money to establish the labor college requested by WSFL President Ohl, Professor Commons hoped that the School for Women Workers in Industry also could serve trade unionists. Thus in 1928 the school was made coeducational. Two top labor leaders, Jacob Friedrick and Henry Rutz attended the 1928 institute to determine its fitness as a trade union school. Their report was favorable and each year more trade unions sent members.

In 1931 the president of the university, Glenn Frank, appointed Jacob Friedrick to the school's Advisory Committee, and by 1932 the School for Workers had become an established trade union school. With the explosive growth of unions in the 1930's and with federal aid to help students and faculty, the School for Workers became, in effect, a national trade union education center to which unions from across the country sent students.

Equally important were the evening classes in trade unionism conducted in all of Wisconsin's industrial cities. In the year 1937–1938, federal subsidies enabled the school to hold sixty-seven classes in twenty-eight different cities, for which twenty-five faculty members were employed. The

WSFL and the Wisconsin State CIO took a serious interest in the school, pushing the legislature for more financial support. In 1937 the CIO, feeling the school was too closely tied to the WSFL, demanded that it, too, have representation on the Advisory Committee and that some faculty with a CIO background be hired to teach CIO classes. Both requests were granted.

Although the University of Wisconsin had for many years offered special training for business leaders in its commerce and engineering schools, for farmers through its College of Agriculture and Cooperative Extension, and for the professions, some of the state's business leaders were unwilling to grant a similar service through the School for Workers. When the 1938 state elections replaced the Progressives with conservative Republicans, the School for Workers became a target for dissolution. The governor, Julius P. Heil, a Milwaukee manufacturer, appointed a new and business-oriented Board of Regents, which soon eliminated the statewide program provided by the school. Amid charges of Communist activity, the entire School for Workers was scheduled for abolition. Labor joined the university in protest, and Rudolph Faupl of the WSFL staff appealed to Reuben Trane, president of the Trane Company of La Crosse, who, according to Faupl, assured his business friends among the regents that labor education was not communistic.[7]

Although they had put an end to the statewide classes, the regents allowed the school's summer institutes to continue at Madison. By the end of World War II, unionism had gained more public acceptance, and in 1945 the Wisconsin legislature authorized re-establishment of the School for Workers extension programs wherever local adult and vocational education boards were willing to finance them. The response was positive, and the statewide labor education program was re-established.

During World War II the School for Workers summer program in Madison was almost the only university-sponsored labor education program in the country. After the war, the Wisconsin pattern for labor education was copied widely by other universities, albeit under varying administrative structures. From 1950 through 1981, education at the School for Workers became more specialized, and the faculty increased from three to ten full-time members.

Since 1925 approximately 50,000 Wisconsin workers have attended trade union classes given by the school. In the state's industrial cities it has become a tradition for local union officers, stewards, and members to attend these classes, held in their hometowns. The tradition could not have become established without the early and full support of the WSFL leadership—Henry Ohl, Jack Handley, and the executive board. Each generation of labor leaders since then has continued that support and urged the legislature to continue adequate funding for the program. While most industrial states now offer this same form of labor education, because of its early start in Wisconsin, the state perhaps has a trade union membership which is better educated in union matters than any other state. This strong faith in education is a clear legacy from Wisconsin's early Socialist union leadership.

After World War II the School for Workers was converted from a part-time summer institute to a year-round university department. Students attending summer sessions from 1925 through 1975 were housed in fraternities or student dormitories which were vacant during summer months. Increasing enrollment made this housing inadequate, and in 1976 the Madison campus opened a year-round adult education center, the Jacob F. Friedrick Center, named after the distinguished Milwaukee labor leader. Funds for the center were provided by a state appropriation which received bipartisan support.

In 1981 the State AFL–CIO sponsored nine institutes at the school, covering collective bargaining, union administration, labor law, labor journalism, time-study, job evaluation, arbitration, worker compensation, and occupational health and safety. In addition, the WSFL has itself conducted programs on local union education and on the environment. Under the Schmitt administration, labor education has become one of the major services of the Wisconsin State AFL–CIO.

Women and Wisconsin Labor

The Wisconsin labor leadership has been portrayed in these chapters as generally having been enlightened. Certainly its Socialist leadership advocated such reforms as the income tax, worker compensation, and unemployment compensation many years before their enactment. Its members were in the forefront of industrial union organizations, and since 1920 the Wisconsin labor movement has been extraordinarily devoted to the education of its members. It has been diligent in organizing to raise wages and improve working conditions for workers throughout the state. But where has it stood on the issue of equality for women?

As described earlier, at one of its first conventions the WSFL passed a resolution in favor of woman suffrage. Through the years the WSFL conventions repeatedly affirmed support of that reform, and in 1912, when the state held a referendum on women's suffrage, the federation was part of a statewide coalition in support of its passage. The alliance included the

State Teachers Association, the Socialist party, the Federation of Women's Clubs, the Wisconsin State Grange, the Farmers' Society of Equity, the Ministerial Association, and the Women's Christian Temperance Union. The referendum was badly defeated, obtaining only 27 per cent of the total vote, losing even in Milwaukee by a two-to-one margin.[8]

The German American Association and the Brewers' Association were the leading organizations openly fighting woman suffrage. Precinct vote figures on the 1912 suffrage amendment, however, point to other anti-suffrage sentiment even among some Socialist and labor voters whose organizations were suffrage supporters. For example, many of the same wards which voted heavily for Victor Berger voted two to one against the suffrage amendment. Victor Berger was himself a strong foe of woman suffrage. His argument was that women more than men are under the domination of reactionary clergy and would vote against Socialism. In this author's opinion it is reasonable to assume that on the suffragist issue brewery workers and their local leadership would have voted with their employers, the Brewers' Association, which clearly felt that women were more likely to vote for prohibition. But for Frank Weber there was no backsliding. Both as head of the WSFL and especially as a legislator, he led assembly debates during the 1913 session in favor of a constitutional amendment on woman suffrage, only to have the bill vetoed by Governor McGovern.[9]

Weber also supported the notion of organizing women into trade unions. His addresses on the subject, however, were confusing at times and would not pass muster in current union circles. At the 1899 convention, he appealed for the organization of women workers, but noted that when women's wages were raised to equal those of men, the employers would hire men instead of women.[10] In his 1905 address to the convention, he referred to the fear which men presumably had that employment of lower-paid women would throw husbands out of work, and advocated as a remedy organizing women and elevating their wages to those of men.[11] In 1906 Weber put forth additional arguments:[12]

> With the complete organization of both sexes affected, we shall find closed most of the avenues leading to prostitution, gone the incentive or need for deviation from the paths of rectitude and virtue; the woman will be the home-keeper not the breadwinner for herself or others; she will be healthy and strong, a happy wife, a willing and joyful mother—while man will have such a home life that the ties thereof will find and keep him and he, too, will be more like the image after which God fashioned man.

It is clear from Weber's words that because women received low wages they were perceived by his listeners to be a threat to employment of men. As we saw in Chapter 2, during the Oshkosh Woodworkers strike of 1898, one of the union demands was for the dismissal of women and children, whose low wages were considered by the union a threat to the employment of men at good wages. Weber accepted the doubtful proposition that if women's wages could be raised through unionization, they would somehow become happy housewives and mothers. As previously noted, when the proposal for a minimum wage and maximum hour law for women came to the state legislature in the 1911–1913 session, Weber opposed it on grounds that a minimum wage law "no doubt would weaken or destroy the unions of women workers. . . . Let us do some good hard work to organize the female workers and then there will be no necessity . . . of a minimum wage law by the state."[13]

Weber's successor, Henry Ohl, who took over the leadership of the WSFL in 1917, was even more supportive of women's rights, recognizing particularly the importance of organizing working women into trade unions. In 1918 the WSFL officers invited Maud McCreery (mentioned earlier in connection with the Milwaukee Labor College), a delegate from Milwaukee Newspaper Writers, Local 9, to address the convention:[14]

> The Chair thereupon introduced Sister McCreery, who gave a splendid talk on the problem that women workers are confronted with, urging that women who were obliged to work in the industries should be organized, and in the same unions with men; declaring against exclusive organizations for women workers, because they would be less educational, less effective to accomplishing real things for the women—and finally, women organizations, apart from the male workers, would not be lasting. Her talk was a straight-from-the-shoulder one, being impressive of real earnest desire to see the ills men and women now endure remedied, and pointing out to the men that the problem must be solved by the workers themselves, urging organization industrially, and political action on election days. She made a plea for support for the suffrage amendment now before Congress, and asked the men to help give woman the ballot. Her address received hearty applause.

McCreery was a union organizer, a Socialist, a militant working-class feminist and suffragist. While her views on the role of women in unions undoubtedly were not shared by most local union leaders or members, she clearly had support from the WSFL leadership.[15]

What was the ratio of men to women in the unions of the WSFL? Normally unions do not keep those records, but for the years 1912–1916 a

WSFL survey did ask for a breakdown of membership by sex. The results are as follows:[16]

	Total Members	Women	Percentage Female
1912	22,856	802	3.5
1913	22,382	1,353	6.0
1914	14,737	1,106	7.5
1915	23,835	1,249	5.3
1916	27,197	1,314	4.8

The report showed that the building trades and metal trades had no women members; unionized women were overwhelmingly employed in certain low-paying industrial jobs. Seventy-eight per cent of union women in the years 1912–1916 were employed in the manufacture of garments and shoes. The large increase in female membership from 1912 to 1913 was due to successful unionization of 400 clothing workers in Racine.[17]

The first woman delegate to a WSFL convention had appeared in 1897, four years after the Federation's founding. She was Miss Angie Haak, a member of the United Garment Workers Union, Local No. 126, from Oshkosh. She secured passage of a resolution urging organized labor everywhere to buy only ready-made garments bearing the label of the United Garment Workers. She served on the press committee and was appointed assistant secretary.[18]

In 1913 the WSFL affiliated with the Women's Trade Union League (WTUL), a national organization, led by middle-class reformers, dedicated to improving conditions for working women.[19] The Women's League sent temporary organizers to Oshkosh in 1915 and into Marinette in 1916 to aid the striking glove workers. Henry Ohl, conscious of the need for women organizers, worked closely with Mrs. Laurel Kosten of the Women's Label League to organize retail salesmen and saleswomen in Marinette in 1916. In 1924 a WTUL representative visited Rhinelander on behalf of the paper mill strikers. In 1926 the League paid the salary of a full-time organizer, Alexia Smith, to work under Ohl's direction. She worked with many groups, in particular the Green Bay Stenographers, Milwaukee Bakery Workers, and Kenosha's Full-Fashioned Hosiery Workers.[20]

On social issues, local and central labor bodies occasionally took stands which the State Federation did not support. A case in point was the issue of firing married teachers. When jobs became scarce, a popular response was to throw married women out of their jobs. Union members seemed particularly prone to push that solution through their local trades councils, as illustrated by the Green Bay Federated Trades Council, which, in

1928, began pressuring the local school board to replace married women teachers. The council president told the body that "he had obtained a list of the city school teachers who are married women and turned over the names for investigation."[21] At the October 14, 1930, council meeting a member of the school board, Dr. W. Webber Kelly, congratulated Mayor John V. Diener, who was attending the meeting, for removing married women teachers from the schools and for stipulating in women's contracts that their positions would be terminated when they married. In 1931 the Green Bay Council again wrote the school board concerning the employment of married teachers.[22]

In the "Report of the General Executive Board" presented to the 1932 convention of the WSFL, an effort was made to counteract such activities. A special section titled "Sex Discrimination" declared:[23]

> In the prevalent confusion and desperation born from the desire to hit upon a cause and to find a cure, or at least some relief, from unemployment, some people sincerely but foolishly believe that relief could be accomplished by depriving married women, particularly those engaged in public service, of the right to work. The suggestion would be merely amusing were it not for the fact that some communities and certain school boards have actually acted upon it. Were a general rule barring all married women from working carried out, we should have cause to regret the loss of some of the best talent. Moreover, it is our opinion that such regulatory discrimination because of sex is not only unwise but socially unjust. In case of emergency employment it is well when engaging labor to give preference to workers with families, but no prohibitive legislation or rules of employment on grounds of sex should receive the support of labor when applied to such employment which is generally accepted as being in the field of women's work.

This executive board opposition to sex discrimination specifically in "employment which is generally accepted as being in the field of women's work" was not an endorsement of equal rights for women in all fields of work as has been advocated by unions in recent years. However, for the 1930's it was clearly an advanced position. The tendency of the Green Bay FTC to use the public schools as a job reservoir for males was quite typical of public opinion in an era when there was no unemployment compensation nor even any systematic public welfare program.

By 1937 it would appear that even the Green Bay FTC had changed its attitude toward jobs for married women. At its November 23 meeting, there appeared a delegation of married women and President Martin

Young from the Cheese Workers Union. The FTC minutes record the event as follows:[24]

>Martin Young President of the Cheese Workers spoke for the ladies. The gist of Bro. Young's talk was about the fact that the majority of the cheese makers local want the married women expelled from the union and their jobs. This especially when many of these married women are charter members of this local. Bro. Young is most decisive in his remarks in support of the married women's contention that they have every right to their jobs. A hearty discussion arose from which it was apparent that the vast majority of the council was in favor of the delegation also.

With the rush of labor organization in the early 1930's, women began joining unions in large numbers. Katherine Hartman Lichter, a member of Milwaukee Local 99 of the Fur and Leather Workers, became a full-time statewide organizer for her international union. Elected to the executive board of the Milwaukee Industrial Union Council, CIO, in 1942, she became the first woman to serve as an officer in a Milwaukee central body. As she attended Wisconsin State Industrial Council conventions and those of her Fur and Leather Workers International Union, she was aware that the number of women participants was very small. Interviewed in 1978, she reported that being the only woman presented no problem in her work as an organizer but that "there was a tendency to assign me to things that were considered of interest to women. I was a little resentful, feeling this is the sort of thing turned over to me because the men feel it's too trivial to bother with or not the kind of thing men are interested in. It was so handy having a woman. . . . This was especially true during the war with various war relief committees."[25]

In 1974 a woman was elected to serve on the executive board of the Wisconsin State AFL–CIO. She was Catherine Conroy, an international representative for the Communications Workers of America. Conroy was very active in the political action committees of her union, and became the first woman to serve on the board of the Wisconsin Department of Natural Resources. In 1982 she was appointed by Governor Anthony Earl to the University of Wisconsin's Board of Regents. Active in the women's liberation movement, she was one of the founders of the National Organization of Women (NOW).

In 1970 the Wisconsin State AFL–CIO supported equal rights for women by establishing the Standing Committee on Women's Activities, chaired by Helen Henson. The committee holds annual statewide conferences and workshops to inform trade union women of their rights and responsibilities and to develop leadership techniques to enable them to participate more fully in union activities. With the establishment in 1974 of the Coalition of Labor Union Women (CLUW), women who are trade union leaders in Wisconsin have been active in organizing the unorganized women, pushing for affirmative action in the workplace, encouraging women to become more active politically to obtain shorter workweeks, supporting child care legislation, and raising the minimum wage.[26]

Until the Civil Rights Act of 1964, wage and job discrimination against women were deeply ingrained. Employers traditionally had separate wage scales for men and women, even when the jobs were similar or identical. As described in Chapter 5, the Retail Clerks' wage demand in the Boston Store strike of 1934 called for $15 for women and $20 for men. This kind of differential was not an invention of the union, but had long been employer policy. Unions, however, struggling for recognition and survival, usually had neither the power nor the will to challenge the practice of discriminatory wage policies. In factories the difference sometimes was made less obvious by labeling women's jobs "light" and men's jobs "heavy." Since union officers generally were men, unions were often content to accept the benefits of employers' discriminatory wages.

In white collar and professional jobs, wage discrimination among men and women was equally common. In the 1920's and 1930's, Wisconsin school boards often had three salary scales, one for women teachers, a higher one for men, and a third, higher still, for married men. Married women usually were dismissed, as described earlier. Because women were in the majority in the teaching profession, unionization there was accompanied by rapid abandonment of discriminatory pay scales.

In the factories little progress was made toward eliminating lower pay for women until the 1964 Civil Rights Act prohibited discrimination in employment on grounds of race, age, and sex. The fear of expensive lawsuits moved both employers and unions to institute single pay scales and thus to remove obvious sex differentials. The more subtle discrimination in fringe benefits, type of job, and equal pay for comparable work are still the subject of long and continuing struggles.

Blacks and the Labor Movement

At the 1959 convention of the national AFL–CIO, President George Meany reported that in 1940, when he became secretary–treasurer of the AFL, there were more than twenty unions out of the approximately 120 in the AFL whose constitutions allowed only whites to join.[27] Such "white only" uses were also common in the Railroad Brotherhoods, which were not AFL affiliates. Meany pointed out that by 1959 all the clauses had been eliminated, with the exception of railroad unions, which just had affiliated with the AFL–CIO and were in the process of deleting the clauses. Meany's statement, however, did not mean that prejudice had evaporated.

Although one of the unions with a white-only policy had been the International Association of Machinists, Wisconsin Machinists had had a long and active record of opposition to the discriminatory policy. In 1892, IAM, Lodge 66, of Milwaukee voted 11 to 2 to abolish the policy.[28] Wisconsin Machinists continued their opposition until the policy finally was abolished in 1947.[29]

Blacks began moving to Wisconsin during the labor shortages of World War I and took heavy industry jobs in Milwaukee and Beloit. Since at that time those industries did not even recognize unions, the problem of union membership did not arise. Wisconsin industry treated the newly arrived blacks as they had treated most previous immigrants—by employing them in the hottest, hardest, and dirtiest jobs in the plant, usually in the foundry. But when immigrants from Europe learned the English language, they gradually were permitted to transfer into the other departments and to be promoted to foremen's positions. Blacks, by contrast, were hired into the foundry and kept there. For example, in 1941 Allis–Chalmers had 101 blacks in its foundry whose seniority dates indicated that they had begun work during World War I and the early 1920's. They had remained in the foundry in the intervening years.[30]

During the labor shortages of World War II and thereafter, many more blacks came to Wisconsin. They, too, were hired into the foundries, but this time the plants were unionized. Under industrial unionism blacks not only were admitted into the unions, but often took the lead in organizing them. The principal union that had spawned the CIO, the United Mine Workers, had a long history of an integrated membership, and the CIO unions generally welcomed blacks.

After passage of the Wagner Act in 1935, unions gained recognition and bargaining rights by winning government-conducted elections, for which they needed the votes of all workers, including those of the blacks in the foundries. With the advent of the CIO in 1936, competition in these elections between it and the AFL put an even greater premium on garnering all possible votes. Blacks and other minorities, therefore, became first-class union members, and gained the benefits of unionization: higher wages, job security, paid vacation, promotion and layoff by seniority, and fringe benefits such as pensions and health insurance.

Yet the new industrial unionism of the 1930's did not stop employers from continuing to give blacks the least desirable jobs. There were several reasons for this.

First, the form of seniority written into labor–management agreements was departmental. Thus, a job opening first was offered to the most senior worker in the same department. Since blacks generally were hired only in the foundry, they could rise to top jobs only in that department. To transfer to another department, a worker had to start at the bottom of the new department, sacrifice his layoff seniority, and take a substantial cut in pay in the new department. In the northern states, departmental seniority for job openings was not invented for purposes of racial discrimination. It had descended from craft unionism in which different unions organized each department of the plant: the foundry was the territory of the Molders' Union, the machine shop the territory of the Machinists, and so on. Departmental seniority long antedated the influx of blacks into northern factories.

Second, as industrial unions won union shops in the 1930's and 1940's it was always on condition that the union would not interfere with management's exclusive right to hire whomever it pleased. The Taft–Hartley Act's (1947) prohibition of the closed shop reinforced management's exclusive control over hiring.

Third, the union surge of the 1930's was primarily a labor upsurge, not a civil rights movement. The abolition of race discrimination in employment would be a prolonged struggle.

In some plants, as late as the 1950's, blacks automatically were hired into the foundry regardless of qualifications. A black high school graduate described his employment at the J. I. Case Company, a large agricultural implement firm which had a plant in Racine.[31]

> When I got out of high school in 1956 I was offered only a custodial job by a leading Racine employer. I refused and later got into the foundry at Case where every black went. Our first "break" came in 1960 when callbacks after the strike were on the basis of plant-wide seniority. Some of us found that outside the foundry there were good paying jobs that were clean and you didn't have to break your back. Pretty soon they made me foreman, but that's where it ends. I left when I couldn't go any higher. Case holds you down to foreman.

In this instance the worker was rescued from the foundry by the United Auto Workers contract ending the Case strike, which called for rehiring on the basis of plantwide seniority instead of departmental seniority.

Affirmative action in job placements and transfers has come about gradually, aided primarily by federal legislation. The Office of Federal

Contract Compliance has made elimination of racial and sex discrimination a requirement for any company receiving federal contracts. The Civil Rights Act of 1964 also greatly advanced racial equality in employment. Union–management contracts now almost universally include a nondiscrimination clause. An example is the clause in the agreement between the United Food and Commercial Workers, Local 538, and the Oscar Mayer and Company, in Madison:[32]

> Neither the employer, the Union or fellow employees shall discriminate against any individual because of his race, age, religion, sex, color, ancestry, national origin or disability with respect to opportunity for or tenure of employment or with respect to any term or condition of employment or any other right, benefit, duty or obligation created and/or protected by the provisions of this Agreement.

Some court decisions have established that where discriminatory hiring has existed, departmental seniority for promotions, rather than plantwide seniority, tends to perpetuate the discrimination. In some unions there consequently has been a move to extend plantwide seniority to promotion as well as layoffs.

The responsibility for racial discrimination in the construction industry—which, historically, was common—must be shared in part by unions, since they usually have participated with management in the selection of apprentices. Since 1967 in Milwaukee, there has been a joint union, management, and government program of affirmative action to recruit and assist minority workers to enter building and construction trades apprenticeships. At the same time, the Building Trades joined with the Urban League to establish a minority recruitment and training program for all skilled trades. It was funded first by the federal government, but in 1984 it was financed by a collectively bargained fund contributed by workers and employers. In 1983 the program employed a director and staff who helped applicants pass tests, get on the waiting lists, and get through apprentice programs. The staff included a full time tutor and part-time tutor. The Wisconsin AFL–CIO also funded a full time building trades expert to assist communities statewide in recruiting minorities.

According to James Elliott, President of the Milwaukee Building Trades Council, since 1967, 1,900 placements have been made into apprentice programs in both building trades and maintenance jobs. In addition, 2,300 non-subsidized minority placements, such as welders, have been made in factories. The deep recession of 1981–1983 in both the construction trades and in factory employment in Milwaukee caused severe cutbacks in minority training placements, and in minority employment. In 1983 the Milwaukee Building Trades Council did not have figures on the number of skilled trade minority apprentice placements who currently were working at their trades.[33]

When the great surge of workers into unions occurred in the 1930's, blacks in Wisconsin factories were some of the staunchest union supporters. But for many years they rarely became top union officers. A very early exception was Eugene Terman, of Steelworker Local 1533 in Beloit. Terman began work in the Fairbanks–Morse foundry at the age of eighteen in 1928. In 1937 and 1938 he was one of the principal leaders of the organization drive. At that time he became the treasurer of Local 1533 and chief grievance officer for the foundry.[34]

By the early 1980's blacks held many top union leadership positions in Wisconsin such as: the presidency of one of the largest industrial unions, Federal Labor Union, Local 19806; the presidency of Steelworkers, Local 1533, in Beloit; the directorship of the State AFL–CIO Human Resources Institute; the Assistant Directorship of United Auto Workers, Region 9; and full-time staff representative positions in several unions. One of the black local presidents, Dee Gilliam, by 1983 was director of the United Steelworkers Department of Arbitration in Pittsburgh. Although by 1982 no black had been elected to the nineteen-person executive board of the Wisconsin State AFL–CIO, this situation could easily change in the light of the union leadership positions now held by blacks.

PART III

Paper Mill Workers:
The Forty-Year Struggle for Unionism

INTRODUCTION TO PART III

With the exception of the brief account (Chapter 2) of the nineteenth century sawmill strikes, the past nine chapters have described the Wisconsin labor movement as it developed in the state's industrial heartland, its southeastern counties. Yet from 1900 on, there occurred an epic forty-year labor–management struggle in the state's single largest manufacturing industry, paper. The locus of this contest was the widely scattered industrial cities along the state's northern river valleys: the Fox, the Wisconsin, the Eau Claire, and the Menominee.

What makes this struggle unique and worthy of national attention is the elaborate employer organization which maintained for over twenty of those years a strict surveillance of employee unionism and which effectively mobilized the wealth and power of some thirty paper corporations against the workers of any plant whenever they strove for union recognition. Across the country there have been numerous employer organizations which fought unions. But for none of them, of which this author is aware, is there detailed and vivid documentation of such employer actions. In Chapters 11–13 the effects of such activity on the unions are observed simultaneously through local newspaper accounts and the complete files of the Pulp, Sulphite, and Paper Mill Workers Union. To the state labor movement the outcome of this forty-year struggle covering the northern half of the state was crucial in regard to any long run security, financial stability, and political influence.

CHAPTER 10

The Fight for Saturday Night Off:
1900–1905

A S DESCRIBED IN Chapter 2, thousands of sawmill workers across Wisconsin's northland struck during the 1880's and 1890's for a shorter workday. By 1900 a new industry, papermaking, had invaded the same northern river valleys. Along the Fox River, papermaking gradually moved in on the sites of the vacated gristmills; along the Wisconsin, the Eau Claire, the Marinette, and the Peshtigo rivers, it took the place of the sawmills for, like them, it used wood, water power, and skilled labor. The production of paper was destined to become one of the state's largest manufacturing industries.

After 1900 the paper workers took up the struggle for the reduction of working hours. The men who worked the sawmills had been as restless and as mobile as the mills themselves, which moved on when the white pines had been devoured. But the paper mills, with their huge factories and highly skilled work force, were permanent residents. Here the struggle between workers and managers was to be long and hard fought.

1902: Victory on the Fox River

Men and women have been making paper in the Fox River Valley since the water of the river first washed through the beater and powered the machine at the C. P. R. Richmond Brothers mill in Appleton in 1853.[1] In October of 1872, about forty people began work at the new Globe mill, which the Kimberly–Clark Paper Company had built on a gristmill site in Neenah. As the wheat fields moved westward during the 1870's, the flour mills often were replaced by paper mills. By the end of the decade there were twenty paper mills along the Fox. In the Wisconsin River Valley, paper mills replaced sawmills as the timber was depleted, and by the early 1900's it, too, was an important paper-producing valley. In 1910, 6,000 people were working in paper mills throughout Wisconsin, along not only the Fox and Wisconsin rivers, but also along the Menominee, Wolf, Oconto, Eau Claire, Peshtigo, and Flambeau rivers.[2]

Before 1901 there were no unions in the paper mills, but there was dissatisfaction. The work was dangerous: "willingness to take risks [was] one of the requisites for a good papermill man."[3] Many had fingers cut off, arms burned, and bodies mangled by the open machinery and the hot rolls and felts that dried and supported the fragile paper as it made its long journey from the beater to the spindles which wound the finished paper. Sometimes the huge boilers exploded. Charity was the only source available to help pay the medical bills, to make up for the loss of wages, and even to compensate for loss of life.

There was a hierarchy among the workers on a paper machine: first came the machine tender, followed by the backtender, third hand, fourth hand, and fifth hand. The highly skilled machine tenders and backtenders were generally the core of the unions. On a Monday afternoon in May, 1892, nine "boys"—backtenders and third hands—walked out of the Thilmany Pulp and Paper Company in Kaukauna. The backtenders demanded that their daily wage of $1.25 be increased to $1.50; the third hands wanted their $1.00 a day to be increased to $1.25. "The boys miscalculated their power, however," reported the Kaukauna *Times,* "and instead of the mill shutting down, everything ran as of yore and their places were soon filled.[4] If wages were low, the hours were long. Because the water which powered the mills flowed twenty-four hours a day, the machinery was operated day and night, six days a week, by an eleven-hour day shift working sixty-six hours a week, and a thirteen-hour night shift working seventy-eight hours a week. The workers alternated shifts on a weekly basis.

The paperworkers especially loathed the Saturday night shift. It was that shift, rather than the physical hazards or wages, which goaded them to organize their first union in Wisconsin. They had a precedent, for at the paper mills in Holyoke, Massachusetts, the Saturday night shift had been the chief irritant that had driven the machine tenders and beater engineers (who supervised the mixing and cooking of the raw pulp) to transform their social club into a labor union, which was chartered by the American Federation of Labor (AFL) in 1893.[5] In 1901 this union, by then a part of the United Brotherhood of Paper Makers (UBPM), AFL, struck successfully to abolish the Saturday night shift and to set a minimum wage of $2.00 per day.

To protect these gains from the competition of the unorganized mills in the Midwest, the UBPM sent their general organizer, William Hamilton, to the Fox River Valley in March, 1901.[6] The Fox Valley workers, hoping to end the Saturday night shift, responded enthusiastically and established lodges in Neenah–Menasha (named the Hamilton Lodge), Appleton, and Kaukauna. By fall they were well enough organized to issue the following demands to all paper manufacturers in the valley:[7]

Gentlemen:

At a meeting of the United Brotherhood of Paper Makers of America, it was voted unanimously to submit the following propositions to the paper manufacturers of the Fox River Valley, viz:

1. To grant tour [shift] workers off from 6 o'clock Saturday night till 7 o'clock Monday morning without any reduction in week's pay for said time off.
2. To grant finishing room help off at Saturday noon without any deduction in week's pay for said time off.
3. To grant time and a half for all Sunday repair work.

The manufacturers were asked to respond on or before December 1. It was understood that "if the request is not granted, a general strike will be instituted."

The manufacturers did not join together in a uniform response. When the president of the Appleton lodge called on Kimberly–Clark, he was told that although the company considered the union demands reasonable, it could not afford to close Saturday night unless all other mills did so.[8] The Gilbert Paper Company at Menasha sent an offer to the Hamilton Lodge:[9]

. . . tour workers in our machine, engine and calender rooms [to be] off from 6 o'clock Saturday night to 7 o'clock Monday morning without deduction of pay. . . . we grant the above January 1st, experimentally . . . we will continue on this basis until the shorter schedule becomes generally adopted or we demonstrate that its working is detrimental to our company, when we haven't the least doubt. . . . you will willingly return to the old schedule.

Two days later, Kimberly–Clark, which had mills in Neenah, Appleton, Kimberly, and Niagara, changed its mind and offered to close on Saturday night, with a specific qualifier: "If the mills competing for the same business that we sell to have by April 1st [1902], granted like favors . . . then this agreement . . . to remain indefinitely. But if . . . not . . ., then the men employed by Kimberly & Clark Company agree to resume work on old basis of working hours and pay." In a fatherly manner President John A. Kimberly added: "we should never cease regretting, if these extra hours were used in dissipation that would lead to a lowering of the morals of our men . . . extra time for rest making you better husbands, fathers, citizens and Christians, . . . appeals to us very forcibly."[10] The Fox River Paper Company in Appleton and the Neenah Paper Company, a mill controlled by Kimberly–Clark, made the same offer.[11]

The Hamilton Lodge voted to accept the Gilbert and Kimberly–Clark offers, but the Appleton lodge held back at first, then accepted the April 1 qualifier and assured Kimberly–Clark that the shorter hours would not only benefit "home and family life," but would result in "more and . . . better work" since "air, sunshine, love, home, recreation and rest make muscles as well as beefsteak."[12] During the next three years the Appleton lodge had cause to wonder if its initial rejection had, in fact, been the right move.

A union committee called on the other paper companies, with dismal results. At 6:00 P.M. on the first Saturday in January of 1902, the mills which had agreed to the request for "Saturday night off" closed down. On Sunday afternoon the Appleton and Neenah–Menasha lodges met to celebrate, but the workers employed at the other Neenah and Menasha mills had worked as usual that Saturday night. Not for long, however; the next Saturday, workers at the Strange, Whiting, Menasha, and Winnebago mills did not report for the night shift. The mills closed, and the strike was on.[13]

The Wisconsin State Board of Arbitration called on the owners of the struck mills and found them not only opposed to the shorter hours, but unalterably opposed to dealing with a union: each owner agreed to meet with his own employees, but only on condition that no union representatives would be allowed to attend. The result of the meetings was that the Strange Company proposed to close Saturday night, but with a comparable reduction in pay; the Menasha Paper Company offered double wages for Saturday night; the Whiting and Winnebago companies warned their employees to return to work before they were replaced.

Ignoring the threats and counteroffers, the Appleton and Neenah–Menasha lodges voted to continue the strike and to present their hours demands to every paper manufacturer in Wisconsin; any company which did not meet these demands within two weeks would be struck. The lodges called their members to a big "Saturday night off" rally, where they spurred them on with the question, "Why do all [paper] mill owners require their help to work seventy-eight hours per week, when all other industrial enterprises require only sixty-six hours of labor?"

The millowners stiffened in their resolve. George Whiting, in Menasha, warned that the next thing manufacturers could expect would be demands for a three-shift, eight-hour schedule. John Strange, also in Menasha, placed guards around his mill.[14] In Appleton, the Patten Company workers announced that they would not return to work on Monday morning.[15] John McNaughton, secretary–treasurer of the company, stated that "it is to the best interests of our men to work Saturday nights. Most of them would visit the saloons. . . . They are much better off in the mill. Then, too, Saturday night is our most productive time, because of the water power." He warned that if the papermakers did strike, he would operate the plant by any means possible.

Nevertheless, the workers struck on Monday morning. After a meeting with McNaughton, William Hamilton, who was there on behalf of the UBPM to help the Fox Valley strikers, announced that "the men have extreme obstinacy to overcome." The UBPM considered the Fox Valley fight so difficult that it levied on every member an assessment of ten cents a week for a defense fund.[16]

For the next three and a half months the Fox Valley strikers tried to keep the mills from operating, with limited success. By mid-January each of the struck mills was managing to run at least one machine with the help of management and backtenders. When the owners began to import workers, the strikers met the newcomers at the railroad station and told them of the strike. Some were willing to return home, especially when the UBPM offered them a return ticket.[17] The townspeople seemed to side with the strikers. The Neenah *Daily Times* reported that the demand for Saturday night off was "regarded with a great deal of favor by the general public." The Oshkosh *Northwestern* editorialized: "To all appearances the workmen seem to have the elements of right and justice on their side."[18] Feelings against the strikebreakers became stronger. In Menasha, boarding house owners who rented to strikebreakers received threatening letters and felt compelled to buy their groceries outside the city.

As the termination date for the trial period, April 1, approached, the continuing strikes put the "Saturday night off" contracts in increasing jeopardy. The United Brotherhood of Paper Makers had achieved Saturday night closings in only four more companies, the Northern Tissue Company and Hoberg Toilet Paper Company in Green Bay, the Combined Locks Paper Company at Combined Locks, and the Wisconsin Tissue Paper Company of Appleton. Consequently, at the end of March, the Neenah–Menasha and Appleton lodges prepared to admit defeat and arranged a meeting with Kimberly–Clark. They were not prepared for the reception which Kimberly himself described:[19]

> We were waited upon Monday by representatives of the Appleton and Neenah lodges. . . . They offered to have the Brotherhood men go back to work in our mills on the long hour plan according to the agreement made last December, but we told them that we would extend our short hour system indefinitely in our mills now operating under it and also in the Neenah Paper Company's mill.

Kimberly also announced that the company would extend the shorter schedule to its Niagara mill as well, even though the employees there had not asked for it. Niagara Lodge No. 43 had been organized earlier in the year by a member of the Neenah lodge. The Gilbert Paper Company and the Fox River Company let it be known that they would continue the shorter-hour schedule "no matter what happened at the other mills."[20]

In April there finally was a break for the strikers at the Winnebago Paper Company in Neenah, who had been out for fourteen weeks. When the United Brotherhood of Paper Makers called on all Wisconsin paper mill workers who were still working on Saturday nights to strike on Saturday, April 5, workers at the Thilmany Pulp and Paper Company in Kaukauna "walked out to a man" and management could keep only one of the company's five paper machines running. Most of the people of Kaukauna sided with the strikers. Thilmany announced that after April 21, the strikers' jobs would be "filled by others."

The truth of that statement was never tested, because on Saturday, April 19, a new figure came into the Fox River Valley, bringing with him a breath of outside air. Monroe A. Wertheimer, from Los Angeles, succeeded Oscar Thilmany as president. On Monday and Tuesday mornings he met with a committee of the UBPM lodge. An agreement was reached, and at noon on Tuesday, April 22, the strikers returned to work.[21] On Thursday, April 24, the co-owner of the Winnebago Paper Company met the president of the Hamilton Lodge and agreed to settle the strike on the "Thilmany terms." The next day, twenty-five of the fifty workers who had been striking the Winnebago mill for almost four months returned to work. The remaining twenty-five had found other jobs.

In mid-June, when all back orders had been completed, the Thilmany and Winnebago mills abolished the Saturday night shift. The Neenah *Times* proclaimed that "the situation among the paper mill circles of Neenah is now as calm as a mid-summer night's dream."[22] It was no dream, however, for the workers who still worked the Saturday night shift at the George A. Whiting Paper Company and the Menasha Paper Company mills.

1902: Defeat on the Wisconsin River

The United Brotherhood of Paper Makers realized that eventually the competition from non-union mills, especially those along the Wisconsin River, would destroy the Fox River Valley gains. As soon as he had arrived, William Hamilton had visited paper mill workers along the Wisconsin River. Workers at Grand Rapids (now Wisconsin Rapids) staged rallies and planned dances for fellow workers from Rhinelander and Nekoosa, but almost no one came. Finally, late in 1901, the United Brotherhood was able to organize a lodge in Brokaw.[23]

The problem was that the Wisconsin River millowners were more determined opponents than many of those on the Fox River. For example, the Wausau Paper Mill Company in Brokaw soon reined in the Brokaw lodge by calling in the men for a talk, which resulted in each individual signing a contract that granted a 10 per cent wage increase coupled with a "no strike" pledge, and stipulated that any signer quitting the mill would give sixty days notice or forfeit ten days' pay.[24] Other Wisconsin River Valley manufacturers used the same tactic, and paper mill workers in the Stevens Point area signed similar agreements.[25]

The Wisconsin River manufacturers also formed an association to counter the union. George Whiting, who had mills in both the Wisconsin and the Fox River valleys, called a meeting in Appleton that was attended by employer representatives from Nekoosa, Grand Rapids, Centralia, Marinette, Menominee, Eau Claire, Wausau, Stevens Point, and seven mills on the Fox River. They established the Northwestern Manufacturers Association, designed to "resist the demands of the union." Whiting was elected president.[26]

Despite the employers' intransigence, some workers continued to meet with Hamilton, and in February and March they formed lodges in Nekoosa, Grand Rapids, and Stevens Point. Nevertheless, even Hamilton acknowledged that there was more bravado than substance behind the ultimatum which he had sent to the Wisconsin millowners in February:[27]

> If the men are permitted to resume work at 7 a.m. Monday, April 7, 1902 it will be taken as . . . your acceptance of . . . the shorter-hour schedule. . . . You are hereby notified that if workmen or women in your employ are discriminated against because of their sympathy with or . . . are members of the United Brotherhood of Papermakers of America . . . it shall be sufficient cause for immediate and concerted action on the part of the United Brotherhood.

The replies from the mill managers in the Grand Rapids and Stevens Point areas had differed only in their degree of disdain. The manager of the Nekoosa Paper Company had responded that "no . . . bloodsucker representing . . . an alleged union will ever be permitted to inject his . . . vile slandering lies between us." The response from George Whiting's Plover mill was to discharge a shipping clerk who had worked at the mill for five years and was trying to organize the plant. "He was discharged for reasons sufficient for the management," declared the mill manager.[28]

The paperworkers held a protest rally at which they formed a new lodge, elected officers whose names they refused to divulge, and demanded that the company reinstate the clerk. When nothing happened, about twenty-five union men shut down the plant and walked out, followed by "some 15 or 20 of the young ladies employed in the finishing room."[29] (A UBPM spokesman noted in April that about one-third of the workers striking the paper mills throughout Wisconsin were "girls employed in the finishing rooms."[30]) At Whiting's mill at Stevens Point, union members also walked out, making about seventy strikers in both mills. According to management, a dozen strikers returned to work within a week and, with some additional replacements, both mills were able to operate fully.[31]

Nevertheless, the struggle continued. Whiting stated that the mills would run if it meant that every man in the plant had to be imported from the East. An organizer from the UBPM national headquarters in Massachusetts came to Stevens Point. AFL President Samuel Gompers sent an organizer from Springfield, Illinois, to explain the strikers' case to the public and to organize Stevens Point workers who were not employed in the paper mills. Frank Weber, head of the Wisconsin State Federation of Labor, came from Milwaukee to organize the paper mill women. The strikes in the Whiting mills led the manager of the Grand Rapids Pulp and Paper Company in Biron to expect a strike "at any moment." He dismissed six of his men, replaced them with a non-union crew, and announced that he would dismiss all union men and make the entire mill non-union.[32]

The union's ultimatum date of April 1 drew nearer. The *Wood County Reporter* warned the workers that if they struck they would "never have an opportunity to return to work" and might "force the paper mills on the Wisconsin River to employ only non-union help."[33] On April 5 the workers made their own decision. Fifty-five at the Nekoosa Paper Company and twenty at the company in Biron did not report for the Saturday night shift, stopping all but one machine in each of these mills. The members of the Brokaw lodge shut down the papermaking division of the Wausau Paper Mills. The Stevens Point and Plover strikers, who had been out since February, appealed to the strikebreakers still working inside these mills to honor the April 5 deadline and join the strike. The AFL organizer and William Hamilton tried to win their support with a special public meeting in Stevens Point, but no one came out of the mills to join the strikers.[34]

By the end of April, 1902, the strikers in the Wisconsin River Valley were defeated. Those strikers who had been living in company houses in Brokaw moved away. A large number of the Biron and Nekoosa strikers now were shoveling sand for the Chicago and North Western Railroad

Company at $1.75 per day—"not in [competition] with the $3.75 a day workers inside a paper mill." The Brokaw, Nekoosa, Stevens Point, and Grand Rapids lodges died.[35]

1902: Defeat on the Eau Claire River

In the course of this drive to extend the shorter-hour contract to all mills, two Neenah paper mill workers took the train to Eau Claire in March, 1902, and talked with the workers employed by the Dells Paper and Pulp Company. They were followed by Hamilton, who established a UBPM lodge and held several meetings with the Dells management. This was done despite of the fact that the Dells management, in recognition of the "condition of affairs in the Fox River Valley," had followed the Wisconsin River tactics and had called its employees together in an early December meeting at which an anti-union agreement was reached. The Dells superintendent described how he later, in April, maneuvered against the union and into a strike:[36]

> One of the men came and told me that two or three of the men wanted to meet me. I told them that I . . . could not meet with them that evening. The men replied that the following day would be perfectly satisfactory. That evening I made a canvass throughout the plant, asking every man and boy to meet me in conference next morning, I agreeing to pay each a half-day's wages in addition for their time at the conference. Next morning I ordered the mill closed down so that night and day forces might attend the conference. All but one man attended—some 250 or more hands.

At the conference, the superintendent asked the workers to await the outcome of a meeting of Eastern paper manufacturers and their employees, scheduled for May 15, at which the shorter-hour schedule was to be discussed. He asked the men to vote on his proposal by moving to the right (for) or left (against) side of the room. All but five moved to the right. Those five then submitted their resignations. The superintendent's narrative continued:

> We supposed everything O.K. until this morning when one machine tender and about fifteen helpers refused to work under existing conditions and were paid off. We shut the mill down, made some much needed repairs, and expected to start our two large machines in the morning. Our beater engineers and helpers to a man, we are proud to say . . . were all at their posts ready for duty . . . . There was no dissatisfaction whatever in our mill until the advent of the organizers.

Hamilton's report of this episode was entirely different:[37]

> Mr. O'Brien [the superintendent] . . . especially abused the officers and influential members of the unions. His language is said to have

been so vile and abusive that five of his machine tenders, helpers and engineers quit on the spot. This action was the cause of a sympathetic strike, a day or two following, which involved almost the entire mill, all except two machine tenders, . . . [another man] and his brother.

According to Hamilton, the Eau Claire police force joined the company against the strikers,

. . . with the chief at the head riding around to the homes of the men and boys, using all kinds of arguments either to persuade or compel them to return to work. These tactics were very effectual . . . and succeeded in driving a few back to work. By this time several scabs had been imported from other points.

When Hamilton returned to Eau Claire, the police went after him. On the afternoon of April 30, Hamilton was writing a letter in the writing room of the Eau Claire House while the chief of police was in the hotel office. Hamilton was called to the phone, and when he returned, the letter was gone. Using this letter as evidence, the municipal judge issued a warrant for Hamilton's arrest. Hamilton was taken to jail for the night. The complaint, read in court the next morning, charged that Hamilton and several others, who were named but never arrested, conspired to close the mill and conspired to cause the employees to go out on strike.

Trial was scheduled for May 6 and bail was set at $400. Hamilton reported that although the strikers took up a collection for the bail, it actually was paid for by Mayor David Hammel of Appleton. At the trial, a witness who earlier had admitted to being a detective now admitted that he had taken the letter. After two days of argument the judge discharged Hamilton. The company lost the case, but the UBPM lost the strike and the Eau Claire lodge died.[38]

Annihilation of the Unions, 1903–1904

The losses in Eau Claire, Menasha, and the Wisconsin River Valley made the gains in the rest of the Fox River Valley untenable. Whistling in the dark, organizer David Sullivan from the International Brotherhood of Papermakers (formed in 1902 when a second union of machine tenders, the International Paper Machine Tenders merged with the UBPM) stated that "a determined effort will be made to bring everyone of the Fox River paper mills into the short hour agreement, though methods different from those in the past will be adopted."[39] As an omen of success he cited the Nicolet Lodge, which he had just organized in De Pere among workers at the American Writing Paper Company. Sullivan expressed faith in the power of the new IBPM union label and in the International Typographical Union's promise to work only on paper bearing that label.

A letter from Kimberly–Clark, however, to the first lodge meetings at Neenah–Menasha and Appleton in the new year, 1903, confronted the paper mill workers with their true situation. The letter, pointing out that Kimberly–Clark's competitors were getting twelve hours more work for the same weekly pay, was a signal that Kimberly–Clark was planning to resume the Saturday night shift.

The Fox Valley lodges joined forces to fight, and throughout January, 1903, presented petitions and counterproposals to Kimberly–Clark, all to no avail. Even their own International president declared that, under the terms of their contract, it was the "duty" of the Fox Valley lodges to return to the Saturday night shift.[40] The papermakers, however, had the support of George Gilbert, President of the Gilbert Paper Company in Menasha, who "assert[ed] the justice of their demand" and continued the shorter hours in his mill.[41] It should be noted that Gilbert's competitors were in the East and consequently were on the shorter schedule. Shorter hours were continued also by the Combined Locks Paper Company, the Union Bag and Paper Company, the Thilmany Pulp and Paper Company, and Shattuck and Babcock, a subsidiary of the American Writing Paper Company in De Pere. The remainder of the Fox Valley paperworkers returned to the Saturday night shift in early 1903.

This was an intolerable reverse for the paperworkers, who, in February, issued an ultimatum demanding reinstatement of the shorter schedule by March 1.[42] The issue was not joined fully until mid-April, when Kimberly–Clark agreed to operate its Neenah mill and the Neenah Paper Company mill on the short schedule without a pay reduction because other mills making that particular type of paper were on short schedules. Kimberly–Clark's Globe mill and its Badger mill, however, would continue to work Saturday nights until mills making their type of paper stopped the Saturday night shift. The lodges replied that they would not consider the proposal, and demonstrated their indignation by agreeing to strike if their demands were not met.[43] But even with new contracts from the Strange, Winnebago, and Neenah Paper companies in hand, the union could not move Kimberly–Clark. A strike against the former champion of the shorter schedule appeared certain.

About forty-eight hours before the scheduled strike time, the State Board of Arbitration stepped in. As the deadline approached, the board came up with a proposal for extending negotiations: if the union would stay out on Saturday night, April 18, the Board would convince

Kimberly–Clark to pay for that one night not worked. With its credibility thus saved, the union could postpone its full strike for one more week.[44]

Kimberly–Clark agreed, but when 600 paper mill workers walked out in Neenah, Menasha, and Appleton on Saturday night, not even they knew if it was a strike or a gesture.[45] Not until Sunday did the union decide to postpone the strike for one week. This was a compromise that paid off, for after several days of sparring with the union at meetings held by the State Board, Kimberly–Clark capitulated and signed a contract granting the "short hour term with full pay for one year from May 1, 1903 to May 1, 1904 with all conditions of wages, hours, etc. to be the same as enjoyed during 1902."[46]

The Hamilton Lodge hosted a victory celebration for 200 paperworkers from Appleton, Little Chute, Combined Locks, and Kaukauna. A "bountiful supper" was served and local delegates gave a report on the Paper Makers' national convention. Euphorically, the Menasha newspaper concluded that it was only a question of time until the men would be granted the eight-hour shift. No one had the ability to foresee that this would be the last celebration for a long time to come.

The victorious workers knew their shorter-hour schedule could not continue if non-union mills across the state continued to operate long hours. So, once more an IBPM organizer, John Malin, traveled up and down the paper mill rivers of Wisconsin, and once more he found the mill-owners on the offensive. Along the Wisconsin River, for example, after Malin had established a local in Stevens Point, one of its twenty-three members was called to the mill office and given an ultimatum by a principal stockholder in the company: "You must either quit the mill or quit the union." The worker quit the mill. The organizer dashed back to Stevens Point in panic, because "a strike would retard us all over the West [Wisconsin]." It took two weeks of negotiation to get this "brother" back to work, but the new local remained intact with twenty members.[47]

In the entire Wisconsin River Valley, however, Malin had only one success. In Port Edwards, "after spending . . . four weeks . . . I formed a local. I had all of the men in Port Edwards and half of those in the Hurlytown mill. . . . The rest . . . were working under a [company] contract," and joined when their contract expired on January 1, 1904.[48]

In Oconto Falls, on the Oconto River, it was Malin himself whom the mill workers feared: "They were under the impression that we or the executive board [of the IBPM] would order them on strike and I could not get it out of their heads." However, the backtenders and third hands wanted to organize and were granted an IBPM charter. They learned, unfortunately, that their lodge could not survive without the skilled papermakers. When required to quit the union or quit the mill, the backtenders and thirdhands chose the latter. The company kept the mill running, and the union died. At Park Falls, on the Flambeau River, Malin "found a good crowd of boys" and organized the Flambeau–Park Falls Lodge. On the Menominee River he organized a new Marinette–Menominee Lodge to replace the one that had lost a strike for "Saturday night off" in April, 1902, but this one also died within a year.[49]

The International Brotherhood of Paper Makers lodges along the Fox River thus continued to stand alone and vulnerable. Furthermore, a significant change in the attitude of the Fox River millowners put not only the short hour schedules, but the very existence of the union in jeopardy. In the crises of 1902 and 1903, each Fox River paper mill owner had acted independently, but when their union contracts expired on May 1, 1904, they united in a determinedly anti-union effort. Charles W. Howard, president of the Howard Paper Company, Menasha, expressed the change succinctly: "I am tired of unionism and will stand with the other manufacturers."[50]

The manufacturers took the offensive by polling their employees individually on whether they would work the longer schedule. In response, the IBPM delivered an ultimatum to the manufacturers on Monday, May 30: "You are hereby notified that in dealing with your employees you cannot deal with them individually but [only] through the International Brotherhood of Papermakers."[51] The ultimatum brought the manufacturers together in a meeting the next day at the Howard Paper Company office. The strength of their anti-union feeling was demonstrated when the superintendent of the Combined Locks Paper Company went directly from the meeting to the mill and ordered all employees to quit the union or call at the office for their pay. Sixty of the workers replied by going out on strike.[52]

Saturday, June 4, was the day when the Saturday-night shift was to be reinstated. Both sides prepared for confrontation. The manufacturers polled employees on whether they would walk out, and offered extra pay to leading union men if they would work during the strike and teach non-union men to operate the machines. Merchants warned that they would not extend credit to strikers. IBPM president George W. Mackey came to Neenah to prepare for a strike. As the 6:00 P.M. deadline neared, the millowners admitted that the "effort to secure union men to run a few machines has been so unsuccessful that no effort will be made to keep them running, until replacements can be slowly secured." The manufacturers threatened to blacklist: "The men who go out tonight will be considered members of the union by the manufacturers. As such, they cannot be again employed in the mills of any of the manufacturers interested in the controversy. This has been agreed upon by the manufacturers who are determined to break up the union."[53]

Undeterred, the workers struck at the Atlas, Vulcan, Tioga, Telulah, Riverside Fibre and Paper, and Wisconsin Tissue mills in Appleton; the Combined Locks Paper Company in Combined Locks; the C. W. Howard Paper Company and the John Strange Paper Company in Menasha; and the Kimberly–Clark and Neenah Paper companies in Neenah. In total, these mills employed about 900 workers. The Gilbert Paper Company in Menasha and the Fox River Paper Company in Appleton continued their shorter-hour schedule; in both cases their Eastern competitors were also on shorter hours. The Winnebago Paper Company in Neenah continued the shorter schedule, instituted after its long strike in 1902.[54]

The State Board of Arbitration found the millowners adamant in their refusal to deal with the union, but willing to pay for the hours added by reinstituting the Saturday night shift; the union rejected this offer. Despite this militant spirit, the first ten days of the strike were peaceful, and none of the struck mills tried to open. President Mackey felt confident enough to leave the Fox Valley and go to Stevens Point to muster support.

But on June 14 the picnic ended: forty men, half of them experienced papermakers brought in from the East and the remainder made up of former Kimberly–Clark employees, reported for work at the Badger mill "amid the jeers of striking papermakers and other union men." The strikers who had planned to camp out for the duration of the strike were called back to town to picket the mill. Probably they had no premonition of the total disaster that awaited them.[55]

While the State Board of Arbitration and a special union committee were searching for a compromise, the strikers were taking direct action. Three hundred gathered at the Russell House in Neenah, where the imported strikebreakers were housed. A band played; the crowd threw eggs. James Kimberly and Frank J. Sensenbrenner, an official of Kimberly–Clark, went to Mayor Charles Schultz's office to ask for protection. The Neenah Common Council debated hiring special police, but the issue so divided the council that it referred the question to the mayor. In Appleton none of the struck mills were able to open. In Menasha, the Howard mill tried to open on Monday, June 20, but only four of the hundred men who had agreed to come to work reported at the mill.[56]

The next day there was shooting in Neenah. About 150 angry strikers followed a group of strikebreakers who were being escorted to the Russell House by a Kimberly–Clark Company guard, Fred Potter, who was either knocked down and kicked or simply fell down amid the surging crowd. He got up and fired his pistol three times from the Russell House steps. He told the police, who promptly seized him: "I am from Chicago and was employed by the millmen to carry supplies to the men at work. I am not a papermaker and know nothing about the business." The police took Potter to Oshkosh immediately "to avoid a lynching."[57]

Violence continued to erupt sporadically in Neenah over the next ten days. Strikers and strikebreakers chased each other, beat each other with shovels, and on one occasion, one fired a gun at another. When a worker from the Kimberly–Clark Niagara mill was seen with a union officer in Neenah, he was called to the central office and fired for being in collusion with the union. In Menasha, union members helped to keep the peace, and in Appleton the strikers avoided confrontation by staying off the streets and away from the mills.[58]

In July, Fred Potter, the Kimberly–Clark guard, went on trial at the Winnebago County Courthouse in Oshkosh. He testified that he worked for the B. H. Holmes agency in Chicago, doing "secret service work," often in the guise of a plant fireman, and that Holmes had put him to work for various midwest companies during strikes and lockouts. Holmes had sent him to do this "secret work" for Kimberly–Clark. The judge dismissed Potter on the second day of the trial.[59]

The Neenah-Menasha millowners continued to import non-union workers. It was rumored that these imports, many of them unskilled, were being paid considerably higher wages than had been paid to the skilled papermakers on strike. The strikers received a weekly stipend from the IBPM, beginning on the first Saturday in July, of five dollars a week for those with families, three dollars for those without. Since there was a labor shortage in Neenah–Menasha, some strikers found other jobs.[60]

The influx of strikebreakers diminished the strikers' strategic position and, consequently, their spirit. When Kimberly–Clark's Badger mill reopened in mid-June, the strikers picketed and demonstrated, but when the Howard and Strange mills opened a month later, they made no move. On the last Saturday in July, twenty-five strikers asked to return to work at the Howard mill. They were accepted, began work at noon, and worked on into the night. Company president Charles Howard said he was working a double crew so that "all the men might be together." The remaining strikers rallied, and during the evening about a hundred of them gathered outside the mill to call out the deserters. Finally, about 4:30 A.M. Sunday morning, the twenty-five walked out of the mill. A union meeting was held then and there, and the strikers decided to continue the strike.[61]

In Appleton the strikers continued to have the sympathy of the community and overwhelmingly had endorsed the strike at every union meeting through early August. But, like their fellow strikers in Neenah–Menasha, they had been unable to keep the Appleton mills from operating. During the first week in August, Kimberly–Clark brought new workers, guarded by five members of the police force and six Pinkerton detectives, into its Atlas mill to operate the last idle machine in that mill. Its Tioga mill was being operated under the protection of Pinkerton guards, and its Vulcan plant was due to open as soon as more outside workers arrived. The apparently limitless supply of outside labor, together with some defections from their own ranks, finally forced the Appleton strikers to surrender. On Saturday, August 13, exactly ten weeks after the start of the strike, they met and voted to accept the Saturday night shift.[62]

The next day, IBPM President Mackey advised all of the Fox Valley strikers to return to work, which most of them did on Monday morning. Kimberly–Clark announced that it would "take back as many as we have places for. Some of the positions are already filled by outside help and these we will retain." By Monday afternoon a majority of the strikers were back at work, and the millowners notified their Eastern agents to stop sending strikebreakers. When some of the local union officials and strike leaders reported for work, they were turned away, and it was rumored that at least five of them never would be hired by a Wisconsin paper mill again. The president of the Appleton lodge, James Tolan, sold his house for $1,015 two days before the vote to surrender. The day after the vote, he left to take a job as machine tender in Fitchburg, Massachusetts.[63]

When the vice-president of the IBPM visited the Appleton and Kaukauna lodges at the end of 1904, he found the meetings were attended chiefly by "brothers placed on the blacklist by the manufacturers of the Fox River Valley."[64] By July, 1905, these two lodges no longer existed. Also dead by this time was the Niagara lodge, to which "every skilled man" in the Kimberly–Clark plant had belonged just the year before.[65]

The Hamilton Lodge of Neenah–Menasha died more slowly. In 1905 it still had enough strength to elect a delegate to the IBPM national convention and to help the Trades Council plan a Labor Day parade and picnic, to which the merchants and businessmen had promised to contribute "quite generously."[66] The next year it sent to the *Paper Makers' Journal* a vigorous declaration of its continuing existence:[67]

> Certain papermakers have been parading around the country claiming to be good union men giving as the reason for being behind in their dues the following stuff and nonsense: They were members of Hamilton No. 18 and went out on strike and Hamilton No. 18 busted up, and the union owed them money, and it will be a long time before they have another local there. . . . Now, Mr. Editor, in justice to our local . . . Hamilton No. 18 has never been out of existence since it was organized over four years ago, and we stand to pay any claim of a member in good standing . . . we reinstated seven members last meeting and we have three applications for next meeting. Who says Hamilton No. 18 busted up?

Despite this bravado, by February of 1907 the Hamilton Lodge was dead, as was the Nicolet Lodge in De Pere. There were no more IBPM lodges in Wisconsin.[68]

The last attempt to obtain Saturday night off came in 1905, when a bill to reduce the weekly hours of the night shift from seventy-eight to sixty-five was introduced and subsequently killed in the Wisconsin legislature. The desire for shorter hours was not expunged, however, and some years later the Wisconsin paper mill workers reorganized and fought again, this time for the eight-hour day.

CHAPTER 11

The Renewed Struggle
for the Eight-Hour Day

IN THE YEARS from 1904 onward, when the Wisconsin paper mill workers again were locked into the shifts of eleven and thirteen hours, many Eastern paper mills changed to eight-hour shifts. During its efforts for shorter hours the International Brotherhood of Paper Makers had opposed eight-hour shifts, even though the American Federation of Labor urged them to join the campaign for the eight-hour day. In the paper industry of that time, the schedule for an eight-hour day would have meant three eight-hour shifts, six days a week. When some of the delegates had proposed this schedule at the 1902 national convention, they were howled down by the majority, which insisted on Saturday night off. Many delegates also feared that management could break a union with the new men it would train for a third shift. Finally, in 1906, the International Brotherhood of Paper Makers endorsed the eight-hour shifts.[1]

By the end of the first decade of the twentieth century, the International was in desperate condition. In 1909 it reported zero assets. President Jeremiah Carey mortgaged his own house for money to keep the union alive, and from 1909 through 1912 he and Vice-President George A. Schneider of Appleton worked for the International without pay. While they struggled to revive the IBPM, they succeeded in organizing lodges in Rhinelander, Merrill, Grand Rapids (now Wisconsin Rapids), Stevens Point, Green Bay, and Niagara.[2]

Rhinelander: The First Three-Tour Paper Mill

Not until 1912 did one of these lodges have the strength to ask for shorter hours again, and then it had President Carey do the asking, first by letter and then in a meeting with the Rhinelander Paper Company. Surprisingly, the company agreed, and on July 8, 1912, paperworkers in Rhinelander began working eight-hour shifts in three "tours" a day.[3] At the same time, the workers at the Consolidated Water Power and Paper Company in Grand Rapids and at the Grand Rapids Pulp and Paper

Company in neighboring Biron also began the three-tour schedule. George W. Mead, the head of these mills and a strong anti-unionist, had not been asked to introduce the eight-hour shift, but he must have been aware of the fact that the IBPM had been organizing in Grand Rapids and that there was great agitation for the eight-hour shift throughout the Midwest.[4]

No other Wisconsin lodges were strong enough at that time to demand the eight-hour day, but its adoption in these mills spurred union organization at other sites. Paperworkers in Nekoosa, Port Edwards, Tomahawk, Wausau, and Eau Claire formed lodges. Even in the Fox River Valley, where all had been quiet since the devastating defeats of 1904, the Appleton and Kaukauna paper mill workers reorganized their old locals for the same reason: they were "not in love with the 14 hour night shift."[5] Neenah, however, remained quiet. It was reported in 1914 that a paper mill worker who tried to organize a lodge in Neenah was fired from the Lakeside Paper Company. Three years later, the International lamented the continuing lack of effective union leadership in Neenah.[6]

Along the Fox and Wisconsin Rivers, the paper manufacturers grew nervous and wary. It seems clear that at least one of the paper industry leaders, David Clark Everest, director of the Marathon Paper Mill Company at Rothschild, on the Wisconsin River near Wausau, had some secret keyhole through which he watched union activity in a number of the mills, and he took it upon himself to alert his fellow millowners to any dangers he noticed in their mills. He warned the Tomahawk Pulp and Paper Company that its machine tenders and beater men, seventeen in all, had an active IBPM lodge. He promised that he would send further information in unsigned letters and asked the company to destroy all of these secret communications.[7] Everest had an even more alarming tip for Lewis M. Alexander, president of the Nekoosa–Edwards Paper Company: men were on their way to get jobs in the Nekoosa–Edwards mill for the purpose of organizing a strike for the eight-hour shift in September, 1913. Everest sent Alexander the names of these men along with an admonition to avoid hiring any of them.[8]

Alexander evidently shared Everest's fears and suspicions. Early one morning, when he went to the Port Edwards railroad station to take a trip north, he saw in the depot a tall, dark man in a long coat, carrying a small satchel. It was well to watch such a man, Alexander thought, because strangers were rare in Port Edwards. He noted that the stranger did not buy a ticket in the depot, but as the train carried them both north, he saw him pay the fare to Wausau, Everest's bailiwick. Without waiting to reach his destination, Alexander wrote to alert Everest to the arrival of this person who, Alexander assumed, must have been wandering about the Nekoosa–Edwards mill all night. Why else, Alexander asked, would a stranger be in the Nekoosa depot at 5 o'clock in the morning?[9]

Even the manager of the Flambeau Paper Company in Park Falls, far off the path of union organizers, was suspicious. Although he had fired two men he feared were labor agitators, the unrest among the remaining workers was so great that he did not dare to work any of them beyond their regular shifts. Instead of hiring new men, he hired six boys, who could not do as much work as men, but weakened the pressure for a wage increase.[10]

In the summer of 1913, workers in three paper mills in Minnesota struck for the eight-hour shift. Everest warned his fellow manufacturers that if the strikers were not defeated in Minnesota, the mills in Nekoosa, Port Edwards, and Stevens Point would be next. He exhorted the Wisconsin owners to do everything possible to aid the struck mills, especially to forward to them job applications they received for machine help of any kind.[11] Everest did not mention that the Wausau Group, an organization of wealthy lumbermen who had hired Everest to start and manage the Marathon Paper Mill Company for them, had money invested in one of the struck Minnesota mills.[12]

The Employers Organize: The Western Paper Manufacturers Association

This rather haphazard mutual support system was formalized into an anti-union network covering three states when paper manufacturers from Michigan, Minnesota, and Wisconsin met at the Hotel Stratford in Chicago in April, 1914, and organized the Western Paper Manufacturers Association (WPMA). Frank J. Sensenbrenner, an executive at Kimberly–Clark and an instigator of the new organization, was elected president. The association's primary purpose was to ensure that a local union which tried to flex its muscle would face the combined financial power of the associated companies—twenty-four in 1914, thirty-two by 1919.

Each company member was assessed for a contribution to the association's strike aid fund in proportion to that company's production. The initial assessment was five cents per ton. If a member company should be shut down by a strike, it would receive aid from the fund in proportion to the tons of production it lost owing to the strike. The rate of compensation was two dollars per ton lost.

The by-laws ensured that the association itself and not the struck company would set policy during the strike: "By accepting aid [strike benefits] from the Association . . . the member binds himself to counsel with and be governed by the decision of the Executive Committee as to the management of the strike." And no member would be allowed to withdraw during the struggle: "No member shall resign [from the Association] during the existence of a strike or a pending settlement of a difficulty between any member of this Association and his workmen without the consent of the Executive Committee."[13]

The association, of course, hoped to keep unions from ever forming, and to this end it hired agents to keep track of agitation in the mills and labor organizers in the communities. In the formal language of the by-laws: "The Executive Committee . . . may . . . employ at the expense of the Association, an agent or agents to assist it in averting and settling possible labor difficulties, and may invest such agent or agents with such authority as it thinks best."[14] Evidently the WPMA members did not want to make public the anti-union work of the association. This is illustrated by the fact that when one of the association members went into receivership in 1925 it dropped its membership in the association so it would not have to reveal in court the purpose of the assessments which it had paid to the WPMA.[15]

In spite of this concerted effort by the paper manufacturers, the International Brotherhood of Paper Makers "organized local after local" in Wisconsin, because the demand for labor in the United States, brought on by increased production during World War I, gave workers across the country a great surge of power.[16] By the spring of 1916, the International Brotherhood of Paper Makers, the Wisconsin State Federation of Labor, and a second paper mill workers' union, the International Brotherhood of Pulp, Sulphite and Paper Mill Workers[17] (which at the time had locals in Appleton, Kaukauna, and Marinette), were able to launch a co-ordinated drive for union recognition and for the eight-hour day in the Wisconsin paper industry.[18] Local unions described the initial success of this eight-hour drive. The IBPM Appleton lodge, practically lifeless since its reorganization in 1913, awoke with new strength:[19]

> [A] general depression in the paper trade at the time [1913] did not give us an opportunity to do anything. We managed to hold together. . . . However, this spring [1916] the time was ripe for action as the paper trade has never been better . . . [IBPM] Vice President George Schneider, and Ohls of the State Federation of Labor, appeared on the scene. We soon had things coming our way.

The Appleton local held a meeting for all shift workers on March 26, 1916; new members signed up, and everyone endorsed the eight-hour day. The union learned that management had decided, prior to the union meeting, "to grant a slight increase in wages to keep their workers satisfied." When the union meeting revealed to management "how things were," management "immediately" called another meeting of its own, "at which they decided to grant the eight-hour day to take effect April 1. This they thought would keep all who were not members from joining the union."[20]

The Kaukauna local appeared to have even greater power:[21]

> Thursday morning and evening we had meetings . . . we took in about fifty new members. The employers, seeing that these meetings were well represented . . . called a meeting of the whole Thilmany Pulp and Paper Co. Friday evening, this included everybody—finishers, girls, and other employees—and we got the surprise of our lives . . . the mill owner, addressed us and told us that as soon as we could get the help . . . he would put us on the eight hour system, something we have been longing for for years. He also told us that the company intended to put up a place of amusement for the employers and their families and also a library connected with it. From the first of the year we were given a 6% bonus, which we thought would be knocked in the head, but we were told that was on yet, too.

The Appleton and Kaukauna successes were not isolated victories. On or about April 1, fourteen Wisconsin paper companies changed to eight-hour shifts.[22] Eleven of the fourteen were members of the Western Paper Manufacturers Association, and the remaining three joined subsequently.[23] In a letter to its members, the WPMA identified this extraordinary changeover in schedule as a deliberate, synchronized move by the association to halt the escalating union activity. In addition, association members raised wages substantially.[24] These concessions caused no cessation in union activity; on the contrary, the union organizers were as active as ever and warned the paper mill workers that the companies would revert to the eleven- and thirteen-hour shifts if union pressure abated. The association begged its member companies to assure the workers that this was not their plan.[25]

An example of the approach newly adopted by the manufacturers was the action taken by Kimberly–Clark. In 1916, workers stoned the company's big plant in Kimberly. Instead of reacting harshly, the company, under the leadership of its treasurer, Frank S. Shattuck, tried to remove the causes of dissatisfaction. To this end it hired its first personnel director. Surprisingly, in that era, the new director was a woman, Mary Baker, a former English teacher at Appleton High School. The company transferred the power to hire and fire the workers from the foremen to Miss

Baker, who replaced the foremen's arbitrary methods with careful, digni-
fied interviews. She also did away with discharges for moderate use of al-
cohol, and when the union staged a parade, she countered with a picnic
and entertainment financed by the company.[26] There were no more violent outbreaks in the Kimberly mill. For many years to come, the
Kimberly–Clark Company continued to use programs such as these to
inoculate its employees against the appeals of union organizers.

Many paper mill workers continued to join unions regardless of the
tactics used against them. For example, the growth of the IBPM local in
Kaukauna was spectacular: "Unionism has certainly made a great stride
in the last six months. Six months ago there was about 25 stickers of the
local in all (you couldn't get any more in if you pulled them in with a rope);
now we have about four hundred and fifty union members in the
papermills here with the Finishers' Local." The IBPM local in DePere reported that it was alive and well: "We now have about 60 members and we
are initiating more at every meeting."[27]

The true measure of the organizing drive's success or failure was
whether the companies now were compelled to deal with these unions as
representatives of their employees. Two strikes measured union strength
in this regard during the summer of 1916. One was against the Interlake
Pulp and Paper Company in Appleton, where employees were still obliged
to work the old eleven- and thirteen-hour shifts while workers in other
Appleton paper mills were working eight hours. The Interlake workers
found this intolerable, so in early June, 1916, Vice-President John P.
Burke of the IBPS&PMW went to the company with the following demands: "Eight-hour shift for tour workers, nine-hour day for day workers, union preference in hiring, union membership mandatory after 15
days on the job, non-union workers the first to go in layoffs, union men to
be laid off by seniority."[28] Interlake refused, and posted a bulletin announcing that it would introduce the eight-hour shifts in three departments and the nine-hour day in one department. The bulletin continued:
"For . . . other workers the hours will remain the same, as usual. . . .
Any man who does not wish to comply with this schedule . . . is at liberty
to go elsewhere."[29]

On the question of union recognition, neither side would yield, as was
made dramatically clear at a subsequent meeting between the Interlake
general manager and five employees. The employees brought with them
Vice-President Burke and an official of the Appleton Trades and Labor
Council. The manager refused to meet with the union representatives; the
five employees refused to meet without them. The next morning, 300 In-

terlake employees refused to go to work, and the strike was on. Two days later the employees of the Riverside Fibre and Paper Company joined the strike for union recognition.[30]

When the confrontation began, Interlake was not a member of the Western Paper Manufacturers Association, but it sought the advice of that group and, the day before the strike began, joined the association. Consequently, when the IBPS&PMW struck Interlake, it took on the entire association. Instituting the eight-hour day had been a relatively painless maneuver for the fourteen WPMA companies which had adopted it in April, because the longer shifts were making it difficult to attract new workers in the tight labor market of World War I. But holding the IBPS&PMW at bay at the gates of Interlake was to prove much more costly.

Before the Interlake strike, the association had been financing its strike fund through an assessment, as mentioned earlier, of five cents for every ton of pulp and paper that each member company produced. The day after the strike began, the association's executive committee met in Appleton and increased this assessment to fifteen cents per ton. At its general meeting a week later, the association increased from $2 to $5 its strike subsidy for each ton of pulp and paper production lost by a company because of a strike. By August the association was paying a strike subsidy to Interlake of $3,000 to $3,500 per week.[31] By comparison, the Appleton local was receiving $50 a week from the State Federation of Labor.[32] To some of the association's members, the strike fund assessment seemed "a helluva lot of money," and they complained bitterly.[33] However, after a special study of the situation, the executive committee confirmed the payment of $5 for every ton of ground pulp production which Interlake lost due to the strike, and so the reimbursement to the company continued.[34]

Henry Ohl of the Wisconsin State Federation of Labor and George Schneider, IBPM vice-president, came to Appleton and held a mass meeting that packed the armory. Burke was "cheered to the echo" and the Appleton press was "roundly roasted" because it "was not open to the union side of the argument." "Incorrect," wrote the Appleton *Evening Crescent,* which went on to defend itself: "Paid advertisement cannot be refused, and the press has not refused to print the strike situation."[35]

As other companies had done in earlier strikes, Interlake brought in strikebreakers from Chicago and housed them in the mill. At the company's request, the sheriff appointed four new deputies with police powers to guard the mill.[36] After the union had been picketing for a month, the municipal court judge handed down an unusually broad injunction, listing by name over a hundred defendants, among them the vice-president of the

IBPS&PMW, each officer of the Appleton local, and each Interlake employee out on strike. The injunction prohibited picketing and inducing present employees to stop work, banned use of the word "scab," forbade "giving advice to unions by defendants regarding the interference of the present workforce," and prohibited "gathering for the purpose of concocting a scheme to in any way injure the interest of the present employees or the firm." In other words, advice from the union officers and the convening of union meetings were prohibited.[37]

In defiance of the injunction, the strikers picketed the next morning, but by noon they had gone. Nevertheless, the strike continued. Two hundred seventy-six pulp workers marched in the Labor Day parade and were "applauded and cheered" by the crowd.[38] Two and one-half months later, in mid-November, the strike ended. Organizer Charles Sample of the IBPS&PMW reported the settlement terms to the International:[39]

> Please to inform you that I settled the strike at the Interlake Mill and part of the men are back at work and the rest will be soon. I didn't get what we should have but have got the boys back and the union intact, which I consider lucky for a Greenhorn at the Business, now we can build it up in the future, they agreed to the eight and nine-hour shift and no discrimination. I don't know as it is anything to brag about but we put the old manager and supt. out of business and the mill has gone into new hands.

The "new hands" were those of George W. Mead, owner of the Consolidated Water Power Company of Grand (Wisconsin) Rapids and the Grand Rapids Pulp and Paper Company in nearby Biron. War in Europe had stopped sulphite pulp shipments to the United States, and Mead bought Interlake to obtain pulp for his mills. It is not surprising that he installed the three-tour (eight-hour shift) system at Interlake, since he had adopted the eight-hour shifts in his two Wisconsin River mills in 1912. In both years he may have made the change in order to weaken the union's appeal, but he did not shorten hours in acknowledgment of the union's existence. The Appleton local was not yet strong enough to gain such acknowledgment.

Interlake was sold and the strike was ended, but the Western Paper Manufacturers Association had to collect two more assessments to erase its Interlake debt. It had been a costly undertaking, the association admitted, but well worth the price. Association members who felt unduly burdened by these additional assessments were advised to take comfort from the fact that the fight had been waged in someone else's mill.[40]

The "General" Strike at Marinette

The second test of the success of the 1916 organizing drive was a strike in Marinette. Labor activity that summer in the twin cities, Marinette on the Wisconsin side and Menominee on the Michigan side, was like popcorn in a hot popper, and a number of labor leaders came to Marinette from around the state to generate some of the heat. A general strike never was called, but before the episode was over, 1,700 workers had struck.

On a Saturday night in mid-June, between six hundred and seven hundred people, including newly organized timber workers from Peshtigo, crowded into the Marinette High School Auditorium to hear Henry Ohl and Frank Weber of the Wisconsin State Federation of Labor; Mrs. Laurel Kosten, organizer for the Women's Label League; Harley Nickerson, organizer for the International Association of Machinists; and Richard L. Drake, secretary of the Michigan Federation of Labor. Some of the speakers assailed the capitalists; all of them called on the working class to organize. There previously had been even larger meetings at the high school, but at this one there were more women than ever before—one hundred fifty—most of whom were already on strike against the Boreal Glove Company.[41]

The Marinette workers were aroused. On the Wednesday following the rally, laundry workers met at Steffens Hall and organized a local consisting of twenty-five members. The following Monday, 200 women met at Germania Hall and organized a chapter of the Women's Label League. Tuesday night the barbers met at the Fabry Shop on Main Street and organized a Barbers Local. On Wednesday night seventy-five "retail salesmen and salesladies" met with Mrs. Koston, Henry Ohl, and Richard Drake to discuss joining the Retail Clerks Union.[42] The Menominee and Marinette Trades and Labor Council had an organizer at work and was able to report "one of the most successful organizing campaigns" to the annual convention of the WSFL:[43]

New unions organized in Marinette, Wis., and Menominee, Mich. and vicinity, since April, 1916:

Timber Workers.	Woman's Union Label League.
Paper Workers.	Stationary Firemen.
Pulp and Sulphite Workers.	Laundry Workers.
Glove Workers.	Federal Union.
Box Makers.	Bartenders.
Reed Workers.	Machinists.
Wood Workers.	Hoisting Engineers.
Teamsters.	Car Workers (Federal, Peshtigo).
Painters.	Timber Workers (Peshtigo).
Lathers.	

Besides the foregoing new organizations, in nearly every instance have the older organizations been largely augmented by new members, while several other crafts are in process of formation.

While these workers were organizing, hundreds in Marinette and Menominee were already on strike. On one morning alone, four hundred workers struck the Peninsular Box Company; thirty-five struck the Central West Coal Company; and forty struck the Crawford Box Company. By June 24, approximately 1,300 workers were striking eight companies in the twin cities—the coal company, the glove company, an iron works, several lumber and box companies, and the Marinette and Menominee Paper Company. Hotel Marinette became headquarters for the state labor leaders who came to assist. Henry Ohl helped direct the strikes. Mrs. Kosten stayed on. George Schneider, IBPM vice-president, came from Appleton, and two organizers, a man and a woman, came from Milwaukee. The State Federation contributed $50 a week to help the striking paper mill workers.[44] The Marinette *Eagle-Star* identified the common cause behind the strikes: "The issue is one of recognition of the union. The manufacturers are not in favor of the closed shop and the men want union recognition. There the matter appears to stand."[45]

The Marinette and Menominee manufacturers banded together in the Menominee River Manufacturers Association, whose main purpose was to deny union recognition and whose strategy was to convince the public, through newspaper publicity, that such recognition was wrong.[46] By early July the paper reported: "Employers and Employees are locked tighter than a drum . . . both quite belligerent," and called it "the worst situation that the two cities have faced in their history."[47]

The unions were equally worried, and the Menominee and Marinette Trades and Labor Council sent the following appeal to the annual convention of the State Federation, held later in July.[48]

Greeting: The Menominee Trades and Labor Council and its affiliated unions are in combat with the organized employers of the Menominee river and their hired gunmen and strikebreakers, it having been decided by the Menominee River Manufacturers' Association that the strikers and locked-out men and women of Marinette, Wis., and Menominee, Mich., must be starved into submitting to the terms of organized capital.

During the period of our general organizing campaign, since early in April, the membership of our unions has increased to thousands where before there were but hundreds. Our success has set the exploiters' organization wild with rage, as they realize that the "good old days" of $1.40 per day of ten to thirteen hours for men, while many women received $3.50 per week and less for ten-hour days, are passing into history.

Arrests are taking place without warrant or cause in an effort to intimidate the locked-out men and women and those who have been forced to strike, whose approximate number has reached 1,700.

The workers of the Twin Cities are facing starvation unless their fellow workers come to their aid to supply the means of subsistence while the battle is in progress. Many are now in distress and unable to procure food through the usual channels, some of the merchants having refused to extend further credit. . . .

We therefore appeal to our sister unions for such financial assistance as is possible for them to extend, so that the families of the men on the firing line may be fed while their husbands, fathers and brothers are in the trenches in combat with the most unscrupulous employers and their hired thugs and gunmen.

Our fight is your fight. If we are to win your response must be immediate. The call is urgent. Send all contributions to Chas. Peterson, 1809 Emma Street, Menominee, Michigan.

                                                          Fraternally,
                                                          Chas. A. Peterson

At the end of July, the strikers began to return to the mills. Some said that they returned "under conditions similar to those desired by the union," but one employer spoke of "our men with whom we arranged to start our mills," and declared: "We are running an open shop and refuse to be governed by any union or its regulations."[49] The agreements between the companies and the strikers (with the exception of the Marinette and Menominee Paper Company settlement) stated that wages would remain the same through May, 1917.

The strikers of the IBPM and the IBPS&PMW still held out against the Marinette and Menominee Paper Company. They had been out since June 14. Unable to obtain a meeting with the company, they sent their demands by registered letter on June 2, asking for an eight-hour day for tour workers, a nine-hour day for day workers, and time and a half for overtime on Sundays, Labor Day, Christmas and New Year's, all to go into effect on June 12. On the deadline date, the company manager was out of town, and the company officials who were in town refused to meet with them. On the morning of June 14, the unions held their own meeting and then struck the company's three mills, including one which already was on the three-tour system. After the mills closed down, the secretary of the company stated:[50]

We thought the men understood. . . . I told a number of them including the secretary, that we would not be in shape to put in the three tour system until July 1 or thereabouts. We will have to install considerable new machinery. . . . I told the secretary last night that the demands would be granted. After the receipt of the communications

> from the men, altho we did not answer it with a communication, the
> men were told of the situation.

The "men" may have been told, but the unions had not, and that was the
essential point.

The unions maintained a strong picket line. Early one morning, seven
or eight carpenters and mechanics came to work in the Marinette and Menominee Company's Park Mill and found fifty to seventy-five strikers barring their entrance into the plant. The strikers would not give way, in spite,
of a foreman's claim that the craftsmen were there to prepare the mill for
the three-tour system. The mechanics and carpenters refused to cross the
picket line even with police escort. Their resolve was not tested; the sheriff
explained: "I did not have force enough to compel the strikers to give way
and I did not know whether it was my place to act. I will consult the district attorney."[51]

The strikers returned to work on August 5. They had won the eight-
hour day for tour workers, the nine-hour day for dayworkers, a wage increase of ten cents a day for all employees, adjustment of grievances by
meetings between company officials and a committee from the "organization," and the rehiring of all strikers without discrimination. When Vice-
President John Burke reported to the IBPS&PMW, he stressed the great
value of Henry Ohl's leadership and the economic and moral support of
the Wisconsin State Federation of Labor. He admitted that the unions had
not won recognition from the Marinette and Menominee Paper
Company:[52]

> We did not secure an all union shop agreement. . . . We lay too
> much stress at times upon the union shop agreement. A good militant
> organization without an agreement is better than a weak local with
> the best union shop contract that was ever written. However, our
> members are going to attend the meetings and pay their dues without
> compulsion because they realize that ORGANIZATION IS THE
> HOPE OF THE WORKING CLASS.

It was evident that class consciousness alone was not sufficient to maintain "a good militant organization." When the Marinette and Menominee
Paper Company filled out its application for membership in the Western
Paper Manufacturers Association four years later, it stated that it had no
union and no labor trouble.[53] However, on Labor Day of 1916, hope still
reigned. A great parade of 3,500 to 4,000 workers, led by two bands, was
cheered along the route, and applauded at the park by the "largest crowds
the park [had] . . . ever held." The parade was a roster of the unions in
Marinette and Menominee that summer: Retail Workers, Laundry Workers, Glove Workers, Vessel Loaders, Barbers, Cigar Makers, Stage Hands,

Timber Workers, Brewery Workers, Shingle Weavers, Teamsters, Machinists, Box Makers, Masons, Carpenters, Lathers, Painters, Paper Makers, Pulp and Sulphite Workers, Bartenders, and the Trades and Labor Council. Harley Nickerson, organizer for the International Association of Machinists, gave an address that praised Senator Robert La Follette for his vote for the eight-hour bill and warned the union members not to join the Marinette Civic and Industrial Association, organized that summer to bring in new industry, because the businessmen would "inveigle them to desert their unions." A team of paper mill workers defeated a team of timber workers in a tug of war, and in the evening a concert was given on Dunlap Square.[54] It was a bittersweet celebration at the end of a hard summer.

Of course, this extensive strike activity in Marinette caused nervousness in Wisconsin's other paper manufacturing communities. The Menasha *Record* tried to ward off trouble in the Fox River Valley. In two long successive front page articles it described in great detail the strikes in Marinette and Menominee from which those communities would "not recover in many months, possibly years." It recalled "the only blotch on this city's industrial escutcheon . . . the strike of paper and pulpmill employees about a dozen years ago [1904]" from which "many did not recover their loss for a year or more and some have not yet recovered." Then it warned the citizens of Menasha:[55]

> . . . some of the labor agitators responsible for the depressing conditions in [Marinette and Menominee] are the same individuals who are making every effort to upset peaceful, prosperous conditions in Appleton, Menasha, Neenah, Kaukauna and other cities of this vicinity.

The *Record* concluded that:

> The older employees for the most part thinking and conservative men are not anxious for a repetition of such an experience. Citizens . . . 'openly deplore the activity of agitators who are endeavoring to again plunge this community into a period of strife, discontent and heavy financial sacrifice."

Although the Wisconsin paper manufacturers had been able to deny the unions recognition during these 1916 confrontations, they were still unable to drive them out of the state. During the fall of 1916 and the following year the IBPS&PMW organized locals in Rhinelander, Oconto Falls, Shawano, and Green Bay, and the IBPM began or reactivated locals in Ashland, Park Falls, and Ladysmith. IBPM delegates attended the State Federation of Labor convention in 1917, coming from the locals of Green Bay, Marinette, Rhinelander, and Ashland.[56]

In the summer of 1917 the local at Ladysmith struck the Menasha Paper Company mill and found, as was often the case, that the Western Paper Manufacturers Association was aiding the company. Alcoholic beverages were illegal in Ladysmith; Tony was the nearest "wet" town. Strikers and strikebreakers fought each other on the road between the two towns. When the strikers were arrested and tried for assault, Ira Beck, executive secretary of the WPMA, appeared in court against the strikers. They lost their strike and were forced to return to work on the eleven- and thirteen-hour shifts.[57] The return to the longer schedule stirred an IBPM member to write in the *Paper Makers' Journal:*[58]

Wake Up Wisconsin!

None should have so soon forgotten [what] the terrible life and discomfort and agony these long hours . . . meant to the employee and his family. . . .

As for him who would deliberately foster . . . a plan to force the old [hours] . . . back upon the workers . . ., there is no place in hell hot enough to scorch his dirty soul and make it clean. Nor is he who would father or belong to an association for that purpose a fit subject for heaven. . . .

Wake up Wisconsin, one of your mills [Ladysmith] has already gone back on the eleven and thirteen-hour day. You may be the next one.

CHAPTER 12

The Fight for Union Recognition: 1919–1923

IN APRIL, 1917, the United States shifted its role from supplier to fighting partner in World War I, and the need for labor became greater than ever. With this security, many more workers dared to join unions. Membership in the American Federation of Labor, which had been about 2,000,000 in 1916, had increased to 3,260,000 by 1919.[1] Because the federal government needed to avoid wartime strikes, it set forth rules to mitigate labor–management confrontation, recommending that employers should recognize unions and not interfere with the workers' right to organize. It did not advocate, however, that employers deal with the unions as bona fide representatives of their employees. It merely endorsed the status quo; existing union shops were to be continued, but no attempt should be made to change non-union shops into union shops.[2]

In their continuing crusade, the International Brotherhood of Pulp, Sulphite, and Paper Mill Workers (IBPS&PMW) and the International Brotherhood of Paper Makers (IBPM) made full use of government's endorsement of the right to organize. From 1918 through 1920, the IBPM formed locals in Neenah, Kimberly, Eau Claire, Wisconsin Rapids (Grand Rapids until 1920), Merrill, Nekoosa–Port Edwards, Green Bay, and Wausau.[3]

The Western Paper Manufacturers Association, on the other hand, continued to interfere with the workers' right to organize, despite the government's pronouncements. It endeavored to keep close tabs on paper mill workers throughout the state, asking each member company to send to the association the names of its machine workers and to report when any one of them left that company, the reason for his leaving, and, if possible, his destination.[4]

A special committee of the association was appointed to study the "handling of labor," and in May, 1919, it recommended a unified strategy: all member companies paying wages below the level prescribed by the War Labor Board were to raise them to that level "promptly," and all member companies still operating the long shifts were to change to the eight-hour shifts "promptly."[5] Thus, union recognition would be the only issue on which the companies would have to confront the union, and, as one member explained, "on the question of the closed shop . . . all of the mills will stand out against . . . the union."[6]

A year later, in April, 1920, the Western Paper Manufacturers Association panicked when it learned that a unionized mill in Kalamazoo, Michigan, had agreed to raise its wages on May 1 and that unionized mills in Green Bay, Wisconsin, might grant the same increases. It sent a list of these new union wage rates to its member companies and warned the mills in the Fox and Wisconsin river valleys that if they, the unorganized mills, did not get together quickly and decide to meet these rates, they would be handing the union organizers a winning issue in their summer organizing drive. It urged its geographically isolated members to take heed.[7]

Association companies met the union threat in various ways. The Flambeau Paper Company, in Park Falls, had some leeway because it was one of the isolated mills. Nevertheless, in April, 1920, organizer George Schneider of the IBPM, whose earlier activities have been described in Chapter 11, made his way to Park Falls and called on the Flambeau employees. The Flambeau manager, Guy Waldo, was surprised to learn that, in spite of a wage increase which had just begun on April 1, Flambeau workers had joined the union. He feared that he would have to increase wages again on May 1 if other Wisconsin paper mills did so. However, the company felt that in its hideaway in rural Wisconsin it safely could defy the general move to eight-hour shifts. Its day employees worked ten hours a day, and its shift workers put in eleven and thirteen hours per shift. The manager saw no problem in continuing this schedule, since these workers were mostly farmers and, as everyone knew, farmers were accustomed to working long hours.[8]

Leaders of four of the association's companies, Frank J. Sensenbrenner of Kimberly–Clark, David C. Everest of Marathon, Judson Rosebush of Nekoosa–Edwards, and Monroe A. Wertheimer of Thilmany, paid two thousand dollars to finance a survey of the industrial relations practices of various companies, which would be conducted by the famed industrial relations economist, John R. Commons, a professor at the University of Wisconsin.[9] During the summer of 1919, seven of his graduate students traveled across the country to study labor–management practices in thirty different companies. That fall the manufacturers were invited to a Monday afternoon seminar in which Commons and his students reported on their summer findings regarding: "1. Strictly open shop; 2. closed shop; and 3.

some profit-sharing basis."[10] Nothing in the report changed the manufacturers' commitment to the "strictly open shop."

Everest and Marathon

Before that study even was begun, David C. Everest, secretary and general manager of the Marathon Paper Mills Company, had to face the International Brotherhood of Pulp, Sulphite and Paper Mill Workers. For years he had been giving advice to his fellow paper manufacturers on measures to stop unions. In March, 1918, he learned that after a union organizer had spent ten days visiting Marathon workers, about thirty-five of the company's 550 workers had joined the union. Shaken by this discovery, Everest sought advice from a Michigan paper manufacturer, Munising Paper Company, which had had a union contract for almost a year. Life under a union contract was terrible, was the response, and Everest should try to avoid it by hiring a detective from the Russell Bureau of Milwaukee who could keep track of what the union organizers were up to day-by-day. Everest replied that he had already tried agents from the Russell Bureau and now employed detectives whom he liked better.[11]

Everest proceeded to ward off the union with a dual program of succor and surveillance. Before 1914 he had installed a bonus system for the machine help and beater engineers, which he credited with keeping the union from getting a toehold in his mill. In 1918 he planned to win the workers away from the union by paying wages equal to or higher than those paid by other Wisconsin manufacturers. To this end he gathered wage records from across the state.[12] For the next twenty-two months, the plan worked. Marathon workers were paid more than any other manufacturing workers in the area, and the Marathon Paper Mills Company operated without a union, or so it seemed.

But in January, 1920, Marathon workers surprised Everest with a petition demanding an increase of eighty cents a day for shift workers and ninety cents a day for day workers. They explained that they could not manage with their present wages. Everest told them that was ridiculous and he held to his strategy. He was planning, he said, to increase wages on April 1, not as enormously as they demanded, but to rates as high or higher than those of competing companies. He promised to discuss the new rates with the employees from the different departments and he invited any worker who thought he could get more elsewhere to leave.

Actually, Everest immediately moved to smother this spark of unionism. Instead of waiting until April 1, he announced a wage increase to begin in two weeks. The new rates were, in some instances, even higher than the union schedule and included a production bonus for machine help. Everest believed that if only he had raised wages on January 1, before the petition, there never would have been a union. In addition to these high wages, the company provided free nursing service and instituted company life and disability insurance plans.[13]

Everest wrote to a fellow manufacturer that this action "may be called paternalistic," and paternalism was exactly what he was aiming for: "I would just as soon put it on a personal basis as to whether the men can depend upon me as being of greatest assistance to them or upon . . . some organizers."[14]

He was correct. This brand of paternalism laced with fear destroyed the local union of Marathon workers which the IBPS&PMW had managed to organize in February, 1920. Many workers saw no need to join the union. The local's recording secretary explained: "We had a good start but too much propaganda was the cause of our downfall, many members dropped out because they could not see the use of any union, because we had an increase in wages a short time before the local was organized. Their remark was, 'We got enough wages, why should we join the union' and all other kinds of damn fool remarks."[15] Those who did join were afraid to recruit others for fear of losing their own jobs. Eighteen months after the Marathon local had formed, when it had only seven members left, its IBPS&PMW charter was revoked. The depression that began after World War I increased the workers' fear.[16]

Not satisfied with preserving the open shop just at Marathon, Everest, with typical fervor, also organized and initially funded the Wausau Open Shop Association to keep Wausau industry on an open shop basis, especially the lumber mills, where unions had made substantial inroads during the war. Almost all of the employers in the Wausau area joined the association, which carried out both overt and covert attacks against the Wausau unions. During 1920 it paid $33,000 to the Russell detective firm, and over $1,000 to the two Wausau newspapers for the association's Saturday advertisement, "Open Shop."[17] This featured, among other things, prizewinning entries in an open shop essay contest the association sponsored, the prizes ranging from $25 for the best essay to $5 for those of lesser merit, all judged on the strength they would lend to the Saturday column. Six of the twelve winners were women. The fact that only twenty-two essays were submitted surprised and disappointed Everest, so he asked the contest chairman not to reveal this number. Everest asked each Wausau employer who had endorsed the open shop drive to contribute fifty cents per employee to pay for the association's work, which he called invaluable to the people of Wausau. The Sulphate Fibre Company and the lumber and box manufacturers made the biggest contributions. By 1922 the Wausau Open Shop Association, greatly aided by the postwar depression, had worked itself out of a job. Unions were no longer a threat in Wausau, and the association dissolved.[18]

Alexander and Nekoosa–Edwards

The International Brotherhood of Paper Makers and the International Brotherhood of Pulp, Sulphite and Paper Mill Workers found that Lewis M. Alexander, president of the Nekoosa–Edwards Paper Company and also one of the sponsors of the Commons study, proved even more difficult than David C. Everest. In February, 1919, Nekoosa–Edwards laid off forty to fifty men. The Grand Rapids *Daily Leader* offered the conventional sympathy of the day: "It will not seriously injure the laboring men in this vicinity as spring is nearly here with all sorts of new enterprises on foot."[19]

The Nekoosa–Edwards workers began a new enterprise of their own that spring, demanding company recognition and collective bargaining for their two locals, the IBPW, and the IBPS&PMW. The company responded with a bristling letter:[20]

To All Mill Employees of the Nekoosa-Edwards Paper Company:

A committee purporting to represent . . . the International Brotherhood of Paper Mill Workers and the International Brotherhood of Pulp, Sulphite and Paper Mill Workers presented itself to the Management of the Company Saturday morning at nine o'clock May 31st, 1919 asking that this company enter into dealings and contracts with such Unions. This we will not do. . . .

If employees . . . desire to take up with the Company any matters respecting their welfare they may do it in person or by representatives of their own number chosen from amongst themselves in a way justly representative . . . fully and freely open to every class. This is the very essence of . . . the democratic spirit which distinguishes AMERICANISM. The CONTRARY principle . . . insisted upon by the Union organizations . . . seeks to force Industry to deal . . . with Committees selected only by members of the Union Organizations. This is . . . AUTOCRATIC and not DEMOCRATIC.

This Company cannot consent to it.

The Company . . . positively will not recognize or deal with a LABOR UNION or OUTSIDE ORGANIZATION.

This invitation to the workers to choose "representatives of their own number . . . from amongst themselves" was similar to offers then being made by other United States companies, which hoped to divert their workers from unions to company-controlled organizations, dubbed "company unions."

For three weeks, prodded by two labor conciliators from the federal government, the company met with the "shop committee," the company's euphemism for the unions' bargaining committee, but continued to offer only a company union and collective bargaining "confined to men in our own employ."[21]

The unions would have no part of the offer and at a meeting on June 22, their members passed a resolution reading: "Whereas, Officials . . . have during the conferences and are as of this date trying to impose upon their employees a substitute organization of their own liking and dictation for the legitimate trade-unions now in existence, therefore be it, Resolved, That we, Members of Unions, . . . stand out from our work."[22] The issue thus was joined—a company union versus "legitimate" trade unions—and on June 23, 800 to 900 workers of the Nekoosa–Edwards Paper Company "stood out from their work." The strike committee posted the notice of the union's demands:[23]

NOTICE! STRIKE!

AT NEKOOSA AND PORT EDWARDS, WIS.

Paper and Pulp Makers, Mechanics and Laborers are on strike.

KEEP AWAY

Eight hour day, increase in wages, overtime pay are asked for. The right to belong to trade unions, and collective bargaining are demanded by the workers.

Post this notice and advise all workers to stay away. Don't be a STRIKE BREAKER or SCAB against your fellow workers.

By order of

Grand Rapids, Wis.   STRIKE COMMITTEE.
July 3, 1919

The strike followed a familiar scenario. Strikers hoed their gardens and went fishing. The company mailed notices to the strikers to vacate the company houses; the strikers returned the notices unopened. Five hundred strikers marched to the Nekoosa plant to collect their back wages and tried to convince the plant railroad switching crews to join their walkout, but with no success. The crews said they would need approval from the national railroad brotherhoods.[24] Edwin E. Witte and George Hambrecht, representing the Wisconsin Industrial Commission, arrived on the scene. As a result of their mediation, Alexander proposed to the strikers:[25]

1. If they seek employment within a week the company will rehire everyone at the same job and wages.

2. No one will be discriminated against for union membership but open shop will be maintained.

3. A committee of employees elected by secret ballot by men performing manual labor will be formed following resumption of work. The committee and management will take up the question of hours, labor and overtime rates and the organization of a joint committee of employees and management.

4. In case of disagreement the question will be submitted to a board of arbitration composed of one representative of the men, one of the company, and a third chosen by both.

Hambrecht said this was the best offer the mediators could arrange, but to the strikers it was the unchanged company union proposal. They voted it down, 174 to 34.[26]

The next scene was played by Nekoosa businessmen, whose efforts at mediation precipitated disaster. The company sent the businessmen a letter of explanation:[27]

We appreciate fully your efforts. . . . The proposal, submitted by you . . . was accepted by us. . . . The men instead of acting promptly on this proposal, as agreed, have referred it to Union Officers. This company has persistently stated our dealings will not be with the Union and its outside official advisors, consequently we withdraw our acceptance of the proposal.

signed,
L. M. Alexander

This was the last demonstration of gentlemanly jousting. The Fox Valley strikers of 1904 would have recognized the scenes of unrestrained combat which followed. First, the company posted the following notices:[28]

NOTICE   July 29, 1919

Former Employees Of The Nekoosa–Edwards Paper Company Wishing To Return To Work Should Make Application To The Employment Department, Or Through Their Superintendent Of Foremen At Once, As The Company Is Hiring Men And Is Desirous Of Giving Preference To Former Employees

Nekoosa–Edwards Paper Company

SPECIAL NOTICE WARNING!

This is to give *SOLEMN WARNING* that this company expects to start its mills at Port Edwards on Monday, August 18th and any attempt to carry out any threat . . . will be met by resistance . . . we have erected barriers . . . any attempt to force these barriers will be a violation of the law and criminal . . . and WE SHALL HOLD THE PROPERTY HOLDERS OF NEKOOSA and PORT EDWARDS FOR ALL DAMAGE DONE as well as the County of Wood and the State of Wisconsin

Nekoosa–Edwards Paper Company
by L. M. Alexander, President
and General Manager

Thirteen strikers returned to work. In the company's words, "the number who responded was comparatively small."[29] Nekoosa–Edwards brought in strikebreakers from Minneapolis and Chicago, some of whom "came in the early hours of the morning, under armed guard, on a train run in here without lights." Some were "squeezed into boxcars which were run into the mill." The company housed them under guard in the mill behind newly erected steel fences. The strikers managed to intercept a few of these "foreign" workers at the railroad station and tell them of the strike. Thirteen of them sued the company for $2,300 for hiring them under false pretenses, and the court awarded them return fare to Chicago. The strikers managed to halt the company's practice of hiring strikebreakers through the U.S. Employment Service in Minneapolis. "We thought there was no strike—just trouble by a few IWW's," explained a Minneapolis Employment Service official.[30]

But these efforts to stop the importation of strikebreakers were as effective as holding one's finger in the hole of a dike when the flood was on. Nekoosa–Edwards filled the company houses and the Port Edwards Hotel, vacated by the strikers, with strikebreakers. By the end of the summer it was building barracks and additions to the hotel to house the workers it continued to bring in.[31]

The company began work inside its Port Edwards mill on the announced date, August 18, while the strikers confronted armed guards outside the mill. Only "near clashes" resulted, but the conflict spread quickly through the villages of Nekoosa and Port Edwards. The president of Nekoosa's board of selectmen deputized company guards, who "paraded about the streets" dispersing groups and arresting strikers. Several citizens were able to stop this, pointing out that the deputized guards were not permanent Nekoosa residents, as required by ordinance.[32]

Strikers hurled rocks and shattered the windows of a train bringing in strikebreakers, and there were rumors that members of the "Daughters of Democracy" threw themselves across the track in front of the train. The Daughters of Democracy, a group organized by the strikers' wives, daughters, mothers, and sisters, cheered the strikers and fed them on the picket line while the men carried on the fight. The Daughters called on strikebreakers' wives in their homes and on the strikebreakers at the Port Edwards Hotel, imploring them to join the strikers. They were condemned by the company and its supporters for being "unwomanly." One evening the

Daughters demonstrated loudly at the railroad station against a Ne-koosa–Edwards Company official and his family, who were welcoming a brother on furlough from military service. The official described the women as a "howling crowd led by a distracted woman from Nekoosa. If it had been a man I would mention her name but I refrain." The women, he said, "hurled . . . such epithets as scab, yellow dog, skunk . . . at this . . . Major . . . who had faced the Boche."[33]

In a public letter the wife of a strikebreaker accused the Daughters of Democracy of frightening young wives and of using "such vile and putrid names that self-respecting women wouldn't write them down. . . . They have drawn the amazed attention of woman-hood all over the state. . . . We wonder if they are not working in the interest of Pro-Germans."[34] This letter writer's sixty-five-year-old husband was beaten by one of the strikers, who was convicted of assault and sentenced to sixty days in jail.[35] The Daughters defended themselves, stating that they hardly could be "ex-pected to sit quietly at home while our Fathers, Husbands, and Brothers are being abused by . . . Gunmen and Professional Strikebreakers brought into our community by . . . the paper company. . . . We have also called a 'scab' a 'scab'"[36]

The strikers were once again up against the financial power of the West-ern Paper Manufacturers Association and its strikebreaking fund. To aid Nekoosa–Edwards, it assessed its members 50 cents per ton of pulp and paper produced per month (the amount was 5 cents when the association organized in 1914) and then 70 cents per ton per month. In December, 1919, the association told its members that an assessment for that month of $1.60 per ton would pay off the Nekoosa-Edwards strike debt. This proved to be overly optimistic. Six months later the association asked its members for a June assessment of 20 cents per ton, part of which would pay the small amount still owed Nekoosa–Edwards for its strike losses.[37]

Meanwhile, the striking Nekoosa Local was in desperate financial straits which its President Patrick O'Brien described in one of his frequent letters pleading for help from his International union:[38]

> . . . The situation remains the same here. At the present time we have no credit whatever and no money. . . . The manager of the Farmer's Co-operative Association store who was extending us credit and whom we now owe $600.00 or more has been discharged because of this fact. . . . There is only one other store in Nekoosa where we can get credit, and, at the present time this man has shut down on us. We now owe him about $900.00. This store keeper does business on a small scale and I personally know that he cannot afford to carry his

account much longer. At the present time he has been forced to discontinue rendering us credit.

   . . . There will be the extra expense of furnishing the pickets with coal and some winter clothing.

A week later O'Brien received the following heartfelt reply from International President Burke.[39]

   . . . I am enclosing a check for $50.00. I am sending this amount for the following reason: I addressed a meeting of Bellow Falls, Local #45 last Sunday and they gave me a present of $50.00 in gold. I believe that the strikers need this money more than I do so this will explain the reason I am sending this amount.

Sporadic contributions of varying amounts—one day $25.00 from the Kaukauna Paper Makers Local, another day $300.00 from the Badger Local at Wisconsin Rapids—came to the Nekoosa Local from unions across the country. During the course of the strike fifteen Wisconsin IBPM Locals contributed a total of $7,358.51, of which $4,740.00 was contributed by the neighboring Badger IBPM Local "which assessed each member one day's pay per month for the Nekoosa–Edwards strikers for as long as the strike lasts." By November, 1920, the Nekoosa Local's fund receipts totaled $19,758.94.[40]

Early in August the company had sought a permanent injunction against picketing. The court denied the request on the grounds that it was unnecessary and in conflict with the new Wisconsin anti-picketing law.[41] In mid-September the company again sought an injunction and named 105 strikers as defendants. This time the judge brought the two parties together. For two days company officials and union attorneys (one of whom was the mayor of Wisconsin Rapids, Charles E. Briere) met with him, but then the meetings ended abruptly. The company would not agree to install the eight-hour shift for a trial period, and insisted on the right to discriminate against any man in employment, which obviously put the strike leaders in jeopardy.[42] Two days later a local union officer reported that seventy strikers had been blacklisted and that the company never would hire them again under any circumstances. Three-fourths of all the strikers, he said, had gone to Janesville to work on the construction of the Sampson Motor and Tractor Company.[43]

Desperate as the situation was, it was not the end of the strike. A year later a striker from the IBPM Nekoosa local wrote to the *Paper Makers' Journal,* reminding "the brothers throughout the paper making industry that we are still holding the picket line and will continue to hold it as long as we get the moral and financial support that we have been getting." He continued: "The pickets certainly get Alec's nanney; the company have tried everything they knew to get the pickets off . . . but . . . can't scare a good Union man." He appended a list of "the scabs working at Nekoosa!"—giving the names of twenty-eight employees and the jobs each one held.[44] The president of the IBPS&PMW local kept insisting the strike still could be won if the international's president, Burke, would send more money for picketing, and organizer Sample made a "stirring speech" at the IBPS&PMW October, 1920, convention pleading for more financial support.

All through 1921 the strike continued. Nekoosa merchants began writing to the International union for payment of bills owed them by the Nekoosa strikers. Finally, in March, 1922, Robert Rogers, Secretary of the Nekoosa local, received word that President Carey of the International Brotherhood of Paper Makers had told a local merchant to whom the picketers owed $2,700.00 to extend no more credit to them. In a panic Rogers wrote to Burke:[45]

> Now what are they going to do without credit or means to live after they have so nobly sacrificed themselves for our benefit?
> From a personal view I think it is wrong to call this strike off just at present. And would suggest that the pickets be allowed a living wage until at least May 1st.

In a tone of defeat and exasperated finality Burke replied:

> . . . I do not see how the International Unions can let these bills get any larger. I realize that the boys at Nekoosa and Port Edwards have put up a splendid fight and have made great sacrifices, but I would call your attention to the fact that you have received very liberal support from the two International Unions and we have reached a stage now where we cannot afford to put any more money into this strike. I would be perfectly willing to allow the pickets a "living wage" if we had the money to pay them. You and all the boys at Nekoosa must realize that there is a limit to the financial resources of labor unions. Our limit has been reached.

Finally, the Nekoosa local decided, on a vote of 18 to 2, that the Nekoosa–Edwards strike would end on June 21, 1922. President Alexander had escaped, without even a company union.

The company was not complacent, however, and the Western Paper Manufacturers Association continued surveillance by means of spies in the mill. In the late 1920's, reports from them indicated the union organizers were completely stymied and the skilled workers were glued to the company by the sticky bonds of bonus pay and ownership of company houses, which Nekoosa–Edwards had encouraged. One spy sensed that, as the Great Depression developed, the workers seemed to cling to the company as a benefactor who was keeping the mill running just for them.[46]

Sensenbrenner and Kimberly–Clark

In the Fox River Valley, another sponsor of the Commons study, Frank J. Sensenbrenner of Kimberly–Clark, demonstrated the use of the company union as a preemptive maneuver to fill the place of a workers' organization, so labor unions could find no opening through which to enter. To this end, Kimberly–Clark established the Mill Council Plan, similar to the company union that had just been established at International Harvester, the huge agricultural implement organization headquartered in Chicago. Under the plan there were "mill councils" in the four cities where Kimberly–Clark had one or more plants—Neenah, Appleton, Kimberly, and Niagara. Workers' representatives, elected in the plants, met monthly with an equal number of management-appointed representatives to discuss wages, worker grievances, safety problems, rents in company-owned houses, and other labor–management problems. The constitution even gave the council power to rule on such problems. Upon occasion, worker and management representatives from all Kimberly–Clark plants met at Neenah in what was called the General Council.[47]

In February, 1920, an average of 80 per cent of the workers in each Kimberly–Clark plant voted, in company-supervised elections, to adopt the Mill Council Plan. Soon after, Sensenbrenner asked David C. Everest to send him all of the wage schedules which had been filed with the Western Paper Manufacturers Association so he would be prepared for any problems which might be brought before the General Council.[48]

Two weeks later, Kimberly–Clark proposed to the General Council a general wage increase of 12.5 per cent, which the council of course voted to accept. It met again only three months later to approve an additional 7.5 per cent wage increase. By using the council as an instrument for granting wage increases, Kimberly–Clark strengthened its company union as a bulwark against the true workers' unions. The company announced to the public that the Mill Council Plan was adopted "to stop bolshevism, IWWism, Socialism, and Sovietism."[49] What it actually accomplished was to keep the IBPM and the IBPS&PMW out of Kimberly–Clark mills for twenty-two years.

Mead and Consolidated: An Employer Accepts Unions

In the midst of these defeats, the two international unions enjoyed one success of far-reaching significance. In the spring of 1919, some of the workers at the Consolidated Power and Paper Company in Wisconsin Rapids wrote to the American Federation of Labor for advice on organizing. George Schneider, vice-president of the IBPM, was sent to Wisconsin Rapids, and on Sunday, March 30, 1919, the Consolidated workers organized Badger Local 187.

George Mead, president of Consolidated, had instituted the eight-hour day in 1912, had granted the eight-hour day and re-employment to the striking Interlake workers at Appleton in 1916, and was not a member of the Western Paper Manufacturers Association. He was, nonetheless, opposed to unions. When, on the following Friday, he learned of the existence of the Badger Local, he ordered the mill to be shut down by two o'clock that afternoon; all employees were then to report to his office. There, according to his employees, he announced that "the mill would remain closed until the men disbanded their union and returned as unorganized workers." Mead explained to the Grand Rapids *Daily Leader* that he was not opposed to a union independent of the AFL, but that he would not be dictated to by outside labor organizations. Calling Mead "un-American and autocratic," the workers voted to stay out until he conceded their right to organize "as recognized by our government."[50]

These were the ingredients for a bitter fight. Schneider was joined by Henry Ohl, organizer for the Wisconsin State Federation of Labor. The company obtained an injunction from the Wood County Circuit Court ordering the workers to desist from acting concertedly to maintain pickets. A few days later, on the evening of April 9, a union mass meeting filled Grand Rapids Amusement Hall.

The next day brought a surprise. The Badger Local received a statement from Mead, quoting the endorsement by the War Labor Board of the workers' right to organize and bargain collectively, and announcing that he would follow this policy in his two Consolidated mills and would reinstate the strikers without discrimination.[51] The local glowingly reported the outcome:[52]

> We organized on March 29th last with 40 charter members. Six weeks later we had all of the members in the two mills except four, or in all 336 members. We have a working agreement signed and in force since May 1—to be in force one year. It being one of the best working agreements in the state, which was not all received through our own efforts but through the generosity of Mr. Geo. W. Mead, president of the company.

The contract that covered the Consolidated Power and Paper Company mills in Wisconsin Rapids and Biron provided a union shop, according to which all new employees were to join the union within fifteen days of employment and all permanent employees were to maintain their membership. In July an identical agreement was made with the locals of both the IBPM and the IBPS&PMW at Mead's United Paper Company at Stevens Point. The union shop provision did not last. The next contract replaced the union shop provision with an agreement that the company would "encourage new employees to become members . . . would not discriminate against union members and would give union members preference in hiring if equally competent to non-union members."[53]

Mead lived up to this agreement, making him in the 1920's a pariah among his fellow manufacturers, who now feared him as much as they feared the union organizers. Through the WPMA they had spent an enormous sum to rid their industry of labor unions, and yet union locals, abetted by Mead, remained at his plants. From this beachhead the unions could reactivate locals all over the state, costing the WPMA another struggle at a future time to again get rid of them. Mead himself reinforced these fears. Attending a WPMA meeting, he spoke in favor of unions. He spoke so eloquently, in fact, that one member complained: "[I]f he had stayed much longer, he might have won them all over to unionism."[54] On a much later occasion, Mead drove up to the picket line in front of a paper mill out on strike and talked with the strikers.[55] In 1926 Mead strongly endorsed unions in a speech given before a group of industrial and social workers:[56]

> The men of our principal plants are organized in their unions and we recognize and deal with the Union. Nothing is said about closed or open shop but in the three plants where we deal with the Unions one hundred percent of our paper makers are members of the Papermakers Union, ninety percent of our pulp workers are members of the Pulp and Sulphite Workers Union, and one hundred percent of our electrical men are members of the Electrical Union. These are all good Unions and our relationship is very harmonious and satisfactory. We have dealt with the Union for nearly eight years. We have found that the Union helps in good management and assists us in the guarantee of a square deal to every man.

His speech caused quite a stir. The IBPS&PMW printed it on the front page of their *Journal*. The Western Paper Manufacturers Association discussed the danger that it would spark union organizing and speculated that Mead would put Consolidated's common labor on a 45 cents per hour, eight-hour day. David C. Everest wrote that he was not afraid of Mead because he was himself already paying 44 cents per hour for eight-hour days, plus a bonus.[57]

As for other members of the association, the organization's informers confirmed their worst fears. One, after spending a winter's evening with a talkative and unsuspecting union organizer, sent back word that copies of Mead's infamous speech were being passed out to the workers in an organizing drive at Interlake Pulp and Paper Company in Appleton, and that Mead's mill manager himself had gone to Appleton to encourage these workers to join a union.[58]

According to other reports from this informer, Mead's contracts with the Consolidated Power and Paper Company unions were being used to show Interlake workers what they could have if they formed a union, and union posters affixed to time clocks at the Interlake mill announced that a delegation of union members from Mead's Consolidated mill would be special guests at a union rally. Even Mead's son was accused of spreading unions; according to the informer, a rousing pro-union speech given by young Mead at Stevens Point brought thirty-eight members into the IBPS&PMW local there.[59]

These reports increased the fears of WPMA members. One believed there was nothing Mead would not do to organize Interlake; another was sure he would get a union at Interlake but felt he at least should be made to fight for it, and begged the Fox Valley paper manufacturers to stop Mead before he spread unions to the rest of the valley.[60] The Interlake Company was doing its part to stave off the union, according to an informer for the WPMA. It was paying a minimum wage of 45 cents per hour, 5 cents higher than any other mill in the area; and the employment official assured Interlake workers that if any mills in the vicinity raised their wages, Interlake would top the increase by 5 cents.[61]

The informer also reported that Consolidated workers were "planted" in the Interlake mill, and described the terms of the new 1929 Consolidated union contract: one week paid vacation for ten-year employees and some form of guaranteed annual wage, all of which was very helpful in organizing. By October, 1929, the informer declared Interlake was 100 per cent organized but could not get a closed shop contract.[62]

The unions, of course, recognized Mead as a true friend. The Wisconsin State Federation of Labor invited him to speak at its 1924 convention, and in 1926 the unions helped to elect him mayor of Wisconsin Rapids. When he won overwhelmingly, receiving 2,060 votes of the 2,832 votes cast, he gave the unions credit for his victory: "All groups, except the Socialists, united in casting a splendid majority in my favor. But it was the Labor Group that nominated me and conducted the campaign to a successful issue. . . . They managed the campaign alone without help from any other group."[63]

What changed Mead from an aggressive opponent to an active friend of labor? John Lennon, a mediator sent in by the U.S. Department of Labor during the lockout, may have been a catalyst. In a discussion with Mead, Lennon pointed out that the right to organize had been granted in most large cities and that it was better to grant this right than to cause frustration which could lead to socialism and Bolshevism.[64] Mead himself explained it this way:[65]

Why I Unionized My Plant

Nine years ago this spring a union-membership campaign gave the papermakers' union a foothold in our Wisconsin Rapids plant. . . . We just about saw red at the thought of having our plant unionized. Why, indeed, should our men want to join with outsiders in organizing against us? . . . We had paid good wages and had voluntarily given the men bonuses when war prices had increased our income. Our plant was pleasant to work in. Our hours were reasonable. . . .

Other plants in Wisconsin were not unionized; if they could keep out the unions we could. So we had what union men would call a lockout. . . . With the plant idle, I myself had time to cool off and do some thinking. I had reacted on an emotional basis. Now I acted on a basis of reason.

Men who had been with us for years were out of work, their families without income. Our mill was idle, our business hazarded if we kept it idle too long. . . . The local community as a whole would suffer. . . . Had I carried this opposition further than was necessary?

The result of my three days' thinking was that I sent word to our men that they could come back if they wished, on these conditions: Any man who wanted to retain his union membership could do so, but they must not expect me or the company to recognize or deal with the union. And they all came back.

As I sat in my office that next morning and watched them come walking past my window with eager step . . ., I gained a new sense of what a man's job means to him. . . . They were just as glad to be back as I was to have them back. . . . So we started work with an "open shop." . . .

We decided . . . to keep on applying the scientific method to our union-labor relations. . . . We would see what would happen if we attempted negotiations with the union. . . .

We were fair with our workers before they were unionized, we thought. And we were generous. But we were not fair or generous in an arrangement to which they were voluntary parties; it was only in a way of our own choosing. In other words we were paternalistic. And paternalism may be generous, which is easy, but it often does not succeed in being just, which is hard.

Wage Cutting: The Depression of 1921–1922

In 1920 at its first postwar convention, President John P. Burke warned the IBPS&PMW delegates that the country was changing: the slowdown of industry and an influx of immigration would bring back the "standing army of unemployed," and the employers would seize this opportunity to attack the unions.[66] In January, 1921, the IBPM and the IBPS&PMW together held a wage conference in Toronto, Canada, coinciding with the IBPM's annual convention. Delegates to the conference were unanimously in favor of demanding a wage increase; the only question was how much.

One of the people attending the conference was an informer for the WPMA, who sent detailed minutes of each day's proceedings back to the association. He reported that Burke cautioned against rushing into a struggle over wage increases which risked disrupting the organization and losing public sympathy. He urged that they use good judgment rather than wield the big club of a strike threat. President Carey of the IBPM was more militant, pointing out that declining dividends would prompt directors and stockholders to demand wage cuts, which had to be forestalled.[67] The IBPM delegates wanted a 5 per cent increase in wages; the IBPS&PMW decided to demand a 10 per cent increase. Looking back on it in 1922, Burke considered the conference request for a wage increase "a grave mistake" because "it became more and more apparent . . . that a wage increase would be impossible to secure."[68]

Events in Wisconsin confirmed Burke's judgment, for the state's paper mill workers had to decide not what wage increase to ask for, but whether to protest wage cuts of 10 to 20 per cent. Comments by one paper manufacturer illustrate what the Wisconsin workers were up against: he speculated that with so many workers of all kinds available, it might be very effective to shut down a machine for a while and thus make the workers even more amenable to wage cuts.[69] Burke warned the Wisconsin locals that they were too weak to contest the cuts and that resistance only would give the manufacturers the excuse they needed to destroy them.[70]

His prediction came true in both Green Bay and Rhinelander that summer. When two Green Bay batteries had returned from the war in 1919, the unions turned out "to give them a welcome such as never was seen before." And yet to "have a lot of men back" also worried the unions, because the mills were working only three or four days a week.[71] Nevertheless, a year later, two paperworkers' locals in Green Bay were still setting the pace for wage increases in Wisconsin.[72] As the war boom changed to bust in the postwar years, the situation reversed.

When workers at the Northern Paper Mills Company in Green Bay approached the time clock on February 28, 1921, they found a notice stating that the next day, March 1, wages would be cut by 16.6 per cent. Stunned, they voted by a 97 per cent margin to go out on strike. Faced with this strong reaction, Northern's board of directors agreed to listen to the IBPM organizer and a committee of workers, then merely apologized for not conferring with them prior to the cut.

On March 19, 500 workers struck Northern and established an elaborate picketing system. Union members, who still were working at the John Hoberg Paper Company and the Green Bay Paper and Fibre Company, gave financial assistance to the Northern strikers. Other unions in Green Bay assessed each member ten dollars to aid the strikers.[73] The Federated Trades Council of Green Bay pledged "moral as well as financial support."[74] Several thousand citizens, led by the city band, marched to show their support of the strikers.

When Northern began to look for new employees it faced union interference, as the Superintendent explained:

> We had a bunch of men coming in from the Miami Valley, but the union here has sent reports out all over the country saying that people are being killed, etc. so these men got "cold feet" and backed out after their tickets were all bought.

However, within two weeks the company managed to hire two hundred new workers. Although they were able to operate two machines, they also caused problems. The Superintendent complained:

> We have more men coming in every day, but they really are not the kind of men we would choose to hire in normal times and of course, the union has several men coming in here to do a lot of under-handed work posing as paper makers who are all strangers to us.

> We have about 30 girls now working, but I think a lot of them would like to do other things besides working, so I presume it will be another cleaning out.

The Marathon Paper Company sent enough sulphite to keep Northern's machines running, but evidently Northern was asking its fellow paper manufacturers for more than pulp, as evidenced in this letter from Marathon Paper Company President, D. C. Everest.

> . . . I have taken up the matter of your membership in the Association and I found that the by-laws provided that we could not accept new members where the mills were on strike, but I have telelphoned some of the other men and while under the by-laws we cannot obligate the members for any financial assistance, still we want to assure you of

the moral support and if there is anything that anyone can do . . .
telephone Frank Sensenbrenner [Kimberly–Clark Company] or C. A.
Babcock [Kimberly–Clark Company] at Neenah."

As conflict developed between strikebreakers and strikers, the sheriff
appointed some strikers as "special deputies" in the hope that they could
keep their fellow men from resorting to violence. The chief of police
threatened to call in the National Guard. The company obtained an injunction from the circuit court prohibiting the use of insulting epithets
such as "scab" and "rat," the distribution of handbills, the spreading of
glass or nails on approaches to the plant, and assaults on company employees. It further specified that there be no more than "one picket within
a space of one hundred feet" on any approach to the plant. In the eyes of
the Superintendent the effect of this injunction, thanks to the Sheriff, was
nil:

 . . . . So far this [injunction] has had the same effect as pouring water
 on a duck's back. The sheriff here is in with the strikers and he has
 gone as far as to tell the strikers that they can tear up their injunctions
 for all they amount to.

Interestingly, in the eyes of the judge who has issued the injunction the
situation seemed to be very different. True, the strikers maintained their
picket line under the injunction, but after 45 arrests were made and several
$50 fines were levied, the judge modified his order.[75]

The John Hoberg Paper Company and the Green Bay Paper and Fibre
Company announced that a 16.6 per cent wage cut would begin May 1.
Northern's superintendent feared the militancy of the Paper and Fibre
workers, who, he wrote, were "very strong for a strike. They have been
100% organized for a long time and would not permit anyone to work in
the mill unless they carried a card . . . it has been strictly a closed shop."[76]
He believed that if the Paper and Fibre and the Hoberg workers did strike,
Northern could not keep running. On May 1, 600 workers struck both
plants.

At the end of May there were serious confrontations between strikers
and strikebreakers at Northern, in which two strikers suffered serious
knife wounds, and a picketeer was knocked down and injured by a company fireman who drove his car through the picket line. When a crowd
gathered outside of the mill, the company took workers from inside the
mill down the Fox River by boat, to an area protected by the police. When
the governor, John Blaine, was asked to send state troops to guard the
mill, he refused, saying that more deputies should be hired. The mayor and

district attorney arranged a meeting of strikers from all three mills and presented a proposal from Northern:[77]

    a. No person in the employ of the mill on Saturday, May 28, will be dismissed to make room for a striker.

    b. Strikers will be rehired without prejudice as fast as work can be provided in view of the present condition of the paper market.

    c. Judication of ill-will, on or off company property toward those who did not strike will be cause for dismissal.

    d. The 16-2/3% wage cut will be in effect.

    e. The present existing grievance committee . . . shall exist and operate . . . until January 1, 1922, and shall pay the same care and attention to grievances of employees, whether union or non-union.

The company's retention of strikebreakers and the slowness of the paper market meant it would be several months before all of the strikers would be called back. The assembled strikers objected to this provision, but the IBPS&PMW organizer and the strike committee already had agreed to the proposal, and urged the strikers to accept it. Finally, on a standing vote, the proposal passed; only three strikers stood against it.[78]

It was July 11 before the Green Bay Paper and Fibre Company mill reopened. The company had mailed to all of its employees a form, together with a stamped, return envelope, reading: "I desire to resume work in my position as of April 30, 1921, wages and working conditions to be as per your schedule of July 1, 1921." Anyone wanting to return to work had to sign and return this admission of defeat. The company reported, nonetheless, that the men returned to work gladly on that first morning and were contented despite their vain attempt to avoid the wage cut.[79]

Although this strike drove unions from the Green Bay paper mills, it did not destroy them completely. Oscar Staniske, who had been a leader of the IBPM local at Hoberg when it had 500 members, now kept its spirit alive when it had a handful. During the strike some of the sympathetic Green Bay merchants had extended credit to the strikers, most of whom were too financially hurt by the long strike to repay these debts afterward, but the diminished union helped repay the money by getting contributions from the Green Bay Federated Trades Council and from individual Green Bay unions. Staniske himself was promoted to superintendent of what became the Hoberg Paper and Fibre Company, but he continued to have the friendship and respect of his union. When he died in 1928 the Green Bay Federated Trades Council eulogized him, chiefly for his previous work as an IBPM delegate to the council.[80]

The defeat of the unions in Green Bay made it easier for other companies to cut wages. When Everest reduced wages at the Marathon Paper Mills Company by up to 20 per cent that summer, Sensenbrenner of Kimberly–Clark sent his congratulations, assuring Everest that the cut would cause no trouble whatsoever because the defeat of the Green Bay strikers had shown that it was futile to protest.[81] That spring, union workers at the Rhinelander Paper Company also learned, as Burke had warned, that they were too weak to protest.

The Rhinelander company, which had acceded to the IBPM demand for a three-shift system in 1912, joined the Western Paper Manufacturers Association when it was formed in 1914, but dropped its membership two years later. In 1919 the IBPM local reported that it had a good contract with Rhinelander: "We worked in connection with . . . the Pulp Sulphite Workers' Union and they also were given an increase of about five cents an hour and an eight-hour day for all day workers with time and a half for overtime after nine hours' work." The union admitted, however, that it had one worry:[82]

> The Company would not grant the Union shop agreement, which we asked for. . . . This is not a signed agreement, but we suppose it amounts to practically as much. This company has been dealing with us that way in the past and has been fair with us. Mr. Hawke [Hanke] has taken Mr. Erbel's place as manager and we dealt mostly with the former. He said he would always meet us half-way and that he wanted us to do the same with him.

Hanke was the company's treasurer as well as manager. His promise to always meet the union halfway lasted for about one year. In the spring of 1920 he wrote to Everest: "We expect a demand from the union here sometime next month, but we are going to stop recognizing the union and will only deal with our employees hereafter." He added: "Our former manager . . . always dealt with the unions, but the writer believes they have gone too far and we cannot continue to deal with them in the future. It may mean trouble for us."[83]

The 1921 depression gave manager Hanke his chance to get rid of the union. The company shut down for six weeks for lack of orders, then resumed with only two of its four machines. In April it cut wages 20 per cent. Eighty-five per cent of the members of the IBPS&PMW local voted to strike, but when the presidents of both internationals counseled against a strike, the two locals sought a meeting with the manager. For several months the company had been firing union workers for "inefficiency" and "agitation within the mill." Now, on April 6, instead of meeting with the locals, the manager locked out all of the workers. Company spokesmen visited each employee and offered him a job provided he would resign from the union.

The lockout was three weeks old when the company, through a newspaper notice, invited all employees to gather on the company's lawn on Monday morning to hear the president and Hanke discuss plans for a company union. That morning, the president and the manager confronted a union picket line, which separated those who had come to hear the speakers into small "committees." The company officials decided not to speak.[84] Some of the union members, financially drained by the layoffs and the lockout, felt compelled to quit the union and return to work. On May 9 the mill opened with these workers and with strikebreakers from outside. Those who refused to leave the union set up a picket line.[85]

On a day late in June, a large crowd attacked the strikebreakers. In Everest's view, the crowd was made up of lumberjacks, members of the Industrial Workers of the World (IWW), and hoboes, brought in by a few radicals to keep the Rhinelander Paper Company employees from going to work. A leader of an earlier timber workers' strike and several others were jailed, Everest said.[86]

In August the strike seemed to be settled, but this proved not to be true, and the strikers headed into a terrible winter. The internationals sent aid almost weekly, and the locals staged fund-raising dances and bake sales. The assistance was not enough to support the strikers. Other jobs were hard to obtain because the Rhinelander Paper Company discouraged the area's sawmills from hiring the strikers. Most of those who did find jobs as lumberjacks could not keep up with the experienced men and were let go. Eventually, John Burke of the IBPS&PMW sent regrets instead of funds, because locals across the country were suffering from layoffs and strikes.

In January, 1922, the company cut wages further and lengthened the hours. For a moment the strikers hoped that those working in the plant would join the strikers, but they did not. In April, 1922, Rhinelander elected a Socialist mayor and Socialist city council. The new mayor created more public works jobs to employ the strikers. This was not enough. Gradually the strikers withdrew from the union and returned to the mill or went to other jobs. By August, 1923, neither the IBPS&PMW nor the IBPM local had a single member and the Rhinelander Paper Company was "open shop."[87]

The internationals had partly discouraged the strikes in Wisconsin because in that summer of 1921 over 12,000 members of these two unions had gone on strike against wage cuts in paper mills in the eastern United States and Canada,[88] straining the internationals' resources to the limit.

Nevertheless, the Wisconsin paper manufacturers were worried. No manufacturer wanted to stand alone in cutting wages, and so they sought protection in concerted action through the Western Paper Manufacturers Association. To make co-ordinated wage cuts possible, the association drew up a "Comparative Wage Schedule," which recorded the wages paid during February, 1923, in sixty-six paper and pulp mills in Wisconsin. The schedule listed the wages being paid in a total of 146 different jobs and nineteen departments within the mills.[89]

The Flambeau Paper Company used a technique which, it expected, would make it more difficult for its workers to act against wage cuts: it encouraged them to own their own homes. To the index card which it kept on each employee for income tax purposes, it added whether the employee owned or rented his home. When Flambeau laid off workers, it did everything it could to protect those workers who were homeowners, hoping that this favoritism would lead other workers to buy homes and thus bring the company closer to its ultimate goal of having all of its workers tied down with home ownership.[90]

The WPMA was particularly interested in the fate of George Mead and the locals at his mills during this retrenchment. The Consolidated Power and Paper Company made two wage cuts in 1921: for common labor, from 56 cents to 40 cents per hour; for skilled labor, from 75 cents to 65 cents per hour.[91] Early in 1922 Consolidated cut common labor back to 32 cents per hour, which was lower than the wage being paid by any of the WPMA mills at that time. Ira L. Beck, administrator of the WPMA, hoped this would discredit the Consolidated unions. Nevertheless, the workers accepted Mead's word that there were only two choices, wage cuts or mill closings.[92] Although Mead cut wages, he continued to recognize the unions and, in fact, maintained compulsory union membership.

By January, 1922, there had been so many wage cuts in the Wisconsin paper industry that the WPMA itself "frankly stated" that wages should not be reduced further, as it was almost impossible for common labor to live on less than $3.15 per day.[93] The truth of this statement was poignantly expressed by a Marathon employee who penciled the following letter to Everest:[94]

> I would just like to tell you a few word the talk is about cutting wages the cut would be all right if the eating stuff would come down all the grocery are high the only thing that is down in eating is egges Because that the farmer has got to sell he get noting for it and of course sugar is low, But we can't live on suger . . . I pay $20.00 month Rent and my Grocery Bill was $20.00 but Paid that make $40.00 my check was $43.00 last payday so could not pay for my Butcher Bill or

noting the $3.00 I use for car far I like to smoke But all I could spend
is 10¢ for 1 package of tobaco I got children going to school and you
got to see that they are clean and the House I live in is only a shak and
I have to work Sunday to fall even and you know Mr. Everest if you
had to live like us Poor man I think you be up the spout the first day
there is no more joy for a poor man . . . Don't cut us 8 Hour Men to
much all this world owes us a living But we are not geting a living and
I hope there will be no Strike For I am no Strike Man For I like to see
my Family live.

Good by
Mr. Everest

The WPMA's compassion was short-lived. By the first of March the
association had a plan for further cuts: "Kimberly–Clark Company expects to meet their men at a conference before the 15th of the month to
take up the question of a wage reduction. The balance of the mills in the
valley . . . expect to follow . . . and make their cut immediately after
Kimberly–Clark have made theirs."[95]

It was expected that the workers at Kimberly–Clark would set a pattern
of accepting additional wage cuts without protest, because the company
union there had proved to be the perfect tool for keeping workers under
management's thumb. For example, during the council's first year,
carpenters at the Niagara mill had submitted to the council a request that
their wages be raised to the level of carpenters at the company's mill at
Kimberly. A special council meeting had been called for December 28,
1920, to consider this request. The company president himself had arrived
to report that the directors had granted the request unanimously. The
carpenters expressed their appreciation. The president went on to an-
nounce that because all construction work was completed, it was necessary to lay off the entire construction crew.[96]

At a council meeting four months later, Kimberly–Clark made a motion for a 20 per cent wage cut. The Mill Council Plan constitution called
for block voting, and in the case of a tie vote, a motion was considered
defeated. If, as would have been expected, a majority of worker representatives had voted against the wage cut and a majority of management delegates had voted for it, the cut would have been defeated by a tie vote of 1
to 1. Instead, the motion passed by a vote of 2 to 0. Why?

During discussion of the proposal, an employee representative asked if
there was a room available in which the worker representatives could discuss the motion privately. A vice-president had replied that there was such
a room, but added that the company must have a poor case if it could not
convince the representatives in an open meeting. The intimidated workers

did not withdraw to a private room. The vice-president then asked each representative to express himself on management's proposed wage cut. The worker representatives admitted the need for a 7 to 10 per cent, but not a 20 per cent, cut. Nevertheless, in a secret ballot eight of the worker delegates voted in favor of the 20 per cent cut, and seven voted against it.[97] After the vote Sensenbrenner phoned all of the paper mills in the state to advise them of the result.[98]

The depression deepened. Three months later Kimberly–Clark sought approval for a second wage cut of 10 to 18 per cent; the unskilled workers were to receive the largest cut. Time-and-a-half for weekday overtime and for regular operating time on Sunday was to be eliminated. On this occasion management violated the spirit, if not the letter, of the Mill Council Plan constitution by not convening the General Council at Neenah. Instead, it presented the proposal to each of the four local mill councils.

When the proposed cuts were put before the Niagara Mill Council, worker representatives, in a spirited discussion, put forth the following arguments: (1) the cost of living had not come down; (2) common labor was least able to bear the brunt of the cuts; (3) they ought to get something extra for Sunday work; and (4) "My constituents have instructed me to not vote for the reduction though personally I can see the justice of the proposition."

A company vice-president stated, just before the vote: "If the vote rejects the cut, we will be forced to employ a new crew of men at a reduced wage or shut the plant down until we have different business conditions. It is a question of voting for the proposed wage reduction in order to keep men in work as full as possible time or if the cut is rejected it means 500 to 600 men will be out of work."[99] The worker representatives voted unanimously to empower the company to cut wages.

It is therefore not surprising that in March, 1922, the Western Paper Manufacturers Association relied on Kimberly–Clark to lead the manufacturers safely through yet a third wage cut. In council meetings at its mills, Kimberly–Clark pushed through a four cents per hour wage reduction. At one point the outcome seemed in doubt: the Neenah–Appleton Council employee representatives first voted 13–0 against the cut; management voted unanimously for the cut. The employees then requested arbitration, which management refused, pointing out that the Kimberly and Niagara Mill Councils already had voted to accept the reduction. The employees' representatives then voted to accept the cut,[100] which went into effect on April 1, 1922. The Neenah merchants issued a supportive statement:[101]

Resolution

We recognized that harmony between manufacturers and employees has existed for the past fifteen years or more.

Conditions which have developed need the hearty co-operation of all merchants, and as such, we will do our utmost to continue the harmonious relations which have existed.

Therefore, we promise to still further reduce prices to meet these changed conditions even to the extent of sacrificing our profits.

However, some of the companies of the WPMA were not as safe as they had anticipated in letting Kimberly–Clark take the lead, perhaps because their workers had not been conditioned by a company union. When wage reductions were made at the Gilbert, Neenah, Lakeview (formerly Lakeside), and Island Company mills in Neenah and Menasha, and at the sulphite mill of the Thilmany Pulp and Paper Company in Kaukauna, workers spontaneously walked out. Only the Gilbert Paper Company and the Thilmany sulphite mill were forced to close, however.[102]

The WPMA expected that these companies would stand united against the strikers, but after a few days the Gilbert Paper Company broke ranks and rescinded the wage cut. The company then entered a claim of $300 against the WPMA strike fund to cover its losses due to the strike. Lewis M. Alexander, still president of the Nekoosa–Edwards Paper Company, presented his view of the claim: "In the case of Gilbert Paper Company I understand they settled their own difficulties by conceding to the strikers just what they wanted and now they ask us to pay a bill for doing the very opposite thing of what we are supposed to have been associated together to do."[103]

An unexpected strike at the Thilmany mill, where 400 workers walked out, caused one union member to exclaim, "Hold 'er, Newt, she is a rearin'."[104] Two years earlier, 90 per cent of the Thilmany workers had been union members, but in April of 1922 they just walked out, unorganized and leaderless. When they asked the Kaukauna Trades and Labor Council for help, it sent for George Schneider, vice-president of the IBPM. He called the strikers to the auditorium and "gave them a talk which they should never forget. . . . About three hundred of those 'deviators' put their John Henry to an application blank."[105]

Consequently, the walkout became a union strike. Pickets surrounded the mill. At a meeting a few days later, the strikers voted to accept the wage cut of 4 cents per hour, with the understanding that if the company made any money during the remainder of the year it would pay its employees a refund retroactive to April 1. They returned to work. Although Thilmany did not make the restoration retroactive, it raised wages on August 16 to an amount at least as high as 4 cents an hour for all employees whose wages had been cut. This action pressured other Fox River Valley mills to do the same and Kimberly–Clark joined Thilmany in the wage increase.[106]

Thus, the great expansion of paper mill unions that started during World War I and led to prolonged strikes at Nekoosa, Wisconsin Rapids, and Green Bay had been snuffed out by 1923. The ensuing prosperity of the 1920's effectively ended unionism for the rest of the decade.

CHAPTER 13

The 1930's: Unionization of Wisconsin's Paper Industry

A S THE DEPRESSION deepened after 1929, successive wage cuts at first increased the paper mill workers' interest in the potential of unions to protect them. But by 1932 massive unemployment and the continued activities of labor spies had frightened them away from union activity.

Spies

In 1922 Ira Beck had pointed out the important role spies had played in combating the unions in the Fox River Valley and in the Marinette–Menominee strike. It had been expensive, he admitted. For the four spies the Association had used in the Fox River Valley, wages and expenses had averaged about $30.00 per day. The spies in the Marinette strike had cost $1,500.00. However, the WPMA considered this money well spent, and during the 1920's and early 1930's it continued to finance a very active network of spies. A constant stream of reports come into the Association from spies No. 15, No. 27, No. 29, No. 32, No. 33, No. 151, and B–431. These reports detailed every phase of union activity both among the workers in Wisconsin paper mills and at the national union conferences held in the East. For example, verbatim reports were sent back to Wisconsin employers from the annual wage conferences held jointly by the International Brotherhood of Paper Makers (IBPM) and the International Brotherhood of Pulp, Sulphite, and Paper Mill Workers (IBPS&PMW). At the 1921 wage conference, informer B–431 reported that President Jeremiah Carey advised the workers to "be on the alert" for strangers in the locals. The spies were, as a rule, the smartest men in the locals, Carey said, and well enough educated to accomplish their purpose, which was to destroy the unions.[1]

The following is an account of how the spies operated to discourage local union organizing. In 1931 John Alexander (the son of Lewis M.), who had become the head of Nekoosa–Edwards Paper Company, sent a frantic appeal to the WPMA: according to No. 15, two organizers from the Brotherhood of Pulp, Sulphite, and Paper Mill Workers were coming to organize in his mill. Alexander feared them because he had had to lay off workers and would have to cut wages just when George Mead was renewing contracts with his unions and probably not reducing wages at Consolidated Power and Paper. Mead's example would give the organizers a compelling argument with which to win Nekoosa–Edwards employees. Alexander requested from the WPMA even more strenuous surveillance of his workers and for immediate reports on the slightest signs of union activity, so he could act quickly to stop any union move into his mill.[2]

On Christmas Eve, Alexander obtained a printed form letter which, he surmised, had been sent by a union organizer to the workers at Nekoosa–Edwards. He sent the letter to the administrator of the WPMA that same night, with a request that the association's informer, who was already in the Nekoosa–Edwards mills, check on it. He suggested his company should "get the goods on one or two men in our employ who are agitators and attempting to organize the men and *fire* these men quickly. . . . this would . . . nip this thing in the bud. . . . P.S. Merry Xmas & Happy New Year."[3] Alexander did not entrust either of the above letters to a secretary, but wrote them himself in longhand. The spy responded on January 11 with a letter that included the following passages:[4]

Appleton, Wis., Jan. 11th., 1932.

Dear Sir;—
I have carefully investigated the Port Edwards and Nekoosa matter regarding letters sent to employes of the Nekoosa–Edwards Paper Company by Matthew J. Burns, President of the International Brotherhood of Paper Makers. . . .
The letters that were sent to the Papermakers were all sent to former ex-members . . . There is a machine tender employed in the Port Edwards mill who is an active member of the International Brotherhood of Paper Makers and who is a paid up member at Headquarters. . . .
I will secure this machine tenders name but have to work very carefully, and it may take a little time. . . . In the meantime I am checking up on all possible members and as soon as they sign up, we will be able to trace them. Also any prominent agitators in these two mills.

The continued effect of the Great Depression was not only to reduce the workers' interest in unions, but also to reduce the financial resources of the members of the WPMA, which began to lose interest in paying spies and in continuing the organization itself. Consequently, WPMA folded in 1932.

In early 1932, when union activity was at a low ebb, No. 15 needed to create an organizing drive in order to maintain the WPMA's committment to his activities. He was not then on the IBPS&PMW payroll, but with great effort he persuaded a very skeptical President John Burke that he could organize a local at the Marathon Paper Mills Company by April 1. Reluctantly, Burke agreed to pay him for a limited attempt. This spy, at the same time, was warning the Western Paper Manufacturers Association that an all-out organizing drive was having great success among Marathon workers. Suddenly, in early April, the WPMA disbanded and Burke called off the Marathon organizing drive.[5] Since he was now in need of a new employer, this informer sent a report directly to Everest.[6]

> At dinner, at the Eagles lunch room, in Wausau, Wis. on Friday, April 1st, Archie Hook, Jacob Stephan and Fred Gehring [president of the Wausau Central Body], decided not to hold the meeting at Eagles Hall tonight. . . . At nine P. M. they left Eagles Hall and went to Gehrings home. . . .
>
> The conference at Gehrings home was also attended by Otto Schmidt, who is a member of the timber workers union and is the active man in the Brokaw mill and by Charles Jaeger, tinsmith, employed in the Rothschild mill, who is the active man employed in the Rothschild mill. . . .
>
> Jaeger gave the organizers, the names of forty employees of the Rothschild mill, that would organize and keep their mouths shut. . . .
>
> Do not discharge this man Jaeger at present, as he can do no more harm now and it would destroy a valuable source of information and create suspicion. Also do not have Schmidt discharged for the present.
>
> The organizers now have a certified list of names amounting to 240 names of employees in the Rothschild, Brokaw and Biron mills. Archie Hook also has the names of all of the machine tenders in the Rothschild, Brokaw and Biron mills and he is also going to write to them through headquarters. . . .
>
> They want to make certain that there are no informers in the members that they are writing up. They trust nobody, that is another reason that they are making a canvass of the employees at their homes.
>
> I am securing a list of names of the organized employees of the Rothschild, Brokaw and Mosinee employees and will mail them as soon as I have the list completed. . . .
>
> Respectively

Everest evidently did not take the bait, because a year later No. 15 named Everest as one of the defendants in his claim against the Western Paper Manufacturers Association.

This system of labor spying appears to have been in direct violation of a Wisconsin law, passed in 1919, requiring detective agencies to register with local fire and police commissions and with the secretary of state. In 1925 legislation was passed that required individual licensing of operatives, thus making it easy for unions to identify labor spies.[7] The Western Paper Manufacturers Association did not comply.

When the WPMA disbanded, several of its spies filed claims for unpaid wages against the Association in the Outagamie and Wood County Courts. No. 15's lawyer wrote to Everest:[8]

Mr. Harry Stutz . . . has consulted me relative to . . . an affidavit covering his activities . . . from 1917 to May, 1932. . . . Said affidavit is . . . to be the basis of a publication concerning the activities of the Western Manufacturers Association and its members . . . I write to you and request confirmation or denial of the following purported facts: . . .

6. Was Harry Stutz, to your knowledge prior to May 10, 1932 an operative of the Western Manufacturers Association known as Operator #15?

7. Was Harry Stutz as Operator #15 active during the Spring of 1932, at Wausau, Wisconsin and relative to the organization of paper makers and pulp makers union in mills of the Wausau territory.?

In the case in the Outagamie Court, Charles H. Sample, Plaintiff vs. Western Manufacturers Association, D. C. Everest, J. B. Nash and John Alexander, Defendants, the court said that a "discovery is necessary" and:[9]

That the points on which such discovery is desired are as follows: . . .

4. The relationship of I. L. Beck to the said Association, . . . and the principle duties of the said I. L. Beck . . .

5. The relationship of Harry Stutz to the said Association.

These actions which threatened exposure of the WPMA's covert activities gave the officers a strong incentive to settle out of court, which they did.[10]

In order to file their claims these informers had to reveal their identities. For example, Charles Sample had been such a strong union leader in the 1916 strike at Interlake that he was hired as an organizer by the IBPS&PMW. The International considered him to be such an effective organizer that when a bona fide organizer for the International failed to reorganize Interlake in 1928, the union unwittingly sent this organizer–spy to replace him.[11]

The Roosevelt Era

After Franklin Roosevelt's election as President in 1932, the federal government began to protect workers from their employers' unfair labor practices. In 1933 Congress passed the National Industrial Recovery Act, whose famous Section 7(a) read:

> (1) employees shall have the right to organize and bargain collectively through representatives of their own choosing, and shall be free from the interference, restraint, or coercion of employers of labor . . . ;

> (2) that no employee and no one seeking employment shall be required as a condition of employment to join any company union or to refrain from joining, organizing, or assisting a labor organization of his own choosing; and

> (3) that employers shall comply with the maximum hours of labor, minimum rates of pay, and other conditions of employment, approved or prescribed by the President.

On this foundation a strong and enduring U.S. labor movement was constructed.

At the time of this turning point in industry–labor relations, the IBPM and the IBPS&PMW had contracts with only two Wisconsin paper companies: George Mead's Consolidated Power and Paper Company in Wisconsin Rapids, and the Hoberg Paper and Fibre Company in Green Bay. As Mead had done, J. M. Conway, the president and manager of Hoberg, set himself apart from the anti-union philosophy exemplified by the WPMA. When delegates from the locals of the two brotherhoods presented their credentials to the Green Bay Federated Trades Council in January, 1931, one commented on the difficult labor situation there, saying that organizing "was slow and required a great deal of faith, or at least enough to move a mountain."[12] On the other hand, the delegate brought a bit of good news: when some of the workers at the Hoberg Paper and Fibre Company had asked Conway if they were allowed to join unions, he had answered that they were welcome to join any church, fraternal organization, or union without interference or danger of losing their jobs.[13]

It was not surprising that at the council's installation of new officers the following month, Conway was an honored guest. In a short talk, he said that industry needed a co-operative effort with labor; in response, the council's treasurer, a Hoberg employee, stated he was proud to be an employee of such a fair and courteous employer as Mr. Conway.[14]

Conway was true to his word. At that council meeting in February the IBPS&PMW organizer, Jacob Stephan, reported that the local was taking in many new members. The WPMA had the company under surveillance, for in May a spy reported: "I have spent the past week in Green Bay, Wis. with Organizer Stephan and Krueger. The Hoberg Mill is strongly organized and is 100%. The work they are now undertaking in Green Bay is the organization of the Northern Mill and the Fort Howard Mill of Green

Bay."[15] In August of 1931 both internationals signed contracts with the Hoberg Paper and Fibre Company. Matthew Burns, president of IBPM, came to Green Bay to sign, and when organizer Stephan signed for the IBPS&PMW, he thanked Conway for his help in obtaining the contracts.[16]

A Mill Council Holds Off Unionism at Kimberly–Clark

By contrast, the Kimberly–Clark Corporation tried, by an effort to resurrect its Mill Council Plan, to forestall organizing among its employees under Section 7(a) of the new labor law. After 1925, Kimberly–Clark had altered the plan so the councils had ceased to have even the appearance of deciding wage policy; they functioned only as a forum for hearing workers' grievances and promoting management's policies. During the Depression years of 1930–1932, when its workers were docile and grateful for any job, Kimberly–Clark had allowed the councils to fade away. That era was ending by 1933, as Frank Shattuck, treasurer of the company, stated to the Neenah Lakeview Mill Council: "There must be more democratic control of industry. This purpose is written into the law because it is the spirit of the times we are living in. . . . Most of us got pretty well fed up on the old Council Plan. Today employee representatives have a definite legal status under the law and they know it."[17]

To comply with the new federal law, the old Mill Council Plan had to be revised to eliminate obvious company domination. The company's new plan, "Council Plan of Employees and Management Kimberly–Clark Corporation," gave the General Council complete control over wages and stipulated binding arbitration when labor and management delegates could not agree on wages. Kimberly–Clark workers, however, had no voice in drawing up the new plan. They were given no opportunity to work as a group to pick their council delegates, and the plan did not provide for a meeting attended exclusively by workers, where they could nominate and elect delegates. Instead, each worker wrote on a secret ballot his choice from a list posted on the shop wall of all those who were eligible. The workers then selected their local council delegates by secret ballot from among these nominees. These delegates then elected from among themselves the employee delegates to the General Council.

Employee delegates could not be council chairpersons; the plan designated each local mill manager as chair of the local councils and the company president as chair of the General Council. The plan also stipulated the company must pay the lost wages and expenses of the employee delegates. Unlike a true labor union, this company organization gave the workers' delegates no access to comparative information on wages and hours and no help from experienced bargainers. There was, of course, no specified procedure for calling a strike or establishing a strike fund.[18]

Frank J. Sensenbrenner, president of Kimberly–Clark, sent a letter to each of the former councils asking it to send delegates to consider the new plan. Nineteen delegates met in Neenah on June 12, 1933. Sensenbrenner assured them that it was Kimberly–Clark's policy not to discriminate against any man or woman because of union membership. However, he warned, no outside organization could secure for Kimberly–Clark employees what management itself could provide for them. It was decided to put the new plan to a vote of all of the company's workers.[19] The plan was approved by secret ballot in each Kimberly–Clark mill.

When the new councils met, the workers stated their complaints and wage demands more vociferously than they had in the past, but management responded with the same rebuttals and threats. For example, a worker delegate from Kimberly–Clark's Niagara Falls (New York) mill complained at the 1936 General Council meeting that other factories in the area were paying higher wages to "girls" than was Kimberly–Clark. She predicted that Kimberly–Clark's "girls" would find jobs elsewhere if they were not given a substantial raise. Vice-President Ernst Mahler asked her if this was the attitude of a majority of the "girls." When she assured him that it was, he responded that on that basis Kimberly–Clark could proceed with its plan to replace girls with boys.[20] Some of the women already had been replaced by boys at the Niagara Falls mill because there were many unemployed youths who could be hired at rates less than those paid to men. These Niagara Falls women soon were caught up in the aggressive spirit which resulted from the victory of the United Auto Workers against General Motors in the sitdown strikes of January and February, 1937.

In March the Steel Workers Organizing Committee, affiliated with the Congress of Industrial Organizations (CIO), signed its first contract with the United States Steel Corporation, calling for a huge (at that time) wage increase of 10 cents per hour. By contrast, the Kimberly–Clark General Mill Council meeting in the same month was a desultory affair that ended with a discussion of vacation plans. This quiet atmosphere was illusory: during that month the CIO began to organize women in the Niagara Falls mill, and the employees came near to striking. A shaken Kimberly–Clark faced the fact that its Niagara Falls wages were low for the area, and that a raise of 10 cents per hour was imperative. The largest increase which Kimberly–Clark ever had given was 6 cents an hour, in 1920, and now it wanted to avoid giving a 10 cent increase in its other mills.

To this end, in each mill a management committee called in the workers, three or four at a time, day and night, for four or five days. These meetings brought "good understanding," Frank Shattuck recounted, except on the only issue which mattered, wages. The employees would not agree to a 10 cent raise for Niagara Falls alone. On the contrary, when the company called a special meeting of the General Mill Council for April 1, a wage committee of employee delegates from the Fox Valley mills placed on the agenda a demand for an increase of 15 cents per hour.

At the council meeting, Sensenbrenner described an earlier depression and warned of future trouble:[21]

> The panic of 1893 was precipitated by conditions pretty much like the present. . . . There were strikes . . . without number. Things got so bad that they burned up entire train loads of freight. Kimberly–Clark Company itself had four cars . . . of paper . . . burned up. . . . Some of you remember . . . the haymarket riots, bomb throwing . . . . Grover Cleveland . . . ordered out the regular army with instructions to shoot to kill if there was any interference with the movement of government property. Not until then was was there any . . . check to the lawlessness that was rampant in the entire nation. . . . Now we are drifting in that panic direction today . . . ladies and gentlemen, keep your heads cool and weigh carefully your statements and your actions.

The employee delegates were in no mood to heed his admonition. A Kimberly mill employee delegate started off: "As you know we have been holding meetings. We recognize what is going on around us. . . . The time is here!" Other employee delegates joined in: "Let's take last Sunday's *Milwaukee Journal*. It's chocked full of progress. . . . But the employees can't see any progress . . . on their checks. . . . We feel there is something haywire someplace and . . . we are going to find out what it is all about."

Sensenbrenner asked the delegates how they had arrived at the 15 cent increase they were demanding. They answered that the American Federation of Labor unions were requesting that amount, and pointed out that "a stronger union," the CIO, would get the increase by violence if the AFL failed. Shattuck warned them about the CIO: "Nothing that we might do under our present social order could be satisfying to an out and out conscientious downright Communist, that seems to be associated with the CIO movement. . . . Their whole strategy is to keep turmoil and confusion boiling to the point where the whole social order can be turned bottoms up."[22]

Management defeated the employees' 15 cent proposal with a unanimous "no" vote and then rejected employee compromises of 12 cents and

10 cents. In contrast to the events of the 1920's, employee delegates voted unanimously against the company offers of 7, 8, and then 9 cents. When the difference narrowed to 10 cents versus 9 cents, Kimberly–Clark's Vice-President Mahler brought out what had been the ultimate weapon in the 1920's: "There is only one practical way out of this and that is that we post notice tomorrow morning that we are granting a 9 cent wage increase and those people who like to work for us for that increase are welcome in our plants. Those that can get 10 cents elsewhere had better go there."

The employee delegates were not intimidated. Instead, one replied, "Under the Council Plan, you can't make a move on rates unless it is with Council agreement." Another added: "My people have told me . . . [i]f you don't get a good substantial increase . . . your council is done for . . . as far as we are concerned it is done for now!" Mahler exploded:[23]

> I can give you my situation cold. I've been holding myself back and have taken a lot of dirt all day long. . . . We . . . considered whether we should come in here with eight cents and we said let's give them everything we've got . . . there are some people here who want to put that extra squeeze on. . . . I tell you flat if people are going to get theirs by squeeze, I don't want my job and I don't give a damn if the company ever makes another pound of paper.

Mrs. Bond, an employee representative from Niagara Falls, jumped in: "Why don't you come down and take care of the situation . . . instead of asking the council to do it? What were we supposed to do when they were ready to strike? I think the attitude that you are taking right now is just what started this whole thing." Mr. Mahler replied: "Mrs. Bond, you don't have to threaten me with anything." And she, in turn: "I'm not threatening you . . . I'm just telling you what the feeling is among the employees in our plant." Shattuck then interjected: "I think perhaps we are all getting tired. Perhaps we had better go home and sleep about it and come back here in the morning," which they did.[24]

The next day, after one more futile attempt by management to confine the 10 cent increase to the Niagara Falls mill, the Council passed that amount of increase for all the mills. In the course of a long concluding speech, Mahler offered: "I may have my little differences with Mrs. Bond but I don't think any less of her and I hope she doesn't think any less of me." The shadow of outside labor organizations still was hovering over the Council. The employee delegates' secretary, who was paid by the company, reported: "People are curious. There were people at my house last night at 10:30, speaking frankly — labor organizers. They wanted to know what was going on in Kimberly–Clark."[25]

The 10 cent increase at Kimberly–Clark had the effect of a bombshell on the Wisconsin paper industry. The size of the increase and Kimberly–Clark's failure to consult with the other paper manufacturers made the other millowners very unhappy. Leo H. Barrette, personnel director of Consolidated Power and Paper Company, said that the "tremendous" increase would affect mills not only in the Fox and Wisconsin River Valleys, but all paper mills east of the Rocky Mountains. He went to Neenah to ask Kimberly–Clark for an explanation. Shattuck explained that CIO organizers had been working in the mills in Niagara, Kimberly, and Neenah, and the company consequently had to give in to the demands of the Mill Council's employee delegates.[26]

In reporting to Stanton Mead, president of Consolidated, Barrette concluded that despite the Kimberly–Clark increase of 10 cents, Consolidated could settle for a 5 cent increase if the other manufacturers also held to that line. Wage records show that hourly wages at Consolidated, which had been above those at Kimberly–Clark throughout the 1920's, now lagged behind.[27] Other Wisconsin paper manufacturers appear to have held the line against the 10 cent increase.

The new aggressiveness displayed by the Kimberly–Clark workers was typical of labor reactions in all of the paper mills which had been members of the Western Paper Manufacturers Association. Perhaps the most dramatic change in labor–management relations occurred at the Marathon Paper Corporation.

Forty Years of Labor Peace

With the passage of the National Industrial Recovery Act, followed by the National Labor Relations Act in 1935, workers at the Marathon Paper Company Mills in Wausau, Menasha, and Marinette swarmed into unions. David C. Everest, president of Marathon and the driving force, as we have seen, behind the anti-union activities of the Wisconsin paper manufacturers, now changed remarkably. Not only did he accept the new unions, but during the ensuing decade he developed a co-operative relationship with them. In 1936 he signed a contract with the two internationals, IBPM and IBPS&PMW, which he had fought for so long. In 1937, seventeen years after he had led Wausau's open shop campaign, he signed union shop agreements in the Marathon plants of Wausau, Rothschild, Menasha, Ashland, Wisconsin, and Menominee, Michigan. When in 1947 the National Planning Association commissioned several scholars to write a monograph series on the "causes of industrial peace," the Marathon Corporation was one of the dozen companies selected as exemplars of good labor–management relations.[28]

Under the terms of the National Labor Relations Act, unions took root and flourished in the mills of all of the other former members of the WPMA. Kimberly–Clark was one of the last to sign a union contract, in 1942; Marathon's first agreements were in 1936. Kimberly–Clark's elaborate organization of mill councils had insulated the company from the changing world over those intervening years. For Sensenbrenner, as for Everest, the signing of the contract marked the end of the unyielding opposition to unions which he had exercised since the violent 1904 strike in Neenah.

If we now look at labor–management relations in the paper industry from the vantage point of Professor Richard Lester's four stage evolution we find the following. Stage one, "union rejection" was dominant through 1935, with the Consolidated Power and Paper Company of Wisconsin Rapids as the major exception. Stage two, "arms length bargaining" was short, lasting not later than 1945. "Genuine acceptance of unionism," characterized by the union shop, began even in the late 1930's with some companies and was the paper industry norm by 1948. Indeed, the paper industry's movement to "acceptance" proceeded quickly and without strikes, a sharp contrast to the long bitter strikes in the state's metal industries.

The fourth stage, full co-operation in collective bargaining instead of confrontation, has not been reached yet. The third stage roughly covering the years 1945–1980, has been a long period of peaceful, constructive relationships. Yet it has not been devoid of occasional strikes. The strikes, however, have been over specific wage or fringe benefit demands by the unions, which the companies deemed too costly. Invariably, they were settled by compromise. Unlike earlier periods, none of the strikes of this period have threatened the very existence of the union.

By the end of World War II, about 95 per cent of the Wisconsin paperworkers were working under union shop agreements. The next thirty-five years saw unparalleled advances for workers in wages, pensions, health and life insurance, job security, and reductions in the yearly hours of work. The early union struggle for Saturday night off and the eight-hour day was transformed, year by year, into a movement pressing for longer vacations and more paid holidays. By 1980, senior employees in paper companies were receiving seven weeks' annual paid vacations and from ten to thirteen paid holidays.

Symptomatic of the dramatic change in industral relations in one city are the labor–management dinners hosted annually since 1948 by the Neenah–Menasha Labor Council. At these events, each local union invites its own employers. In alternate years the speaker is from labor and then from management. Pioneered by George Mead at Consolidated in 1919, employers' granting of full recognition to unions became the normal industry pattern after the 1930's.

CHAPTER 14

In Retrospect and in Prospect

WHEN UNITED STATES unions are compared with those of western Europe, significant differences appear in their goals and political tactics. Historically the goal of the European unions was a socialist state modeled after the concepts of Karl Marx and/or Ferdinand La Salle. By contrast, American unions generally have accepted private ownership of industry but have demanded that unions be recognized as a countervailing power to business. Politically, the European unions have established their own labor parties, such as the Social Democratic Party of Germany and the Labor Party of Great Britain. The American unions almost universally have followed the policy of their long-time president, Samuel Gompers, who advocated that labor should not be a part of any political party, but should back those particular candidates who supported labor's policies regardless of their party affiliation. We have seen that, during its forty years of Socialist leadership, the Wisconsin State Federation of Labor was an exception to this rule since it followed the European pattern of class-conscious ideology and third-party tactics, thus opposing Gompers' political policy. Its delegates voted against Gompers for President of the AFL at the national AFL conventions. In Wisconsin it supported the Socialist party through 1934 and then organized and supported another third party movement, the class-oriented Farmer–Labor Progressive Federation.

With the slowing of European immigration and the consequent lessening of American workers' class consciousness, and with other cultural and economic changes, the WSFL's Socialist leadership no longer could pass along its political ideology to the majority of the next generation of workers.

The legacy to Wisconsin of forty years of socialist labor leadership was not socialism which, of course, never was achieved, but, ironically, certain lasting reforms in the capitalist system. Wisconsin's pioneering worker compensation and unemployment compensation legislation was initiated by the socialist labor leadership and enacted by its temporary coalition with the La Follette Progressive Republicans. The enactment of the Wisconsin Labor Relations Act, which gave "Wagner Act" protection to Wisconsin workers in intra-state industries, was the work of the Farmer–Labor Progressive Federation which was organized and led by the socialist-controlled WSFL. The socialists' belief in the importance of public education for everyone began the WSFL's continuous championing of strong public financial support for local schools, for the University system, and for vocational and adult education.

The end of Socialist control in the WSFL was also the end of Wisconsin labor's class-oriented third party politics. In 1940 the WSFL adopted the pragmatic political policy of the rest of the United States labor movement and, in a vote at its 1940 convention, declared it would reward its political friends and punish its political enemies, regardless of party affiliations. The Wisconsin labor leaders, however, could not agree on how to carry out this new policy. Consequently, for about ten years the WSFL endorsed no candidates in statewide races.

In the 1950's the WSFL, the Wisconsin State CIO, and after 1958 the Wisconsin State AFL–CIO gradually became more effective politically, endorsing candidates and giving them financial support and publicity. Since the 1960's, in many of the state's election districts the endorsement and support from the labor movement has become substantial enough to give a candidate his margin of victory in some elections. Instead of the all-or-nothing legislative control which the Wisconsin labor movement experienced in 1937 and 1938, it has a steady, strong voice in the state legislature. Its agenda of desired legislation is considered seriously and gains have been made in each session. Wagner Act protections have been extended to public employees—including teachers—and the levels of benefits for injured and unemployed workers have been improved regularly.

While political activity has been the primary responsibility of the state central labor body, organizing and collective bargaining have been the primary responsibilities of the national and local unions. The history of these latter can be divided neatly into two time periods, pre- and post-1935—the year the Wagner Act was passed. In the pre-1935 period, labor's universal problem was to convince employers to recognize the union and to bargain with it regarding hours of work, wages, and job security. Even in the last century, the building trades unions had had considerable success in achieving these goals. But big industry almost universally refused to recognize or bargain with unions. Thus, labor history was a series of periodic strikes which occurred whenever the union tried to bargain. Invariably superior financial resources enabled the employer, abetted by court injunctions, labor spies, and imported strikebreakers, to starve out the workers and crush their unions.

The national political revolution of the 1930's, however, brought the Wagner Act, which outlawed the common anti-union policies of the pre-1935 period. Previously restrained workers now rushed to join unions. While the Wisconsin State CIO unions distinguished themselves by successfully organizing the large, formerly anti-union, metalworking plants, the AFL paper unions miraculously brought to the bargaining table the companies which had fought them for thirty-five years.

For the next forty-five years, labor and management bargained together with only occasional strikes. Hours were cut, and paid vacations, holidays, and personal days were established. Pensions and medical and dental insurance plans were set up. Wages were raised annually and purchasing power was maintained by cost-of-living payments.

In Prospect

The fate of the labor movement in Wisconsin can be expected to mirror that of the national labor movement. There is little in this account of the history of unionism in Wisconsin to support explicitly a prediction of an imminent rise or fall in union membership. For all the merits of the study of history, we know it tells us little about the future. For example, had this history been concluded before 1981, the prediction of the future of unions would have been an optimistic one of continued economic gains in worker wages and fringe benefits. But the depression of 1982–1983 has seen cuts in workers' wages and benefits similar to those of the depressions of 1929–1933 and earlier. In addition, some now predict a decline of union membership nationally, especially in the northern industrial states such as Wisconsin.

This prediction is based upon several possible developments: (1) a structural shift of industry away from durable goods and machinery which, except for paper, dominates Wisconsin industry, and toward the high-technology industries involving computers and communications, causing unions to decline primarily because blue collar jobs would be replaced by white collar jobs which are not as heavily unionized; (2) a shift of industry to the Sunbelt states because of better climate, state subsidies, lower taxes, fewer unions (and thus lower wages), and, in part, because of anti-union legislation in some of these states; (3) a worst-case trend, in which Wisconsin industries would move to foreign countries in search of lower wages, lower taxes, and/or foreign government subsidies, or, Wisconsin industry might be wiped out by the competition from foreign imports made by foreign workers paid very low wages.

These three trends are not new and have been operating for many years. They appear to be intensifying, but counteracting tendencies do exist. A decline in the value of the dollar would curtail foreign imports and stimulate Wisconsin's exports. Resource-based industries centering on agriculture, papermaking, and even a possible new mining industry, cannot flee the state.

To a large extent, these trends and countertrends are the result of national and even global economic forces which can be affected in a very limited way, if at all, by the labor movement, except to the extent that it discerns and supports correct national public policy. Outside of these forces, however, Wisconsin unions are in a better position than ever before to recover and expand union membership and strength in the years ahead.

First, as Chapter 5, "Growth," pointed out, the Wisconsin labor movement has been anchored firmly since about 1950 with 27 per cent of the state's non-agricultural work force covered by union contracts. Most of these contracts, in both the private and public sectors, call for compulsory payment of union dues after a thirty to ninety day probationary period. Thus, as employment picks up from the depression of the early 1980's, recalled and new workers automatically will become union members.

Second, union contracts specifying wages and hours, wage increases geared to the cost of living, vacations, health insurance, pension plans, and protection from arbitrary dismissal are an accepted institution in much of Wisconsin industry. It certainly can be expected that, if Wisconsin industry survives the possible dislocations set forth above and again prospers, Wisconsin's well-established unions will be able to improve these contract provisions.

Third, we have seen that unionism generally grows during periods of prosperity. Before 1935, unions largely were wiped out during depressions and time and again organizing had to begin from nothing. Today, unions are on-going institutions with proven accomplishments and ready financial and organizational resources with which to organize new workers. The fastest growing unions in Wisconsin in the 1970's were those in government. These unions easily could grow another 50 per cent as Wisconsin's economy improves. It is interesting to note that in Great Britain, during the inflation of the 1950's, white collar employees joined unions in such numbers that union membership grew to be 50 per cent of the non-agricultural work force as compared with about 22 per cent in the United States.

Fourth, in Chapter 8, "Political Action," we noted that the Wisconsin labor movement is now one of the major political forces in the state. The same is true nationally of the AFL–CIO. While political fortunes frequently rise and just as frequently fall, it is likely that as large a segment of the electorate as that composed by unions will be able to maintain present favorable labor legislation and enact further reforms in the years ahead. This could provide the possibility of further spurts in organizing.

One facet of modern personnel management predicts that management, without the pressure of unions, may offer workers everything that unions have achieved in the past: annual raises in wages, longer vacations, improved health and retirement benefits, job security that respects seniority rights in case of layoff, and more. The experience of the serious depression of 1981–1983, however, demonstrated it is very unlikely that these benefits would be offered by employers without the pressure of union bargaining. Employers who had not cut wages since the 1930's reduced them. This time it was the non-union clerical, professional, and supervisory employees, unprotected by union contracts, who frequently experienced the earliest and deepest cuts, often in the form of enforced early retirement.

Competing effectively on the world market while simultaneously achieving full employment and improved living standards is obviously a joint task for labor, management, and government. It is here that stage four, "genuine labor–management co-operation," in Richard Lester's terms, discussed in Chapters 6 and 13, should be given consideration. Stage three, "management acceptance of permanent unionism"—the current mode in Wisconsin—still may be too adversarial to achieve the best in increased productivity and quality control.

In the improbable event that stage two, "arm's length bargaining," or stage one, "management rejection of unions," were to recur, Wisconsin would be thrown back into the wasteful periodic industrial "wars" which characterized the early years of its industrial history.

APPENDIX

Union Leaders at the National Level Who Began Their Leadership Careers in Wisconsin

The Wisconsin labor movement has contributed substantially to the leadership of the national unions and to the staff of the AFL–CIO. Joseph Padway, a lawyer for the WSFL, also represented the AFL under Samuel Gompers. William Cooper, earlier mentioned, became the national secretary–treasurer of the Building Service Union, now the Service Employees Union. Al Hayes, a railroad machinist on the Milwaukee Road, rose to the presidency of the International Association of Machinists in 1948. Hayes was instrumental in effecting the merger of the AFL and CIO and was responsible for the anti-raiding pact between the Machinists and the United Auto Workers. Walter Burke, whose history we have chronicled, became regional director of the United Steelworkers and then secretary–treasurer of the national union. In that election Burke ran on an anti-incumbent slate headed by I. W. Abel as the presidential candidate. It was a hard-fought campaign against an administration headed by David J. McDonald. The victory of Abel and Burke marked the first, and so far only, successful challenge to an incumbent Steelworker administration.

In the building trades, Peter Schoemann of Milwaukee Plumbers and Gasfitters, Local 75, became president of the international union of Plumbers and Pipefitters in 1953. Schoemann had distinguished himself as head of the Milwaukee Building Trades Council and was probably the single most important leader in the drive, starting in 1939, to enlarge the influence of the building trades in the WSFL.

In 1980 Raymond Majerus was elected secretary–treasurer of the United Auto Workers. He had been director of UAW Region 9, with offices in Milwaukee. Originally he came out of UAW Local 833 at Kohler, then served as a UAW staff representative. Until he moved to Detroit, he was on the University of Wisconsin's Board of Regents.

Milan Stone, a member of the Rubber Workers Local in Eau Claire, went from local leadership to the union's national staff and then, in 1981, to the presidency of the United Rubber Workers.

Andrew Biemiller of Milwaukee served as a top political lobbyist and right-hand political adviser to George Meany, president of the AFL, from 1953 to 1978. As mentioned before, in the 1930's Biemiller was a staff assistant to Milwaukee's Socialist Mayor, Daniel Hoan, and was education director of the Wisconsin's Socialist party. During the Socialist–Progressive alliance, he was elected to the State Assembly, where he became floor leader for the Progressive party in the mid-1930's. Because of the value of his legislative leadership to the labor movement, Henry Ohl put him on the WSFL staff as a part-time organizer in the period when workers were flocking to unions. In 1944 and 1948, Biemiller was elected to the U.S. Congress. His experience in the Wisconsin labor movement, in the state legislature, and in Congress brought him to Meany's attention.

Hilton Hannah, a Jamaican immigrant, attended the University of Wisconsin during the 1930's, and after the war became executive assistant to the president of the Amalgamated Meat Cutters and Butcher Workmen of North America. Hannah, a union journalist, wrote for his union's monthly paper, was speechwriter for the president, and was co-author of a history of his union, *The Picket and the Pen*. He also served as a member of the executive board.

One international union, the Allied Industrial Workers, with headquarters in Milwaukee and a substantial portion of its members in Wisconsin, has had three chief officers from Wisconsin: Carl Griepentrog, president from 1957 to 1970; Anthony Doria, secretary–treasurer, 1943–1956; and William Salamone, secretary–treasurer from 1979 to the present.

Reference already has been made, in Chapter 5, to the role of Wisconsin's Arnold Zander in founding AFSCME. He served as national president from 1936 through 1964. Another Wisconsinite, Gordon Chapman, served as secretary–treasurer of AFSCME from 1944 to 1965. William R. Connors, from Madison Bricklayers, Local 13, was secretary–treasurer of the Bricklayers International Union from 1966 to 1971. Harvey Brown, of the International Brotherhood of Electrical Workers, Local 494, in Milwaukee, served as the union's international president from 1939 through 1949.

NOTES

Full bibliographical citations for works given in shortened form may be found in the Bibliography.

CHAPTER 1

1. Gavett, *Development of the Labor Movement in Milwaukee*, pp. 6–7.
2. *Ibid.*, p. 24.
3. *Ibid.*, pp. 22–23.
4. *Iron Molders Journal*, 12 (August, 1876), 73; Racine *Advocate*, August 19, 1876.
5. Lescohier, *Knights of St. Crispin*, pp. 7, 33; Gavett, *Development of the Labor Movement in Milwaukee*, pp. 21–22.
6. Taft, *Organized Labor*, pp. 76–83.
7. Merk, *Economic History*, pp. 178–182.
8. Gavett, *Development of the Labor Movement in Milwaukee*, p. 36.
9. *Ibid.*, p. 58.
10. *Ibid.*, pp. 58, 59. Gavett is also the source of the description of the disturbances of May 2–5.
11. Milwaukee *Daily Sentinel*, May 11, 1886; quoted in Amy Louise Ignatius, "Milwaukee Polish Labor Strike," pp. 12–13, a student paper in possession of the author.
12. Milwaukee *Daily Sentinel*, May 5, 1886; quoted in Ignatius, "Milwaukee Polish Labor Strike," p. 11.
13. Milwaukee *Sunday Telegraph*, May 16, 1886; quoted in Ignatius, "Milwaukee Polish Labor Strike," pp. 13–14.

CHAPTER 2

1. Eau Claire *Free Press*, July 19, 1881.
2. Jensen, *Lumber and Labor*, p. 51.
3. Wisconsin Bureau of Labor Statistics, *First Biennial Report, 1883–1884*, p. 151.
4. Eau Claire *News*, July 30, 1881.
5. Oshkosh *Northwestern*, July 30, 1881.
6. Madison *Daily Democrat*, July 29, 1881.
7. Wisconsin Bureau of Labor Statistics, *First Biennial Report, 1883–1884*, pp. 152–153.
8. Reported in Madison *Daily Democrat*, July 30, 1881.
9. Marinette *Eagle*, September 23, 26, 1885.
10. Wisconsin Bureau of Labor and Industrial Statistics, *Second Biennial Report, 1885–1886*, p. 246.
11. Rhinelander *Vindicator*, August 3, 1892.
12. *Lincoln County Advocate*, issues of July 26 through August 2, 1892.
13. Oshkosh *Northwestern*, August 2–6, 1892; Wausau *Pilot Review*, August 9, 1892; Wausau *Torch of Liberty*, August 4, 1892; Rhinelander *Vindicator*, August 31–September 21, 1892.
14. La Crosse *Morning Chronicle*, April 26, 1892.

15. *Ibid.*, April 26–May 10, 1892; Oshkosh *Daily Northwestern,* May 9, 1892; Wisconsin Bureau of Labor and Industrial Statistics, *Fifth Biennial Report, 1891–1892,* pp. 122–123.
16. Lee Baxandall, "Furs, Logs, and Human Lives: The Great Oshkosh Woodworkers Strike of 1898," in *Green Mountain Quarterly,* 3 (May, 1976). Unless indicated otherwise, the facts of the Woodworker strike are from this article.
17. Personal communication from Julia Morgan, Assistant Archivist at Johns Hopkins University, to Barbara Morford, August 1, 1977.
18. Oshkosh *Labor Advocate,* November 30, 1894.
19. Wisconsin State Board of Arbitration, *Second Biennial Report, 1897–1898,* p. 28.
20. *Ibid.,* p. 32.
21. Stone, *Clarence Darrow,* p. 110.
22. Baxandall, "Furs, Logs and Human Lives: The Great Oshkosh Woodworkers Strike of 1898," p. 49.
23. *Ibid.,* p. 59.
24. Weinberg, *Attorney for the Damned,* p. 326.
25. Glaab and Larsen, *Factories in the Valley,* pp. 240–241.
26. Wisconsin State Board of Arbitration and Conciliation, *Third Biennial Report, 1899–1900,* pp. 39–40.

CHAPTER 3

1. Gavett, *Labor Movement in Milwaukee,* pp. 80–81.
2. Minutes of May 20, 1901, Lodge 66, International Association of Machinists, Milwaukee, Minute Books at Lodge headquarters.
3. Williamson and Meyers, *Designed for Digging,* pp. 61–63.
4. Perlman, *The Machinists,* p. 31.
5. *Machinists' Monthly Journal,* 13 (1901), 525.
6. Job, *Tale of Two Cities,* p. 5. It should be noted that Job was secretary of the Employers' Association of Chicago.
7. Beloit *Labor Journal,* March 21, 1903.
8. Wisconsin State Board of Arbitration, *Fourth Biennial Report, 1900–1902,* p. 24; Beloit *Labor Journal,* March 14, 1903.
9. Wisconsin State Board of Arbitration, *Fifth Biennial Report, 1902–1904,* p. 16.
10. Job, *Tale of Two Cities,* p. 13.
11. Eliot, in *Harper's Magazine,* March, 1905, as cited in Perlman and Taft, *History of Labor,* vol. 4, p. 136.
12. Gavett, *Development of the Labor Movement in Milwaukee,* pp. 122–123.
13. *Iron Molders Journal,* 42 (1906), 839.
14. *Machinists' Monthly Journal,* 18 (1906), 1138–1139.
15. Minutes of July 1, 1892, Lodge 66, International Association of Machinists, Milwaukee, Minute Books at Lodge headquarters.

CHAPTER 4

1. *Wisconsin Vorwaerts,* June 5, 1893 (translation by the WSFL).

2. Oshkosh *Labor Advocate,* June 21, 1895.
3. *Ibid.,* June 17, 1893.
4. *Wisconsin Vorwaerts,* June 9, 1893 (translation by the WSFL).
5. Oshkosh *Labor Advocate,* June 5, 1894.
6. Racine *News,* June 12, 1896.
7. *Ibid.*
8. *Wisconsin Vorwaerts,* June 11, 1896
9. Wisconsin State Federation of Labor, *Proceedings of the Sixth Annual Convention,* 1898, in *WSFL Directory, 1899–1900,* pp. 54, 55.
10. *Ibid.,* p. 63.
11. Milwaukee *Sentinel,* June 15, 1900.
12. WSFL, *Proceedings.* Reports of per capita payments by the Credentials Committees, 1898, 1900, 1901, converted into membership by the author.
13. WSFL, *Proceedings,* 1898, 1900, 1901, 1903. The percentages used were calculated by the author from per capita payments by locals as reported by the Credentials Committee by city and by craft.
14. Frederick I. Olson, "The Milwaukee Socialists, 1887–1941" (Ph.D. dissertation, Harvard University, 1952), pp. 15–16, 93–94.
15. Edward Muzick, "Victor L. Berger, A Biography" (Ph.D. dissertation, Northwestern University, 1960), p. 117.
16. Gavett, *Development of the Labor Movement in Milwaukee,* pp. 100–101, 116–117.
17. *Wisconsin Vorwaerts,* June 11, 1893 (translation by the WSFL).
18. *Wisconsin Vorwaerts,* June 18, 1899.
19. Olson, "Milwaukee Socialists," pp. 94, 97.
20. WSFL, *Proceedings,* 1920, p. 40.
21. Olson, "Milwaukee Socialists," pp. 18–19.
22. Gavett, *Development of the Labor Movement in Milwaukee,* pp. 102–103.
23. Superior Trades and Labor Assembly Minute Book, Vol. 3, entry for January 25, 1911. Superior ARC.
24. *Lumber Workers Industrial Bulletin,* Union 500 IWW, Chicago, 1918–1920.
25. Miller, *Victor Berger,* p. 18.
26. Olson, "Milwaukee Socialists," pp. 191–192.

CHAPTER 5

1. Average annual membership figures are calculated from annual per capita dues receipts, as reported in the annual WSFL convention *Proceedings.* These figures are charted in Figure 2, p. 63.
2. WSFL, Papers, Minutes of the Executive Board, January, 1920, SHSW, Box 3. The executive board reported a January, 1920, WSFL membership of 41,247, higher than the one shown in the chart because it is not an annual *average.*
3. WSFL, *Proceedings,* 1901, and Minutes of the Federated Trades Council of Milwaukee, 1901, in FTC papers, Milwaukee ARC, Box 1.
4. Percentages calculated from membership figures are based on per capita dues receipts as reported by the WSFL. The Milwaukee brewery locals are recorded

in the papers of the Federated Trades Council of Milwaukee, Minutes of the Executive Board, Milwaukee ARC. It should be noted that the word "International" in a union name usually refers, outside of the United States, to Canada and perhaps Hawaii, but not Europe; these were basically U.S. unions.

5. See previous note for sources of information.
6. John Schmitt, interview with the author, January 20, 1980.
7. United Brotherhood of Carpenters and Joiners of America, Local 161, Kenosha, Wisconsin, Minute Books, entries of December 3, 1898; March 5, November 1, 1900; February 21, 1901, November 6, 1903; January 5, 1905; December 22, 1907; March 19, April 16, May 7, June 10, December 10, 1908; March 3, 1910. Parkside ARC, 18, Vols. 1 and 4; 19, Vol. 1.
8. Gavett, *Development of the Labor Movement in Milwaukee*, pp. 20–21.
9. Bricklayers, Masons, and Plasterers International Union, Local 8, Milwaukee, Wisconsin. The English *Minutes* book for 1905–1910 lists in audit reports names of members to whom the union has granted mortgages. An example is the audit report of January 4, 1908, showing four members who have received mortgages from Local 8. Milwaukee ARC.
10. Secretary's letterbook, May 12, 1902, Bricklayers . . . Local 8. SHSW.
11. *Ibid.*, May 20, 1902.
12. Shaw, *Cooperatives in the Northwest*, pp. 319–20; Wisconsin Bureau of Labor and Industrial Statistics, *Second Biennial Report, 1885–1886*, pp. 213–216; Gordon A. King, "A Short History of Milwaukee Plumbers & Gasfitters' Union, Local 75" (in possession of the author).
13. Gordon A. King, telephone interview with the author, August 24, 1983.
14. Sheet Metal Workers International Association, Local 42, Superior, Wisconsin, Records, Minutes of January 12, 1906. Superior ARC, Box 5, Vol. 1.
15. United Brotherhood of Carpenters and Joiners of America, Local 161, Kenosha, Wisconsin, Minute Books, June 20, September 5, 1912; June 29, 1915. Parkside ARC, Vols. 5 and 6.
16. Sheet Metal Workers International Association, Local 42, Superior, Wisconsin, Minutes, November 24, 1905. Superior ARC, Box 5, Vol. 1.
17. Gavett, *Development of the Labor Movement in Milwaukee,* p. 133.
18. Calculated from per capita dues receipts, reported in WSFL, *Proceedings,* 1930, pp. 110–123; see also note 2, above.
19. Federated Trades Council of Milwaukee, Papers, Weber to William B. Coleman, May 8, 1929. Milwaukee ARC, Box 1.
20. Weber's obituary, Milwaukee *Sentinel,* February 5, 1943.
21. Federated Trades Council of Milwaukee, Papers, Coleman to Max Binner, October 1 and November 11, 1930; Weber to Anton Dick, February 24, 1931. Milwaukee ARC, Box 1.
22. *Ibid.,* Coleman to Weber, November 12, 1929.
23. This account of the Allen-A Hosiery Workers strike is taken from John B. Bailey, "Labor's Fight for Security and Dignity," in *Kenosha County in the Twentieth Century,* ed. by John A. Neuenschwander, pp. 237–246, and from Daryl O. Holter, "Labor Spies and Union-Busting in Wisconsin, 1892–1940" (an unpublished paper in possession of the author, 1983), p. 25.
24. Louis Adamic, "Collapse of Organized Labor," in *Harpers Monthly Magazine,* 164 (1932), 167.

25. Calculated from per capita dues receipts reported in WSFL, *Proceedings,* 1933, pp. 104–113.
26. Gavett, *Development of the Labor Movement in Milwaukee,* p. 137.
27. Wisconsin State Federation of Labor, Minutes of the Executive Board, January, 1932. SHSW, Box 4.
28. *Ibid.,* January, 1933.
29. Gavett, *Development of the Labor Movement in Milwaukee,* p. 155.
30. U.S. Bureau of Labor Statistics, *Handbook of Labor Statistics* (Washington, D.C., 1980), 412.
31. Kenosha *Labor,* September 4, 1936.
32. Fine, *Automobile Under the Blue Eagle,* pp. 208–209.
33. *Ibid.,* pp. 240–242.
34. *Ibid.,* p. 242.
35. Elmer Yenny, oral history interview April 24, 1961, Archives of Labor and Urban Affairs, Wayne State University, Detroit.
36. Henry Traxler, "I Went Through a Strike," in *Public Management* (April, 1937), 100–101.
37. Gavett, *Development of the Labor Movement in Milwaukee,* p. 85.
38. Frank Ranney, interview with the author, July 28, 1982.
39. Tom Rodel, "The Establishment of Federal Labor Union No. 18684" (unpublished student paper in possession of the author, 1975).
40. Helen Branch, "Boston Store Strike" (student paper in possession of the author, 1980), 4.
41. Bill Cooper, tape recorded interview, December 4, 1951, Tape 62A. SHSW.
42. *Ibid.*
43. Sheboygan *Times,* May 4, 11, 18, June 1, 1895; Sheboygan *Democrat,* May 16, 1895.
44. Uphoff, *Kohler on Strike,* pp. 3–6.
45. Transcript of the meeting, as quoted in Uphoff, *Kohler on Strike,* pp. 32–33.
46. Uphoff, *Kohler on Strike,* p. 90.
47. *Ibid.,* pp. 99–100.
48. U.S. Bureau of Labor Statistics, *Handbook of Labor Statistics* (Washington, D.C., 1980).
49. Kramer, *Labor's Paradox—The American Federation of State, County, and Municipal Employees, AFL–CIO,* p. 3.
50. *Ibid.,* pp. 5–6.
51. Wisconsin Employment Relations Board Case I, No. 8991 MP-4, Decision No. 6544, November 19, 1963, University of Wisconsin Law Library.

CHAPTER 6

1. Wisconsin State Board of Arbitration and Conciliation, *Biennial Report, 1899–1900,* pp. 16–18; *Iron Molders Journal,* 38 (1902), 157; 43 (1907), 299–300.
2. Frank J. Sahorske, transcript of oral history interview conducted by Jack W. Skeels, August 14, 1961, Wayne State University, Archives of Labor and Urban Affairs, Detroit.

3. *Ibid.*
4. *Ibid.*
5. Larry Carlstrom, telephone interview with the author, January 7, 1976. Notes in possession of the author.
6. Carl Griepentrog, interview with the author, November 7, 1977, Hartford, Wisconsin.
7. Clifford Matchey, interview with the author, July 1, 1977.
8. This account of the Harnischfeger strikes is based on Christopher Coakley, "The Start of Unionism at the Harnischfeger Corporation" (unpublished student paper in possession of the author, 1975).
9. Walter Burke, telephone interview with the author, April 27, 1976.
10. *Ibid.*
11. Rudolph Faupl, telephone interview with the author, September 16, 1976.
12. Harold Newton, interview with the author, October 6, 1976.
13. Milwaukee *News–Sentinel,* July 24, 1938.
14. Wisconsin CIO, *Proceedings of the Annual Convention,* 1939, p. 17.
15. Wisconsin CIO, *Proceedings of the Annual Convention,* 1940, p. 36.
16. Wisconsin CIO, *Proceedings of the Annual Convention,* 1941, pp. 219, 220.
17. *Ibid.,* pp. 226, 227.
18. *Ibid.,* pp. 221, 226, 457.
19. *Ibid.,* p. 451.
20. Wisconsin CIO, *Proceedings of the Annual Convention,* 1940, p. 39.
21. Milwaukee *Journal,* March 5, 1972.
22. Quoted in Gavett, *Development of the Labor Movement in Milwaukee,* p. 184.
23. *Ibid.,* pp. 186–190.
24. Milwaukee *Journal,* December 14, 1946.
25. Milwaukee *Journal,* December 13, 1946.
26. Madison *Capital Times,* December 14, 1946, and Milwaukee *Journal,* December 15, 1946.
27. Milwaukee *Journal,* December 15, 1946.
28. Richard A. Givens, "Milwaukee Brewery Strike of 1953" (M.A. thesis, University of Wisconsin, 1954), pp. 9, 10.
29. *Ibid.,* p. 26.
30. Lester, *Labor and Industrial Relations,* pp. 206–207.
31. Gary A. Cameron, "Labor Relations at J.I. Case" (unpublished paper for the Graduate School of Business, University of Chicago, 1965; paper in possession of the author), p. 10.
32. *Ibid.,* p. 16.
33. Excerpt of speech given by Walter Reuther at the Wisconsin Industrial Union Council, CIO, Tenth Annual Convention, December 5–7, 1947, Milwaukee, *Proceedings,* p. 342.
34. Uphoff, *Kohler on Strike,* p. 103.
35. *Ibid.,* p. 110.
36. E.H. Kolhagen, interview with the author, June, 1952, Madison.
37. Uphoff, *Kohler on Strike,* p. 127.
38. *Ibid.,* pp. 188, 190.
39. *Ibid.,* pp. 107.

CHAPTER 7

1. WSFL, *Proceedings*, 1916, Resolution no. 4, p. 113.
2. WSFL, *Proceedings*, 1918, Resolution no. 1, p. 91.
3. *Cooperation* (Kimberly–Clark house organ), May, 1920.
4. Miller, *Victor Berger*, pp. 206–207, 212–217.
5. WSFL, *Proceedings*, 1920, p. 56.
6. WSFL, *Proceedings*, 1921, p. 56.
7. Gavett, *Development of the Labor Movement in Milwaukee*, p. 131.
8. WSFL, *Proceedings*, 1917, pp. 42, 99.
9. Calculated from per capita dues receipts as reported in the *Proceedings* of WSFL annual conventions.
10. Harold Newton, telephone interview with the author, January 9, 1981. Newton was then (1941) a member of the executive board.
11. Paul J. Smith, letter to Charles Heymanns, July 1, 1943, Heymanns' private files, Sheboygan, Wisconsin.
12. Rudolph Faupl, telephone interview with the author, September 16, 1976.
13. Paul J. Smith, letter to Charles Heymanns, September 28, 1943, Heymanns' private files, Sheboygan, Wisconsin.
14. Harold Newton, telephone interview with the author, January 9, 1981.
15. "An Open Letter to the Delegates to the 1944 Convention of the Wisconsin State Federation of Labor," signed "Campaign Committee," in Heymanns' private files, Sheboygan, Wisconsin.
16. Calculated from per capita dues receipts as reported in WSFL, *Proceedings*, 1943.
17. "Is This Dual Unionism?" Campaign document in WSFL presidential contest of 1944. Heymanns' private files, Sheboygan, Wisconsin.
18. Milwaukee *Journal*, August 23, 1944.
19. Gregory Wallig, telephone interview with the author, October 18, 1977; Carl Griepentrog, interview with author, November 10, 1977, Hartford, Wisconsin.
20. Gregory Wallig, telephone interview with the author, October 18, 1977.
21. James Johnson, "Labor in Wisconsin Politics, 1887–1940" (unpublished student paper in possession of the author, 1976), p. 60.
22. George Hall, interview with the author, October 18, 1977, Green Bay, Wisconsin.
23. Frank Ranney, telephone interview with the author, July 28, 1982.
24. George Hall, interview with the author, October 18, 1977, Green Bay, Wisconsin.
25. William Cooper, interview with the author, December 4, 1951, Milwaukee, Wisconsin.
26. WSFL, *Proceedings*, 1907, Preamble, p. 6.
27. WSFL, *Proceedings*, 1947, pp. 140, 141, 142, 144–145, 146, 150–151.
28. *Ibid.*, pp. 143–44.
29. *Ibid.*, pp. 42–63.
30. Membership figures calculated from per capita dues as reported in WSFL, *Proceedings*, 1956, pp. 42–63.
31. State AFL–CIO, *Proceedings*, 1964, pp. 67–68.

32. Salary of Herman Steffes in 1947, former President of the Wisconsin State CIO, was obtained from him in a telephone interview with the author, October 7, 1983. Salaries of George Haberman are from the WSFL Constitution in WSFL *Proceedings* for 1944, p. 8, and 1956, p. 6, and from the Wisconsin State AFL–CIO constitution in *Proceedings, 1964*, p. 7. Report of the Constitution Committee to the 18th Annual Convention of the Wisconsin Industrial Union Council, December 8–11, 1955, *Proceedings*, p. 175. SHSW Microfilm.
33. Milwaukee *Journal*, August 5, 7, 1966.
34. Memo, John Schmitt to author, February, 7, 1983, in possession of the author.
35. Uphoff, *Kohler on Strike*, p. 107.

CHAPTER 8

1. Commons, *History of Labor in the United States*, p. 156, and Margulies, *Lenroot of Wisconsin*, pp. 75–76.
2. James Johnson, "Labor in Wisconsin Politics," 1887–1940 (unpublished student paper in possession of the author, 1976), p. 39.
3. R. Asher, "Workmen's Compensation in the United States, 1880–1935" (Ph.D. dissertation, University of Michigan, 1971), p. 380.
4. Haferbecker, *Wisconsin Labor Laws*, pp. 40–41.
5. Paul Raushenbush and Elizabeth Raushenbush, "Our 'U.C.' Story" (unpublished manuscript in possession of the author, 1978), p. 16.
6. Haferbecker, *Wisconsin Labor Laws*, pp. 92–97.
7. WSFL, *Proceedings*, 1913, p. 67.
8. Haferbecker, *Wisconsin Labor Laws*, pp. 99–100.
9. Nelson, *Unemployment Insurance*, pp. 108–109.
10. Haferbecker, *Wisconsin Labor Laws*, pp. 123–124.
11. Nelson, *Unemployment Insurance*, pp. 115–116.
12. Raushenbush and Raushenbush, "Our 'U.C.' Story," pp. 15–16.
13. Nelson, *Unemployment Insurance*, pp. 121–128; Haferbecker, *Wisconsin Labor Laws*, pp. 125–127.
14. Haferbecker, *Wisconsin Labor Laws*, pp. 160–161.
15. Transcript of radio address, Social Democratic Party of Wisconsin, 1934 papers, Milwaukee County Historical Society.
16. Lester M. Schmidt, "The Farmer–Labor Progressive Federation: The Study of a 'United Front' Among Wisconsin Liberals, 1934–1941" (Ph.D. dissertation, University of Wisconsin, 1954), p. 2.
17. *Ibid.*, pp. 17–18.
18. *Ibid.*, p. 89.
19. *Ibid.*, pp. 50–62.
20. Taft, *Organized Labor*, p. 384.
21. Schmidt, "The Farmer–Labor Progressive Federation," pp. 84, 176.
22. *Ibid.*, pp. 177–188, 211.
23. *Ibid.*, p. 210.
24. *Ibid.*, pp. 219–221.
25. Milwaukee *Journal*, May 27, 1938.
26. *Ibid.*, May 27, 1938.

27. *Ibid.,* June 6, 1938.
28. Schmidt, "The Farmer–Labor Progressive Federation," pp. 70–74.
29. *Ibid.,* pp. 301, 297, 300.
30. *Ibid.,* p. 261.
31. *Ibid.,* p. 300.
32. Haferbecker, *Wisconsin Labor Laws,* p. 164.
33. Schmidt, "The Farmer–Labor Progressive Federation," p. 272.
34. WSFL, *Proceedings,* 1939, p. 34.
35. *Ibid.,* 1940, p. 139.
36. Johnson, "Labor in Wisconsin Politics," p. 111.
37. WSFL, *Proceedings,* 1940, p. 138.
38. Harold Newton, interview with the author, October 6, 1976.
39. Oshinsky, *McCarthy and the Labor Movement,* pp. 43–44.
40. *Ibid.,* pp. 17–18.
41. *Ibid.,* p. 16.
42. *Wisconsin Blue Book,* 1948; Haferbecker, *Wisconsin Labor Laws,* pp. 174–175.
43. State AFL–CIO, *Proceedings,* 1958, pp. 133–134.
44. Bayley, *McCarthy and the Press,* p. 92.
45. Adamany, *Financing Politics,* p. 179.
46. Wisconsin State Elections Board, *Biennial Report,* 1979, vol. 2, calculated from data on pp. 5–276 and 5–301.
47. Adamany, *Financing Politics,* p. 205.

CHAPTER 9

1. Barbara Morford, "Women Workers and Organized Labor" (unpublished paper in possession of the author, n.d.), p. 36.
2. Federated Trades Council, Green Bay, minutes of November 22 and December 13, 1927; January 24, February 14, March 13, 1928. Green Bay ARC.
3. *Ibid.,* minutes of June 21, 1932, June 13, 1933.
4. Superior *Evening Telegram,* August 23, 1913.
5. Superior Trades and Labor Council, minutes, October 14, 1913.
6. David Clark Everest papers, December 1, 1927, SHSW, Box 5, folder 2.
7. Rudolph Faupl, telephone interview with the author, September 16, 1976.
8. John D. Buenker, "Politics of Mutual Frustration: Socialists and Suffragists in New York and Wisconsin," in *Flawed Liberation,* ed. by Sally M. Miller, pp. 130–131. (Buenker's Ph.D. dissertation, Harvard University, 1952.)
9. *Ibid.,* and Olson, "Milwaukee Socialists, 1897–1941," p. 116.
10. Janesville *Daily Gazette,* June 13, 1899.
11. WSFL, *Proceedings,* 1905, pp. 41–42.
12. *Ibid.,* 1906, p. 18.
13. *Ibid.,* 1913, p. 67.
14. *Ibid.,* 1918, p. 37.
15. See *ibid.,* 1920, pp. 23–24; Buenker, "The Politics of Frustration," p. 138.
16. WSFL, *Labor Conditions in Wisconsin,* 1917, p. 4.
17. *Ibid.,* p. 4.
18. Wisconsin *Vorwaerts,* June 8, 1897.

19. WSFL, *Proceedings,* 1913, p. 133.
20. Women's Trade Union League, *Convention Proceedings,* 1926, p. 34.
21. Federated Trades Council, Green Bay, minutes of November 13, 1928. Green Bay ARC, Vol. 8.
22. *Ibid.,* minutes of October 14, 1930; May 12, 1931, Vols. 9, 10.
23. WSFL, *Proceedings,* 1932, pp. 110–111.
24. Morford, "Women Workers and Organized Labor," p. 35.
25. Katherine Hartman Lichter, interview with Barbara Morford, February 16, 1978.
26. Wisconsin State AFL–CIO, *Officers' Report,* 1974, pp. 101–105.
27. AFL–CIO, *Proceedings of the Third Constitutional Convention,* 1959, p. 59.
28. Minutes of International Association of Machinists, Lodge 66, January 5, 1892. Minutes in possession of Lodge 66, Milwaukee.
29. Al Hayes, President Emeritus of the International Association of Machinists, interview with the author, May 5, 1980, Waukesha, Wisconsin.
30. Ozanne, *Negro in Industries,* p. 22.
31. *Ibid.,* p. 81.
32. Agreement of Oscar Mayer & Co., Madison Plant, and Local 538 of the Amalgamated Meat Cutters and Butcher Workmen of North America, AFL–CIO, p. 1, 1976–1979. (In possession of the author.)
33. James Elliott, interview with the author, October 20 and December 7, 1983.
34. After forty-five years in the foundry, Eugene Terman spent ten years as an internal security lieutenant. Telephone interview with the author, December 21, 1983.

CHAPTER 10

1. Glaab and Larsen, *Factories in the Valley,* p. 225.
2. Clark, *Chronicles of Wisconsin,* Vol. 15, "The Wisconsin Pulp and Paper Industry," pp. 6–8.
3. Glaab and Larsen, *Factories in the Valley,* p. 225.
4. Kaukauna *Times,* May 20, 1892.
5. Matthew Burns Papers, manuscript entitled "History of the International Brotherhood of Paper Makers" (1966), p. 2. SHSW.
6. Glaab and Larsen, *Factories in the Valley,* p. 245.
7. Appleton *Weekly Post,* November 21, 1901.
8. Neenah *Times,* November 27, 1901.
9. Appleton *Weekly Post,* December 5, 1901.
10. *Ibid.*
11. Glaab and Larsen, *Factories in the Valley,* p. 248; Appleton *Evening Crescent,* December 10, 1901.
12. Appleton *Weekly Post,* December 12, 1901.
13. Oshkosh *Northwestern,* January 13, 1902. The full names of these mills are: John Strange Paper Company, George A. Whiting Company, Menasha Paper Company, and Winnebago Paper Company.
14. *Ibid.,* January 16, 1902; Menasha *Evening Breeze,* January 13, 1902.
15. Neenah *Daily Times,* January 17, 1902.

16. Oshkosh *Northwestern*, January 21, 22, 1902; *Paper Makers' Journal*, 1 (June, 1902), 5.
17. Oshkosh *Northwestern*, April 16, 1902; Burns, "History of the International Brotherhood of Paper Makers."
18. Neenah *Daily Times*, January 6, 1902; Oshkosh *Northwestern*, January 20, 1902.
19. Appleton *Weekly Post*, March 27, 1902.
20. *Ibid.*
21. Kaukauna *Times*, April 11, 18, 23, 1902.
22. Neenah *Times*, April 29, 1902.
23. Stevens Point *Daily Journal*, January 14, 1902; *Wood County Reporter*, February 6, 13, 1902; *Paper Makers' Journal*, 1 (December, 1901), 22.
24. *Paper Makers' Journal*, 1 (May, 1902), 4.
25. Stevens Point *Daily Journal*, February 7, 1902.
26. Appleton *Crescent*, April 5, 1902; *Wood County Reporter*, April 10, 1902.
27. *Wood County Reporter*, February 27, 1902; *Paper Makers' Journal*, 1 (February, 1902), 22; 1 (March, 1902), 6; 1 (April, 1902), 22.
28. *Wood County Reporter*, February 27, 1902; Stevens Point *Daily Journal*, February 25, 1902.
29. Stevens Point *Daily Journal*, February 25, 1902.
30. *Wood County Reporter*, April 19, 1902.
31. Stevens Point *Daily Journal*, March 3, 1902.
32. *Ibid.*, March 15, 17, 1902.
33. *Wood County Reporter*, April 3, 1902.
34. Wausau *Pilot*, April 8, 1902; Stevens Point *Daily Journal*, April 3, 7, 1902.
35. *Wood County Reporter*, April 17, 1902; *Paper Makers' Journal*, 2 (December, 1902), 21; 2 (January, 1903), 21; 2 (February, 1903), 22; 2 (March, 1903), 21.
36. Eau Claire *Leader*, April 24, 1902.
37. *Paper Makers' Journal*, 1 (June, 1902), 18.
38. *Ibid.*, 1 (November, 1902) 20; Eau Claire *Telegram*, May 2, 1902.
39. Menasha *Evening Breeze*, September 8, 1902.
40. *Paper Makers' Journal*, 2 (March, 1903), 1.
41. Menasha *Evening Breeze*, April 18, 1903.
42. Kaukauna *Times*, February 13, 1903.
43. Menasha *Evening Breeze*, April 17, 1903.
44. Wisconsin State Board of Arbitration, *Biennial Report, 1904–1906*, p. 14.
45. Kaukauna *Times*, April 24, 1903.
46. Wisconsin State Board of Arbitration, *Biennial Report, 1904–1906*, p. 15.
47. *Paper Makers' Journal*, 2 (September, 1903), 7; 3 (June, 1904), 46.
48. *Ibid.*, 3 (June, 1904), 46.
49. *Ibid.*, 3 (June, 1904), 46; 2 (November, 1903), 22; 3 (September, 1904), 29.
50. Oshkosh *Northwestern*, May 3, 1904.
51. *Ibid.*, May 31, 1904.
52. *Ibid.*, June 1, 2, 1904.
53. *Ibid.*, June 4, 1904.
54. *Ibid.*, June 6, 1904; Kaukauna *Times*, June 10, 1904.
55. Wisconsin State Board of Arbitration, *Biennial Report, 1904–1906*, p. 30; Oshkosh *Northwestern*, June 4, 11, 1904.

56. Oshkosh *Northwestern*, June 15, 1904; Menasha *Citizen*, June 20, 1904.
57. Oshkosh *Northwestern*, June 21, 24, 1904.
58. Appleton *Evening Crescent*, August 15, 1904.
59. Oshkosh *Northwestern*, July 7, 8, 1904.
60. Menasha *Citizen*, July 5, 20, August 23, 1904; Neenah *Daily Times*, June 29, July 8, 1904.
61. Menasha *Citizen*, August 1, 1904.
62. Appleton *Evening Crescent*, August 1, 6, 15, 1904.
63. *Ibid.*, August 15, 1904.
64. *Paper Makers' Journal*, 4 (June, 1905), 11.
65. *Ibid.*, 4 (June, 1905), 53.
66. *Ibid.*, 4 (May, 1905), 25.
67. *Ibid.*, 5 (April, 1906), 16, 18.
68. *Ibid.*, 6 (February, 1907), 32.

CHAPTER 11

1. Burns, "History of the International Brotherhood of Paper Makers," pp. 65, 91, 92, 105, 155, 167.
2. *Ibid.*, p. 157; *Paper Makers' Journal*, 7 (December, 1907), 47; 7 (February, 1908), 32; 7 (June, 1908), 31; 7 (July, 1908), 32; 9 (November, 1910), 39.
3. *Paper Makers' Journal*, 11 (March, 1912), 17; 11 (July, 1912), 22.
4. Edward Paddock Sherry Papers, Flambeau Paper Company, Guy Waldo to Sherry, July 2, 1912. Milwaukee ARC, Box 150.
5. *Paper Makers' Journal*, 11 (September, 1912), 31; 12 (December, 1912), 17; 12 (May, 1913), 37; 12 (July, 1913), 32.
6. *Ibid.*, 13 (March, 1914), 10; 16 (June, 1917), 1.
7. David Clark Everest Papers, Everest to Burt Pride, June 4, June 16, 1913. SHSW, Box 5, folder 7.
8. *Ibid.*, Everest to L.M. Alexander, August 20, August 23, 1913. Box 3, folder 6.
9. *Ibid.*, L.M. Alexander to Everest, June 5, 1913.
10. Sherry Papers, Guy Waldo to Sherry, May 28, August 11, 1913. Box 150.
11. Everest Papers, Everest to Burt Pride, June 4, June 16, 1913. Box 5, folder 7.
12. Steven Burton Karges, "David Clark Everest and the Marathon Paper Mills Company: A Study of a Wisconsin Entrepreneur," (Ph.D. dissertation, University of Wisconsin, 1968), p. 205.
13. Everest Papers, Western Paper Makers Association (hereafter WPMA), 1914–1919, By-laws, Articles IX and X. Box 6, folder 9.
14. *Ibid.*, Article VII.
15. Everest Papers, L.B. McDermott to Ira L. Beck, October 28, 1925.
16. The *Journal*, 5 (August, 1916), 11. The *Journal* was the official organ of the International Brotherhood of Pulp, Sulphite and Paper Mill Workers. Henceforth indentified as the *Journal*.
17. The International Brotherhood of Pulp, Sulphite and Paper Mill Workers was organized in 1906 by pulp and sulphite workers who seceded from the International Brotherhood of Paper Makers after bitter fighting within the IBPM between themselves and the skilled machine tenders. After years of jurisdictional

disputes between this new IBPS&PMW and the IBPM, jurisdictional lines were agreed upon and the IBPS&PMW was chartered by the AFL in 1910.

18. Burns, "History of the International Brotherhood of Paper Makers," pp. 180, 199; the *Journal*, 5 (July, 1916), 23.
19. *Paper Makers' Journal*, 15 (May, 1916), 18.
20. *Ibid.*
21. *Ibid.*, 15 (April, 1916), 34.
22. Burns, "History of the International Brotherhood of Paper Makers," p. 180.
23. Everest Papers, WPMA, 1914–1919, membership rolls and applications. Box 6, folder 13.
24. Everest Papers, James A. Stilp to WPMA members, June 24, 1916.
25. Everest Papers, WPMA to its members, May 3, 1916.
26. Mary Baker, interview with the author, April 28, 1960.
27. *Paper Makers' Journal*, 15 (September, 1916), 27; 15 (October, 1916), 25. The Finishers' Local, No. 56 of the IBPM, was a local of unskilled workers. The skilled workers in the same plant were in Local 20.
28. Appleton *Evening Crescent*, June 20, 1916.
29. Appleton *Daily Post*, June 20, 1916.
30. *Ibid.*, June 20, 23, 1916.
31. Everest Papers, WPMA, Membership Application; minutes of the annual meeting, February 11, 1916; minutes of executive committee meetings, June 21, 27, 1916, all in Box 6, folder 13; J.E. Thomas to Everest, August 12, 1916.
32. *Paper Makers' Journal*, 15 (September, 1916), 8.
33. Everest Papers, Everest to J.E. Thomas, Treasurer, August 12, 1916.
34. Everest Papers, WPMA, 1914–1919, minutes of the special meeting of the executive committee, September 20, 1916. Box 6, folder 13.
35. Appleton *Evening Crescent*, July 1, 1916.
36. Appleton *Daily Post*, June 20, 23, 1916; the *Journal*, 5 (September, 1916), 8.
37. Appleton *Evening Crescent*, August 1, 1916.
38. The *Journal*, 5 (October, 1916), 5.
39. IBPS&PMW Papers, Sample to Malin, November 14, 1916. SHSW, Microfilm, Box 1.
40. Everest Papers, Lewis M. Alexander to Everest, December 15, 1916, Box 3, folder 6. Everest to Harry Fletcher, December 16, 1916; Frank J. Sensenbrenner to J.H. Fromback, January 8, 1917.
41. Marinette *Eagle–Star*, June 12, 1916.
42. *Ibid.*, June 17, 20, 22, 1916.
43. WSFL, *Proceedings*, 1916, p. 132.
44. Appleton, *Evening Crescent*, June 24, 1916; Marinette *Eagle–Star*, May 20, June 26, 30, July 22, 1916; the *Journal*, 5 (September, 1916), 8.
45. Marinette *Eagle–Star*, June 28, 1916.
46. *Ibid.*, June 27, 28, 1916.
47. *Ibid.*, June 28, July 7, 1916.
48. WSFL, *Proceedings*, 1916, pp. 131, 132.
49. Marinette *Eagle–Star*, July 22, 24, 1916.
50. *Ibid.*, June 14, 1916.
51. *Ibid.*, June 27, 1916.
52. The *Journal*, 5 (September, 1916), 7.

53. Everest Papers, WPMA, 1914–1919, membership application, Marinette, and Menominee Paper Company. Box 6, folder 13.
54. Marinette *Eagle–Star,* September 5, 1916; Menasha *Record,* June 21, 24, 1916.
55. *Paper Makers' Journal,* 15 (September, 1916), 29, 31; 16 (January, 1917), 17; the *Journal,* 5 (October, 1916), 5; 6 (May, 1917), 19; 7 (December, 1917), 32. WSFL, *Proceedings, 25th Annual Convention,* 1917, p. 15.
56. *Paper Makers' Journal,* 16 (June, 1917), 15; 17 (January, 1918), 15; *Rusk County Journal,* September 14, 1917.
57. *Paper Makers' Journal,* 17 (January, 1918), 14, 15.

CHAPTER 12

1. U.S. Department of Commerce, Bureau of the Census, *Historical Statistics* (Washington, D.C., 1975), p. 97.
2. Taft, *Organized Labor,* pp. 317–318.
3. *Paper Makers' Journal,* 19 (March, 1920), 21–23. In January, 1920, Grand Rapids changed its name to Wisconsin Rapids. In 1931 the Post Office also changed its name to Wisconsin Rapids. To avoid confusion, the city will be referred to in the text as "Wisconsin Rapids," regardless of the date.
4. David Clark Everest Papers, Everest to Ira L. Beck, May 1, 1918. SHSW.
5. Everest Papers, Western Paper Makers Association (hereafter WPMA), 1914–1919, Minutes, May 17, 1919, Box 6, folder 13.
6. Edward Paddock Sherry Papers, Flambeau Paper Company, Guy Waldo to Sherry, May 19, 1919 and March 24, 1920. Milwaukee ARC, Box 150.
7. Everest Papers, WPMA, 1914–1919, Ira L. Beck to "Gentlemen," Chicago, April 30, 1920.
8. Everest Papers, Guy Waldo to Everest, April 20, 23, 1920; Sherry Papers, Flambeau Paper Company, Guy Waldo to Sherry, May, 1919, Box 150.
9. Everest Papers, M.O. Wertheimer, President of Thilmany Paper Company, to Everest, July 30, 1919, Box 5, folder 10.
10. Everest Papers, Justice Marvin Rosenberry to Everest, November 6, 1919, Box 4, folder 7.
11. Everest Papers, Everest to Charles G. Oberley, March 11, 26, 1918; Oberley to Everest, March 18, 1918, Box 2, folder 12.
12. Everest Papers, Everest to Frank J. Sensenbrenner, September 11, 1914; Everest to M. Harry Ballou, April 26, 1916; Everest to Charles Oberley, March 26, 1918, Box 2, folder 12.
13. Everest Papers, Everest to Ira L. Beck, February 4, 1920; Everest to employees of the Marathon Paper Mills Company, January 13, 1920; Everest to Charles J. Winton, January 21, 1920; Box 15, folder 5; Everest to Tomahawk Pulp and Paper Company, Attention: Burt A. Pride, April 19, 1920.
14. Everest Papers, Everest to Consolidated Power and Paper Company, Attention: C.E. Jackson, Employment Manager of Consolidated, March 3, 1920; Everest to A.J. Stewartson, Secretary of the Wrapping Paper Manufacturers Service Bureau, February 27, 1920, Box 15, folder 10.

15. International Brotherhood of Pulp, Sulphite and Paper Mill Workers (IBPS&PMW) Papers, Marathon Pulp Workers Local, Leslie Nickel to John P. Burke, August 12, 1921. SHSW, Microfilm, Box 1, 1921, Reel 3P.
16. *Ibid.,* Fred Linden to Burke, December 29, 1920.
17. Everest Papers, Open Shop Association, 1920–1922, Everest to Brooks and Ross Lumber Company, July 20, 1920, Box 12, file 14; Sherry Papers, Flambeau Paper Company, George Waldo to Sherry, March 3, 1920, Box 150.
18. Everest Papers, Open Shop Association, 1920–1922, Everest to Wausau Open Shop Association members, July 20, 1920; Association financial statement prepared by Howard W. Russell, President, Howard W. Russell, Incorporated [detective agency], Milwaukee, Wisconsin, Box 12, file 14.
19. Grand Rapids *Daily Leader,* February 12, 1919.
20. *Ibid.,* July 28, 1919.
21. *Ibid.,* June 3, 20, September 12, 1919.
22. *Ibid.,* June 23, 1919.
23. Everest Papers, union leaflet dated July 3, 1919.
24. Grand Rapids *Daily Leader,* June 25, 26, July 1, 1919.
25. *Ibid.,* July 12, 1919. The Wisconsin Industrial Commission was a state agency established by the legislature in 1911 to administer all labor–management relations legislation, principally, worker compensation, minimum wage, safety inspections, and mediation of industrial disputes. Not all of the above duties were given to the Commission in 1911.
26. *Ibid.,* July 14, 1919.
27. *Ibid.,* July 25, 1919.
28. *Ibid.,* July 30, 1919.
29. *Ibid.,* August 30, 1919.
30. *Ibid.,* July 30, August 5, 8, 23, September 2, 20, October 15, 1919.
31. *Ibid.,* September 17, October 8, 1919.
32. *Ibid.,* August 19, 20, 1919.
33. *Ibid.,* July 28, 1919.
34. *Ibid.,* August 26, 1919.
35. *Ibid.,* September 4, 15, 1919.
36. *Ibid.,* August 23, 1919.
37. Everest Papers, letters from WPMA to members, September 4, December 23, 1919; June 6, 1920.
38. IBPS&PMW Papers, Patrick O'Brien to Burke, November 10, 1920, Box 1, 1920, Reel 3P.
39. *Ibid.,* Burke to O'Brien, November 19, 1920, Box 1, 1920, Reel 3P.
40. *Ibid.,* Audit Statement of Nekoosa Strike Fund, Box 1, 1920, Reel 3P; Burns, "History of the International Brotherhood of Paper Makers," p. 19; *Paper Makers Journal,* 19 (September–October, 1920), 17.
41. Grand Rapids *Daily Leader,* August 6, 8, 1919.
42. *Ibid.,* September 11, 19, 24, 1919.
43. IBPS&PMW Papers, George Chapley to Burke, September 26, 1919, Box 1, 1919, Reel 2P.
44. *Paper Makers' Journal,* 19 (September–October, 1920), 17–18.
45. IBPS&PMW Papers, Robert Rogers to Burke, March 22, 1922, Burke to Rogers, April 4, 1922, Box 1, 1922, Reel 3P.

46. Everest Papers, report from no. 15, October 22, 1928; report from No. 33, March 24, 1929, April 24, 1931, Box 91, folder 12. Labor spies working for the Western Paper Manufacturers Association signed their reports only with a number, thus preserving their secrecy if a letter was discovered. Since Wisconsin had a law prohibiting unlicensed labor spies it may have also been aimed at legal protection. Not even the employer in whose mill the spy worked knew the identity of the spy who reported to Ira L. Beck, the manager of the Association.
47. Kimberly–Clark Company, "Mill Council Plan," February 18, 1920 (constitution for the plan, pamphlet in possession of the author).
48. Everest Papers, Sensenbrenner to Everest, February 21, 1920.
49. *Cooperation,* May, 1920 (the Kimberly–Clark Company magazine).
50. Grand Rapids *Daily Leader,* April 5, 7, 1919.
51. *Ibid.,* April 10, 1919.
52. *Paper Makers' Journal,* 18 (June, 1919), 17.
53. Consolidated Power and Paper Company, company records, Wisconsin Rapids, Union Agreements of 1919 and 1921, from memo of L.H. Barrette.
54. Sherry Papers, Flambeau Paper Company, Waldo to Sherry, May 8, 1919, Box 150.
55. Everest Papers, Lewis M. Alexander to Judson G. Rosebush, April 10, 1928, Box 59, folder 2.
56. The *Journal,* 12 (December, 1926), 1.
57. Everest Papers, notes from WPMA annual meeting, March 15, 1927; Everest to Ira L. Beck, March 9, 1927.
58. Everest Papers, report from No. 15, January 24, 1927, Box 59, folder 2.
59. *Ibid.,* August 25, 1927; March 31, 1928; January 24, 1927.
60. Everest Papers, Alexander to Rosebush, April 10, 1928, Box 59, folder 2; John Alexander to Lewis M. Alexander, April 20, 1928, Box 59, folder 2.
61. Everest Papers, reports from No. 15, March 31, April 12, 1929, Box 59, folder 12.
62. *Ibid.,* reports of August 12, October 9, 1929.
63. *Consolidated News,* publication of the Consolidated Power and Paper Company, April, 1926, in possession of the company.
64. Grand Rapids *Daily Leader,* April 10, 1919.
65. Bakke and Kerr, *Union Management and the Public,* pp. 289–294.
66. IBPS&PMW Papers, "Proceedings," October 3–5, 1920, Box 1, Reel 14P.
67. Everest Papers, 1920–1921, minutes from Wage Conference, Toronto, Canada, January 22, 25, 1921, signed B–431.
68. IBPS&PMW Papers, "Proceedings," October 3, 1922, Box 1, Reel 14P.
69. Sherry Papers, Flambeau Paper Company, Waldo to Sherry, January 29, 1921, Box 150.
70. IBPS&PMW Papers, Burke to George A. Schneider, May 4, 1921, Box 1, 1921, Reel 5P.
71. *Paper Makers' Journal,* 18 (June, 1919), 26.
72. Sherry Papers, Flambeau Paper Company, Ira L. Beck to WPMA members, April 30, 1920, Box 150.
73. Everest Papers, Everest to Ballou, March 28, 1921.

74. Federated Trades Council, Green Bay, minutes, March 22, 1921. Green Bay ARC.
75. Burns, "History of the International Brotherhood of Paper Makers," pp. 253, 255; Everest Papers, William A. Kelly, General Superintendent, Northern Paper Mills, Green Bay, to Everest, March 18, 1921, Box 11, folder 1; Everest to Kelly, March 18, 1921, Box 11, folder 1.
76. Everest Papers, William Kelly, General Superintendent, Northern Paper Mills, Green Bay, to Everest, April 26, 1921.
77. Green Bay *Press–Gazette,* June 3, 1921.
78. *Ibid.*
79. Everest Papers, letter from John Welsh, General Manager, Green Bay Paper and Fibre Company, to Marathon Paper Mills Company, July 16, 1921.
80. Federated Trades Council, Green Bay, minutes, March 15, 1928. Green Bay ARC.
81. Everest Papers, Sensenbrenner to Everest, June 11, 1921, Box 10, folder 23.
82. *Paper Makers' Journal,* 18 (August, 1919), 53.
83. Everest Papers, H.C. Hanke, Treasurer and Manager, Rhinelander Paper Company, to Everest, March 29, 1920.
84. Burns, "History of the International Brotherhood of Paper Makers," p. 256.
85. Brian K. Sheldon, "A Brief History of the Rhinelander Paper Company" (unpublished student paper in possession of the author, 1978), pp. 9–10.
86. Everest Papers, Everest to A.J. Stewartson, July 8, 1921, Box 15, folder 10.
87. Sheldon, "Rhinelander Paper Company," pp. 10–15.
88. New York *Times,* June 30, 1921.
89. Everest Papers, "Comparative Wage Schedule" by F.G. Lesnick, February 27, 1923–1924.
90. Sherry Papers, Flambeau Paper Company, Guy Waldo to Sherry, May 12, October 25, 1921, Box 150.
91. Leo H. Barrette, "History of Company's Bargaining with Hourly Unions," memorandum is possession of the Consolidated Water Power and Paper Company, 1957.
92. Everest Papers, Ira L. Beck to Everest, January 25, 1922; Thomas M. Love, "The Struggle to Unionize the Wisconsin River Valley Paper Industry" (unpublished student paper in possession of the author, 1963), p. 16.
93. Everest Papers, Beck to Everest, January 25, 1922.
94. Everest Papers, worker to Everest, April 1, 1922, Box 11, folder 14.
95. Everest Papers, WPMA, Beck to Everest, March 6, 1922.
96. Kimberly–Clark Company, minutes of the Niagara Mill Council, December 20, 1920; papers in possession of the company, Neenah, Wisconsin.
97. Kimberly–Clark Company, minutes of the General Mill Council, April 28, 1921; minutes in possession of the company, Neenah, Wisconsin.
98. Sherry Papers, Flambeau Paper Company, Waldo to Sherry, April 30, 1921, Box 150.
99. Kimberly–Clark Company, minutes of the Niagara Mill Council, August 10, 1921; minutes in possession of the company, Neenah, Wisconsin.
100. Kimberly–Clark Company, minutes of the Neenah–Appleton Mill Council, March 14, 1922; minutes in possession of the company, Neenah, Wisconsin.
101. Kaukauna *Times,* April 13, 1922.

102. Appleton *Post–Crescent,* April 3, 4, 5, 1922.
103. Everest Papers, WPMA file, Alexander to Everest, July 11, 1922.
104. Appleton *Post–Crescent,* April 4, 1922.
105. *Paper Makers' Journal,* 21 (May, 1922), 27.
106. Everest Papers, WPMA file, Beck Report to WPMA for April, 1922, April 4, 1922; Appleton *Post–Crescent,* August 10, 1922.

CHAPTER 13

1. David Clark Everest Papers, Ira L. Beck to Everest, December 26, 1922; minutes of the Wage Conference, Toronto, Canada, joint session of IBPM and IBPS&PMW, January 25, 1921, signed B–431. SHSW.
2. Everest Papers, John Alexander to Ira L. Beck, April 22, 1931, Box 91, folder 12.
3. Everest Papers, Alexander to Beck, December 24, 1931, Box 91, folder 12.
4. Everest Papers, No. 15 to Dear Sir, January 11, 1932, Box 100, folder 9.
5. IBPS&PMW Papers, Burke to Fred Gehring, President Wausau Central Body, March 10, 1932; Jacob Stephan, Organizer, to Sample, Organizer, March 17, 1932; Burke to Stephan, April 9, 1932, Box 2, 1932, Reel 1P; and Everest Papers, reports of January 11, April 3, 21, 1932, to D.C. Everest from No. 15, Box 100, folder 9.
6. Everest Papers, report from No. 15, April 3, 1932, Box 100, folder 9.
7. Haferbecker, *Wisconsin Labor Laws,* p. 176; State of Wisconsin, Department of Regulation and Licensing, Direct Licensing, Applications for Private Detectives and Agency Licensing Series 1881. SHSW, Box 1, folders 1919–1929, 1930–1939.
8. Everest Papers, Gustave J. Keller, attorney to Everest, May 5, 1933; State of Wisconsin: In Circuit Court: For Wood County, Charles H. Sample, Plaintiff, vs. Western Manufacturers Association, defendant's Summons, Box 108, folder 14.
9. Everest Papers; State of Wisconsin: In Circuit Court: For Outagamie County: Charles M. Sample, Plaintiff, vs. Western Manufacturers Association, July 5, 1933; Box 108, folder 14.
10. Everest Papers, Beck to Everest, May 3, 1932, Edward Dempsey, attorney to Nash, Nekoosa-Ewards Paper Company executive, August 31, 1933.
11. IBPS&PMW Papers, Malin, Organizer, to Sample, Organizer, July 26, 1916, SHSW, Microfilm, Box 1, 1916 Reel 1P; Everest Papers, report from No. 32, to Dear Sir, June 12, 1928, Box 59, folder 2.
12. Federated Trades Council, Green Bay, minutes, January 13, 1931. Green Bay ARC.
13. *Ibid.*
14. *Ibid.,* February 10, 1931.
15. Everest Papers, report to Dear Sir, May 10, 1931, Box 91, folder 12.
16. *Ibid.,* August 8, 1931.
17. Kimberly–Clark Corporation, minutes of the Lakeview Mill Council, December 5, 1933; minutes in possession of the company, Neenah, Wisconsin.

18. "Council Plan of Employees and Management, Kimberly–Clark Corporation," in possession of the corporation, Neenah, Wisconsin.
19. Kimberly–Clark Corporation, minutes of the General Council meeting, June 12–13, 1933; minutes in possession of the corporation, Neenah, Wisconsin.
20. Kimberly–Clark Corporation, minutes of the General Council meeting, November 3, December 3–4, 1936; minutes in possession of the corporation, Neenah, Wisconsin.
21. Kimberly–Clark Corporation, minutes of the General Council meeting, April 1–3, 1937; minutes in possession of the corporation, Neenah, Wisconsin.
22. *Ibid.*
23. *Ibid.*
24. *Ibid.*
25. *Ibid.*
26. Barrette, memo in files of the Consolidated Power and Paper Company, Wisconsin Rapids.
27. Consolidated Power and Paper Company, personnel file, "Contract Negotiations," in possession of the Company, Wisconsin Rapids, Wisconsin. Kimberly–Clark records in possession of the author.
28. Flemming and Witte, *Causes of Industrial Peace and Collective Bargaining: Marathon Corporation*, National Planning Association, 1950.

BIBLIOGRAPHY

SHSW = State Historical Society of Wisconsin
ARC = Area Research Center

ARCHIVAL MATERIAL

Bricklayers, Masons, and Plasterers International Union, Local 8. Minutes in English and German, Milwaukee, Wisconsin. Milwaukee ARC, 1884–1925.

Burns, Matthew. Editor of *Paper Makers' Journal* and president of the International Brotherhood of Paper Makers. Papers, manuscript titled "History of the International Brotherhood of Paper Maker," 1 box. SHSW.

Cooper, Bill. Tape-recorded interview, December 4, 1951. 1 reel. SHSW.

Everest, David Clark. Papers, 1891–1957. 320 boxes. SHSW. During the years of this study the Everest Papers were re-catalogued by the State Historical Society. Some of the footnotes bear the new locations including box and folder numbers. Some of the footnotes still bear the earlier designations, without box and folder numbers. Since the the new cataloguing is chronological, sources can be located by using the old designation.

Federated Trades Council, Green Bay. Various materials, 1907–1940. 5 boxes incl. 18 vols. Green Bay ARC.

Federated Trades Council of Milwaukee. Papers, 1900–1950. 6 boxes, incl. 15 vols. Milwaukee ARC.

International Brotherhood of Pulp, Sulphite and Paper Mill Workers. Papers, 1906–1957. Microfilm 43. 284 reels. SHSW.

The *Journal* of the International Brotherhood of Pulp, Sulphite, and Paper Mill Workers. Microfilm 1914–1921; not published 1921–1926; bound February, 1926–December, 1965. SHSW.

The *Paper Makers' Journal* of the United Paper Makers. Microfilm December, 1901–November, 1914; bound volumes December, 1944–1957.

Sheet Metal Workers International Association, Local 42, Superior, Wisconsin. Records, 1904–47. 5 boxes incl. 5 vols. and 1 carton. Superior ARC.

Sherry, Edward Paddock. Papers, 1890–1941, Flambeau Paper Company. 191 boxes and 1 volume. Milwaukee ARC.

Superior Trades and Labor Assembly, Superior, Wisconsin. Records, 1892–1929. 4 vols. in 1 box. Superior ARC.

United Brotherhood of Carpenters and Joiners of America, Local 161, Kenosha. Minute books, 1897–1921. 7 vols. in 2 boxes. Parkside ARC.

Wisconsin State AFL–CIO. Mimeographed minutes of the Executive Board meetings of the Wisconsin State AFL–CIO, 1960–1962 (Box 3). SHSW.

Wisconsin State CIO. *Proceedings* of the Annual Convention, 1939–1957. Microfilm of typescript. 19 vols. on 8 reels. SHSW.

Wisconsin State Federation of Labor. Papers, 1911–1953. 16 boxes incl. 14 vols., and 1 vol. SHSW.

Women's Trade Union League of America Convention. *Proceedings,* 1926.

CORPORATION AND PRIVATE PAPERS

Barrette, L. H. (Director of Personnel and Labor Relations.) "History of Company's Bargaining with Hourly Unions." Consolidated Power and Paper Company, memorandum in possession of the company, April 29, 1957, Wisconsin Rapids.

Consolidated Power and Paper Company, *Consolidated News,* in possession of the company, Wisconsin Rapids.

Cooperation, Kimberly–Clark company magazine, in possession of the company, Neenah, Wisconsin.

Heymanns, Charles. Formerly AFL Regional Director, Private Files, 2 boxes of letters, photos, exhibits, in possession of Charles Heymanns, Sheboygan, Wisconsin, 1936–1970.

International Association of Machinists, Lodge 66. Minute Books. Lodge Headquarters, Milwaukee, 1890–present.

Kimberly–Clark Corporation corporate files. Mill Council Minutes, 1920–1937, "Council Plan of Employees and Management," constitution and minutes of General Council, Lakeview Mill Council, wage records, in possession of the company, Neenah, Wisconsin.

BOOKS, JOURNAL ARTICLES, AND PUBLIC DOCUMENTS

Adamany, David. *Financing Politics: Recent Wisconsin Elections.* Madison: University of Wisconsin Press, 1969.

Adamic, Louis. "The Collapse of Organized Labor." *Harpers Monthly Magazine,* 164 (1932), 167.

Bailey, John W. "Labor's Fight for Security and Dignity." In John A. Neuenschwander, ed., *Kenosha County in the Twentieth Century: A Topical History.* Kenosha, Wis.: Kenosha County Bicentennial Commission, 1976.

Bakke, Wight, and Kerr, Clark. *Union Management and the Public.* New York: Harcourt, Brace, 1948.

Baxandall, Lee, ed. "Furs, Logs and Human Lives: The Great Oshkosh Woodworkers Strike of 1898." *Green Mountain Quarterly,* No. 3 (May, 1976), 15–92.

Bayley, Edwin R. *Joe McCarthy and the Press.* Madison: University of Wisconsin Press, 1981.

Buenker, John D. "The Politics of Mutual Frustration: Socialists and Suffragists in New York and Wisconsin." In Sally Miller, ed., *Flawed Liberation: Socialism and Feminism.* Westport, Conn.: Greenwood Press, 1981.

Clark, James I. "The Wisconsin Pulp and Paper Industry." *Chronicles of Wisconsin.* Madison: SHSW, Vol. 15, 1955–1956.

Commons, John R. *History of Labor in the United States.* Vol. 4. New York: Macmillan, 1935.

Fine, Sidney. *The Automobile Under the Blue Eagle: Labor, Management, and the Automobile Manufacturing Code.* Ann Arbor: University of Michigan Press, 1963.

Fleming, Robben W., and Witte, Edwin E. *Causes of Industrial Peace and Collective Bargaining: Marathon Corporation.* Washington, D.C.: National Planning Association, 1950.

Frey, John P. *History of a Criminal Conspiracy to Defeat Striking Molders: Lawless Method of Employers Uncovered through Court Records.* Cincinnati: International Molders Union of North America, 1907[?].

Gavett, Thomas W. *The Development of the Labor Movement in Milwaukee.* Madison: University of Wisconsin Press, 1965.

Glaab, Charles N., and Larsen, Lawrence H. *Factories in the Valley: Nee-nah–Menasha, 1870–1915*. Madison: State Historical Society of Wisconsin, 1969.

Haferbecker, Gordon M. *Wisconsin Labor News*. Madison: University of Wisconsin Press, 1958.

Jensen, Vernon H. *Lumber and Labor*. New York: Farrar and Rinehart, 1945.

Job, Frederick W. *A Tale of Two Cities*. Chicago: Employers' Association of Chicago, 1904[?].

Kampelman, Max M. *The Communist Party vs. the CIO: A Study in Power Politics*. New York: Praeger, 1957.

Kramer, Leo. *Labor's Paradox: The American Federation of State, County, and Municipal Employees, AFL–CIO*. New York: John Wiley, 1962.

Lescohier, Don D. *The Knights of St. Crispin, 1867–1874: A Study in the Industrial Causes of Trade Unionism*. Bulletin of the University of Wisconsin, no. 335. Economic and Political Science Series, Vol. 7, No. 1. Madison, 1910.

Lester, Richard A. *Labor and Industrial Relations*. New York: Macmillan, 1951.

Margulies, Herbert F. *Senator Lenroot of Wisconsin*. Columbia: University of Missouri Press, 1978.

Merk, Frederick. *Economic History of Wisconsin During the Civil War Decade*. Madison: Wisconsin State Historical Society, 1916.

Miller, Sally M. *Victor Berger and the Promise of Constructive Socialism, 1910–1920*. Contributions in American History, No. 24. Westport, Conn.: Greenwood Press, 1973.

Nelson, Daniel. *Unemployment Insurance: The American Experience, 1915–1935*. Madison: University of Wisconsin Press, 1969.

Oshinsky, David M. *Senator Joseph McCarthy and the American Labor Movement*. Columbia: University of Missouri Press, 1976.

Ozanne, Robert. *The Negro in the Farm Equipment and Construction Machinery Industries*. Wharton School of Finance and Commerce, Industrial Research Unit, University of Pennsylvania. Philadelphia: University of Pennsylvania Press, 1972.

Perlman, Mark. *The Machinists: A New Study in American Trade Union-ism.* Cambridge: Harvard University Press, 1961.

Perlman, Selig. *A Theory of the Labor Movement.* 1928. Reprint. New York: Augustus M. Kelley, 1949.

Perlman, Selig, and Taft, Philip. *History of Labor in the United States, 1896–1932.* Labor Movements, Vol. 4. New York: Macmillan, 1935.

Shaw, Albert. *Cooperatives in the Northwest.* Herbert B. Adams, ed., Johns Hopkins University Studies in Historical and Political Science. Baltimore: Johns Hopkins University Press, 1888.

Stone, Irving. *Clarence Darrow for the Defense: A Biography.* Garden City, N.Y.: Doubleday, Doran, 1941.

Taft, Philip. *Organized Labor in American History.* New York: Harper and Row, 1964.

Traxler, Henry. "I Went through a Strike." *Public Management,* April, 1937.

Uphoff, Walter H. *Kohler on Strike: Thirty Years of Conflict.* Boston: Beacon Press, 1966.

Weinberg, Arthur, ed. *Attorney for the Damned.* New York: Simon and Schuster, 1957.

Williamson, Harold F., and Meyers, Kenneth H. *Designed for Digging: The First 75 Years of Bucyrus–Erie Company.* Evanston, Ill.: Northwestern University Press, 1955.

Wisconsin Bureau of Labor and Industrial Statistics. *Biennial Report of the Bureau of Labor and Industrial Statistics.* First report, 1884, is by the Wisconsin Bureau of Labor Statistics. Reports for 1892–1896 are by the renamed Bureau of Labor, Census, and Industrial Statistics.

Wisconsin State AFL–CIO. *Proceedings of the Annual Convention.* Milwaukee. Published annually by the State AFL–CIO, available starting with 1901.

Wisconsin State Board of Arbitration and Concilation. *Biennial Report of the State Board of Arbitration.* Published every other year, beginning in 1897 (report for 1895–1896).

Wisconsin State Election Board. *Biennial Report.* Vol. II, Campaign Statistics Report, June, 1979.

Wisconsin State Federation of Labor. *Labor Conditions in Wisconsin: Fifth Report of the Executive Board.* Milwaukee: WSFL, 1916.

Wisconsin State Federation of Labor. *Proceedings of the Annual Convention.* Milwaukee: published annually by the WSFL. The proceedings for 1898 were published a year later in a *WSFL Directory* of local unions. Earlier proceedings may be found in newspapers.

UNPUBLISHED PAPERS, THESES, AND DISSERTATIONS

Asher, R. "Workmen's Compensation in the United States, 1880–1935." Ph.D. dissertation, University of Minnesota, 1971.

Branch, Helen. "The Milwaukee Boston Store Strike." Unpublished student paper in possession of the author. 1980.

Burns, Matthew. "History of the International Brotherhood of Paper Makers." Unpublished manuscript, SHSW, 1966.

Cameron, Gary A. "Labor Relations at J. I. Case." Unpublished paper, Graduate School of Business, University of Chicago, 1965. In possession of the author.

Coakley, Christopher. "The Start of Unionism at the Harnischfeger Corporation." Unpublished student paper in possession of the author. 1975.

Givens, Richard A. "The Milwaukee Brewery Strike of 1953." Master's thesis, University of Wisconsin, 1954.

Holter, Daryl O. "Labor Spies and Union Busting in Wisconsin, 1892–1940." Unpublished paper in possession of the author. 1983.

Ignatius, Mary. "The Milwaukee Polish Labor Strike of 1886." Unpublished student paper in possession of the author. 1975.

Johnson, James. "Labor in Wisconsin Politics, 1887–1940." Unpublished student paper in possession of the author. 1976.

Karges, Steven Burton. "David Clark Everest and the Marathon Paper Mills Company: A Study of a Wisconsin Entrepreneur." Ph.D. dissertation, University of Wisconsin, 1968.

King, Gordon A. "A Short History: Milwaukee Plumbers and Gasfitters Union, Local no. 75." 2 pp. Mimeo. Written ca. 1939 in Milwaukee; copy in possession of the author.

Love, Thomas M. "The Struggle to Unionize the Wisconsin River Valley Paper Industry." Unpublished student paper in possession of the author. 1963.

MacKay, Todd. "The 1921 Strike of the Northern Paper Mills." Unpublished student paper in possession of the author. 1980.

Morford, Barbara. "Women Workers and Organized Labor." Unpublished paper in possession of the author. 1979.

Muzick, Edward. "Victor L. Berger: A Biography." Ph.D. dissertation, Northwestern University, 1960.

Olson, Frederick I. "The Milwaukee Socialists, 1897–1941." Ph.D. dissertation, Harvard University, 1952.

Perlman, Selig. "History of Socialism in Wisconsin." B.A. thesis, University of Wisconsin, 1910.

Raushenbush, Paul A., and Raushenbush, Elizabeth Brandeis. "Our 'U.C.' Story." Manuscript in possession of the author. 1978.

Rodel, Tom. "The Establishment of Federal Labor Union No. 18684." Unpublished student paper in possession of the author. 1975.

Schmidt, Lester M. "The Farmer–Labor Progressive Federation: The Study of a 'United Front' Movement Among Wisconsin Liberals, 1934–1941." Ph.D. dissertation, University of Wisconsin, 1954.

Sheldon, Brian K. "A Brief History of the Rhinelander Paper Company." In possession of the author. 1978.

NEWSPAPERS

*The Wisconsin newspapers cited here are
available at the State Historical Society of Wisconsin.*

Appleton *Daily Post.*
Appleton *Evening Crescent.*
Appleton *Post–Crescent.*
Ashland *Daily News.*
Beloit *Daily Journal.*
Beloit *Free Press.*
Eau Claire *Free Press.*
Eau Claire *Leader.*
Eau Claire *News.*

Eau Claire *The Telegram.*
Grand [Wisconsin] Rapids *Daily Leader.*
Green Bay *Gazette.*
Jefferson *Banner.*
Kenosha *Labor.*
La Crosse *Chronicle.*
Madison *Daily Democrat.*
Marinette *Eagle.*

Marinette *Eagle–Star*.

Menasha *Record*.

Milwaukee *Journal*.

Milwaukee *News–Sentinel*.

Milwaukee *Sentinel*.

Milwaukee *Sunday Telegraph*.

New York *Herald*.

New York *Sun*.

Racine *Advocate*.

Oshkosh *Labor Advocate*.

Oshkosh *Northwestern*.

Racine *News*.

Sheboygan *Times*.

Superior *Evening Telegram*.

Wisconsin Vorwaerts.

INTERVIEWS

All interviews were conducted by the author, who has the interview notes in his possession. Below is a list of the persons interviewed.

From these persons specific information was obtained which has been used in the text:

Mary Baker. Former Personnel Officer, 1916, Kimberly Mill, Kimberly–Clark. Interview, April 28, 1960, Hudson, Wisconsin.

Walter Burke. Former Secretary–Treasurer, United Steel Workers of America. Telephone interview, April 27, 1976.

Larry Carlstrom. Staff Representative, United Auto Workers. Telephone interview, January 7, 1976.

William Cooper. Former Secretary–Treasurer, Building Service International Union. Interview, December 4, 1951, Milwaukee, Wisconsin.

James Elliott. President, Milwaukee Building and Construction Trades Council. Telephone interview, October 26, 1983.

Rudolph Faupl. Former Grand Lodge Representative for International Affairs, International Association of Machinists. Telephone interview, September 16, 1976.

Carl Griepentrog. Former President, Allied Industrial Workers. Interview, November 10, 1977, Hartford, Wisconsin.

George Hall. Former Secretary–Treasurer, WSFL. Interviews April 8, 1976, and November 28, 1981, Green Bay, Wisconsin.

Al Hayes. Former President, International Association of Machinists. Interview, May 5, 1980, Waukesha, Wisconsin.

Gordon King. Former Head Business Agent, Milwaukee Plumbers and Gasfitters, Local 75. Telephone interview, October 19, 1983.

E. H. Kolhagen. Worker and leader of United Auto Workers, Local 833, at Kohler, Wisconsin. Interview, June, 1952, Madison, Wisconsin.

Clifford Matchey. Former Regional Director, Allied Industrial Workers. Interview, July 1, 1977, Coloma, Wisconsin.

Harold Newton. Former publisher of Kenosha *Labor Press.* Interview, October 11, 1976, Eau Claire, Wisconsin. Telephone interviews, October 27, 1976, and January 9, 1981.

Frank Ranney. Former President of Teamsters, Local 200. Telephone interview, July 28, 1982.

John W. Schmitt. President, Wisconsin State AFL–CIO. Telephone interview, February 9, 1983.

Herman Steffes. Former President, Wisconsin State Industrial Union Council. Telephone interview, October 7, 1983.

The following persons were interviewed by the author and gave very helpful background information but were not quoted directly:

Andrew Biemiller. Chief Legislative Assistant to President George Meany, AFL–CIO. October 11, 1976, Eau Claire, Wisconsin.

Matthew Burns. Former President of the International Brotherhood of Paper Mill Workers. August 8, 1962, Albany, New York.

James Doyle. Former State Chairman of the Democratic Party of Wisconsin. September 12, 1983, Madison, Wisconsin.

Robert Durkin. Former Vice President of the Milwaukee County Labor Council. April 14, 1981, Madison, Wisconsin.

Charles Eubank. Formerly of the Personnel Department, Kimberly–Clark. May 11, 1962, Neenah, Wisconsin.

John Heidenreich. Former assistant to the President, Retail Clerks International Association. Telephone interview, May 3, 1983.

Charles Heymanns. Former Regional Director, American Federation of Labor. June 18, 1976, and March 6, 1977, Sheboygan, Wisconsin.

Helen Henson. President of Office and Professional Workers Union. Local 9. Telephone interview, March 1, 1977.

Sophie Holtz. Former Office Manager, International Brotherhood of Electrical Workers, Local 494. Telephone interview, March 1, 1977.

Frederick Kranhold. Former Superintendent of Manufacturing, Kimberly–Clark Company. November 20, 1958, Neenah, Wisconsin.

Roy Kubista. Staff Representative, American Federation of State, County, and Municipal Employees. April 6, 1978, Madison, Wisconsin.

Kathryn Hartman Lichter. Former Staff Representative of Milwaukee' Local of Fur and Leather Workers Union. Telephone interview, January 25, 1984.

John Lawton. Attorney and lobbyist for several Wisconsin public employee unions. Telephone interview, September 14, 1983.

Bertram McNamara. Former Regional Director, Region 32, United Steel Workers of America. February 12, 1982, Madison, Wisconsin.

Murray Plopper. Former Assistant to the President, Retail Clerks International Association of Machinists. Telephone interview, October 11, 1983.

S. Frank Shattuck. Former Treasurer, Kimberly–Clark Corporation. April 14, 1958, Neenah, Wisconsin.

Paul Whiteside, Sr. Former member of WSFL Executive Board. Telephone interview, October 11, 1983.

Frank Zeidler. Former Mayor of Milwaukee and Socialist Party Activist. Telephone interview, February 2, 1981.

INDEX

AFL. *See* American Federation of Labor

AFL–CIO: rivalry and jurisdictional disputes, 85–86, 95, 107, 112, 116, 117, 140–141; merger, 102, 116, 117–119. *See also* American Federation of Labor; Congress of Industrial Organizations

AFSCME. *See* American Federation of State, County, and Municipal Employees

Adamic, Louis, 59–60

Adamany, David, 148

Adelman, Meyer, 84–85, 87, 93

Affirmative action, 163–165

Alexander, John, 229, 232

Alexander, Lewis M., 189–190, 206–209, 212

Alfonsi, Paul, 137

Allen–A Hosiery plant: strike of 1928–1929 in Kenosha, 58–59

Allen–Bradley Company, 86

Alliance movement: Janesville autoworkers, 65

Allied Chemical and Dye Company, 57

Allied Industrial Workers (AFL–CIO), 83, 248

Allis, E.P., Company, 5, 8

Allis–Chalmers, 31, 32, 50, 79, 86, 89, 91, 97–99, 137, 162

Amalgamated Association of Iron and Steel Workers, 7

Amalgamated Clothing Workers Union, 143

Amalgamated Woodworkers (AFL): 19–20, 25; Local 95, 25

American Federation of Full-Fashioned Hosiery Workers, 58–59, 158

American Federation of Government Employees, 73

American Federation of Labor (AFL): 13, 18, 22, 26, 29, 34, 37, 59–60, 72–73, 109, 114, 124, 130, 236; Building Trades Department, 43; federal labor unions, 62, 64, 78, 79–80, 107, 114, 115–116, 120

American Federation of State, County and Municipal Employees (AFSCME): 71, 72–76 *passim*, 108–109, 113; founded in Wisconsin, 72; Local 270, 74; struggles in small towns and rural counties, 74–75

American Federation of State, County, and Municipal Workers: Wisconsin's largest union, 75

American Federation of Teachers (AFT): locals organized in Milwaukee, 76; Local 223, 76

American Federationist, 124

American Motors Company. *See* Nash Motor Company

"American Plan," 57

American Railway Union, 23, 44

American Writing Paper Company, 180, 181

Amlie, Thomas, 133, 134

A.O. Smith Steel Works, 57, 78, 86, 111

Appleton *Evening Crescent,* 194

Appleton Labor College, 153

Appleton Trades and Labor Council, 193

Ashland *Daily News,* 18

"Assumption of risks," 125, 127

Automobile Labor Board, 64

Auto Workers Union (AFL), 79

Babcock, C.A., 220

Baker, Mary, 192–193

Barlow and Seelig Manufacturing Company (Speed Queen), 85

Barrette, Leo H., 238

Bayley, Edwin, 146

Bay View. *See* North Chicago Rolling Mills plant

Beck, Ira, 201, 224, 229, 232

Beloit: open shop drive, 28–31; union membership figures (1903–1904), 30

Beloit Citizens' Alliance, 30

Beloit Employers' Association, 30

Beloit *Free Press,* 15

Beloit *Labor Journal,* 29

Bell Telephone System, 94–95

Berger, Victor L.: 36–38; views on political action, 37, 42, 43; influence among blue-collar Milwaukee Germans, 37, 38, 42, 44, 118–119; Milwaukee FTC board member, 41; WSFL activities, 37, 38, 42; Socialist ideology, 42, 43; influence in Wisconsin labor movement, 42, 44; opposes Gompers, 42–44; relations with Frank Weber, 43–44; relations with Debs, 44; anti-IWW views, 44; victim of "Red Scare," 104–